Constructing the Field

Ethnographic fieldwork is traditionally seen as what distinguishes social and cultural anthropology from the other social sciences. This collection responds to the intensifying scrutiny of fieldwork in recent years. It challenges the idea of the necessity for the total immersion of the ethnographer in the field, and for the clear separation of professional and personal areas of activity. The very existence of 'the field' as an entity separate from everyday life is questioned.

Fresh perspectives on contemporary fieldwork are provided by diverse case studies from across North America and Europe. These contributions give a thorough appraisal of what fieldwork is and should be, and an extra dimension is added through fascinating accounts of the personal experiences of anthropologists in the field.

Constructing the Field is a timely contribution to a highly topical debate. Accessible and comprehensive, it will be an essential resource for both students and scholars of anthropology.

Vered Amit is an Associate Professor at Concordia University in Montreal, Canada.

European Association of Social Anthropologists

Series facilitator: Jon P. Mitchell
University of Sussex

The European Association of Social Anthropologists (EASA) was inaugurated in January 1989, in response to a widely felt need for a professional association which would represent social anthropologists in Europe and foster cooperation and interchange in teaching and research. As Europe transforms itself in the 1990s, the EASA is dedicated to the renewal of the distinctive European tradition in social anthropology.

Other titles in the series:

Conceptualizing Society
Adam Kuper

Other Histories
Kirsten Hastrup

Alcohol, Gender and Culture
Dimitra Gefou-Madianou

Understanding Rituals
Daniel de Coppet

Gendered Anthropology
Teresa del Valle

**Social Experience and
Anthropological Knowledge**
Kirsten Hastrup and Peter Hervik

Fieldwork and Footnotes
*Han F. Vermeulen and Arturo
Alvarez Roldan*

Syncretism/Anti-Syncretism
Charles Stewart and Rosalind Shaw

Grasping the Changing World
Václav Hubinger

Civil Society
Chris Hann and Elizabeth Dunn

Nature and Society
Philippe Descola and Gisli Pálsson

The Ethnography of Moralities
Signe Howell

Inside and Outside the Law
Olivia Harris

Locality and Belonging
Nadia Lovell

Recasting Ritual
*Felicia Hughes-Freeland and
Mary M. Crain*

**Anthropological Perspectives
on Local Development**
Simone Abram and Jacqueline Waldren

Constructing the Field

Ethnographic Fieldwork in the Contemporary World

Edited by Vered Amit

London and New York

First published 2000
by Routledge
11 New Fetter Lane, London EC4P 4EE

Simultaneously published in the USA and Canada
by Routledge
29 West 35th Street, New York, NY 10001

Routledge is an imprint of the Taylor & Francis Group

© 2000 selection and editorial matter, EASA; individual chapters,
the contributors

Typeset in Galliard by
BC Typesetting, Bristol
Printed and bound in Great Britain by
MPG Books Ltd, Bodmin

British Library Cataloguing in Publication Data
A catalogue record for this book is available from the British Library

Library of Congress Cataloging in Publication Data
Constructing the field: ethnographic fieldwork in the contemporary
    world/edited by Vered Amit.
        p.   cm.
    Includes bibliographical references.
    1. Ethnology–Fieldwork.   1. Amit, Vered, 1955–
GN346.C64   1999
305.8′007′23–dc21   99-24309
                                                CIP

ISBN 0–415–19829–1 (hbk)
ISBN 0–415–19830–5 (pbk)

Contents

List of contributors   vii

1 **Introduction: constructing the field**   1
   VERED AMIT

2 **At 'home' and 'away': reconfiguring the field for
   late twentieth-century anthropology**   19
   VIRGINIA CAPUTO

3 **Home field advantage? Exploring the social
   construction of children's sports**   32
   NOEL DYCK

4 **Here and there: doing transnational fieldwork**   54
   CAROLINE KNOWLES

5 **The narrative as fieldwork technique: processual
   ethnography for a world in motion**   71
   NIGEL RAPPORT

6 **'Informants' who come 'home'**   96
   SARAH PINK

7 **Phoning the field: meanings of place and involvement
   in fieldwork 'at home'**   120
   KARIN NORMAN

8 Access to a closed world: methods for a multilocale
   study on ballet as a career   147
   HELENA WULFF

9 Locating yoga: ethnography and transnational
   practice   162
   SARAH STRAUSS

   Index   195

Contributors

Vered Amit, Associate Professor, Department of Sociology and Anthropology, Concordia University, Montreal, Canada.

Virginia Caputo, Assistant Professor, Department of Women's Studies, Carleton University, Ottawa, Canada.

Noel Dyck, Professor, Department of Sociology and Anthropology, Simon Fraser University, Burnaby, Canada.

Caroline Knowles, Lecturer, Department of Sociology and Social Policy, University of Southampton, Southampton, UK.

Karin Norman, Senior Lecturer, Department of Social Anthropology, Stockholm University, Stockholm, Sweden.

Sarah Pink, Lecturer, School of Education and Social Science, University of Derby, Derby, UK.

Nigel Rapport, Professor, Department of Social Anthropology, University of St Andrews, St Andrews, Scotland.

Sarah Strauss, Assistant Professor, Department of Anthropology, University of Wyoming, Laramie, USA.

Helena Wulff, Lecturer, Department of Anthropology, Stockholm University, Stockholm, Sweden.

Chapter 1

Introduction

Constructing the field

Vered Amit

In the joint anthropology and sociology department where I teach, students have frequently asked me somewhat hesitantly, assuming they ought to already know the answer, 'What, after all, is the difference between sociology and anthropology?' I usually tend to talk vaguely about general orientations versus absolute disciplinary boundaries but, if a flurry of recent publications are correct, in answering the same question most anthropologists would be likely to invoke ethnographic fieldwork as the quintessential hallmark of social and cultural anthropology. According to Akhil Gupta and James Ferguson (1997: 1):

> the single most significant factor determining whether a piece of research will be accepted as (that magical word) 'anthropological' is the extent to which it depends on experience 'in the field.'

So what is 'experience in the field'? Much as fieldwork is the most commonly cited defining criteria of anthropology, intensive participant observation in turn is frequently treated as defining anthropological fieldwork (see Clifford, 1992). You have to actually be physically present in the field, assert Kirsten Hastrup and Peter Hervik (1994a: 3). Long-distance methods of communication will not do. Ethnographic field-work must be experienced as performed rather than just communicated in dialogue (ibid.). Duration is also critical, according to Judith Okely (1992). The bounded periods of sociological versions of ethnography, she argues, bear no comparison to the long-term and thorough immersion of anthropological fieldwork, 'a total experience, demanding all of the anthropologist's resources, intellectual, physical, emotional, political and intuitive' (ibid.: 8). But of course, this is fundamentally a social rather than a solitary experience mediated by and constituted through the fieldworker's relationships with others (ibid.: 2). The scope of activities which an ethnographer can observe and in which s/he can participate, his/her vantage point and premise of involvement are contingent on the nature of the relationships s/he is able to form with those engaged in these situations. Finally, fieldwork has generally incorporated an expectation of travel away from the researcher's ordinary place of residence and work or 'home' (Gupta and Ferguson, 1997).

Thus in this composite but familiar portrait, 'fieldwork' involves travel away, preferably to a distant locale where the ethnographer will immerse him/herself in personal face-to-face relationships with a variety of natives over an extended period of time. While this is a familiar representation, as the chapters in this volume illustrate, it is a rendering of ethnographic 'fieldwork' that in one respect or another no longer suffices even as a serviceable fiction for many contemporary ethnographers. The contributors to this volume are hardly alone in their discomfiture with the gap between the experience and archetype (Gupta and Ferguson, 1997) of fieldwork, as the latter is subjected to increasing critical scrutiny by anthropologists (ibid.; Flinn *et al.*, 1998; Hastrup and Hervik, 1994b; Okely, 1996; Okely and Callaway, 1992; Robbins and Bamford, 1997). In this introductory chapter I want to examine some of the paradoxes embedded in the anthropological tradition of fieldwork. While these dilemmas reflect epistemological variabilities that are not amenable to overly generalized solutions, how we respond to them has the possibility of either opening up or alternatively limiting the scope of anthropological enquiry. It is to the former orientation that this book is dedicated.

Compartmentalizing fieldwork

One of the peculiarities of participant observation as ethnographic fieldwork is the way in which the researcher and his/her personal relationships serve as primary vehicles for eliciting findings and insight. There is surely no other form of scholarly enquiry in which relationships of intimacy and familiarity between researcher and subject are envisioned as a fundamental medium of investigation rather than as an extraneous by-product or even an impediment. This onus towards comradeship, however incompletely and sporadically achieved, provides a vantage point imbued at once with significant analytical advantages as well as poignant dilemmas of ethics and social location. On the one hand, it encourages ethnographers to see people as rounded individuals, as multifaceted social beings with involvements, experiences and stories reaching far beyond the limited purview of any research project. It makes it difficult, if not impossible, for fieldworkers to regard the people with whom they are conducting research merely as one-dimensional research subjects. Hence the discomfiture many anthropologists have with using terms such as informant, respondent or research subject as textual references for people they have known as friends, neighbours, advisers, etc. Nonetheless, opting instead for the latter terms of reference may not resolve the problem that however sincere and nuanced the attachment they express, ethnographic fieldworkers are still also exploiting this intimacy as an investigative tool. Participant observation is therefore often uneasily perched on the precipice between the inherent instrumentalism of this as of any research enterprise and the more complex and rounded social associations afforded by this particular method.

The tension between the personal and the professional aspects of fieldwork has, however, extended both ways, equally raising concern about the integrity of anthropologists' claims of professionalism. Judith Okely is undoubtedly correct that anthropologists have tried to respond to pressures for scientific detachment (1992: 8) as a marker of professionalism. But the effort to separate work and home or the professional and the personal is responsive to a much more pervasive structural bias in capitalist, industrial societies extending well beyond the university gates. Anthropologists whose principal methodology has rested on a maverick if sometimes uneasy melding of these domains have nonetheless attempted to uphold their overall separation by compartmentalizing fieldwork spatially, temporally and textually. The result has been a set of epistemological conventions which have both reproduced and camouflaged key contradictions in anthropological practices. There is now a copious literature attesting to the distortions and contradictions involved in one of these efforts: the absence of the ethnographer as an active and embodied participant in the social relationships and situations described in published texts. Drawing on Johannes Fabian's analysis of the disjunction between fieldwork and text contrived by textual conventions, Helen Callaway notes that 'ethnographic research involves prolonged interaction with others, yet anthropological discourse conveys the understanding gained in terms of distance, both spatial and temporal' (1992: 30).

Another device for establishing distance has been more literal, involving a convention for choosing fieldwork sites that are 'away', preferably far away from the ethnographer's usual place of residence and work. Gupta and Ferguson argue that this convention has resulted in a 'hierarchy of purity of field sites' (1997: 13).

After all, if 'the field' is most appropriately a place that is 'not home', then some places will necessarily be more 'not home' than others, and hence more appropriate, more 'fieldlike'.

Ironically, however, anthropology has also traditionally been dedicated to the cause of contextualizing the exotic and unfamiliar so effectively that it is rendered explicable and unexceptional. Fieldwork has focused on the ordinary, the everyday and mundane lives of people and often relegated more exceptional and unique circumstances to the province of sensation-seeking journalists (Malkki, 1997). Thus anthropological conventions regarding the selection of fieldwork sites have first insisted on cultural, social and spatial distance as a gauge of ethnographic authenticity but then measured the craft of anthropology through the capacity of its practitioners to render the distant familiar. The nearby is assumed not to require this alchemy and is thus treated as ethnographically unproblematic. As Virginia Caputo's chapter in this volume illustrates, in spite of a post-Said decade replete with anthropological atonement for the sins of orientalism, the disciplinary bias towards the distantly exotic as more valid sites for fieldwork continues to shape training and hiring practices at the very least in North American and British anthropology departments. In designing her doctoral study of children's songs and narratives in Toronto, the city in which she resided, Caputo had assumed that a concept of fieldwork as defined by a journey to distant and specific places no longer held sway in anthropology. And yet the notion of journey and geography subtly recurred in the assumption that doctoral students would adopt a regional specialization, an assumption that appeared in record-keeping practices and comprehensive examinations. In applying for academic positions, Caputo also found that 'geographic area' continued to be a crucial criterion for judging candidates and that her own specific choices of 'field' and 'fieldwork' had become limiting factors.

On the sliding scale of recent efforts to reform fieldwork practices over the last fifteen years, anthropologists have subjected the artifices of textual distantiation to the most sustained introspection and revision. They have sought atonement for representational exoticisms but continue to embed them in their locational strategies. Nonetheless, they appear to have been least inclined to relinquish some long-standing presumptions about what makes the experience of fieldwork truly anthropological. Tellingly, some of the critics who have been most concerned with reshaping ethnographic conventions have also been among the most insistent that anthropological fieldwork must continue to be exemplified by thorough immersion in the daily practices and face-to-face relationships of a particular set of people (Hastrup and Hervik, 1994a; Okely, 1992). Thus Judith Okely has been a long-standing critic of the exoticist bias in anthropological orthodoxies which artificially position 'field' versus 'home'. She has argued strongly for the importance of an autobiographical reflexivity as an integral element of ethnographic fieldwork. Indeed, Okely has gone so far as to subject episodes of her own childhood experiences in an English boarding-school to a retrospective ethnographic analysis (1996). Yet she insists that the quintessence of what makes ethnographic fieldwork anthropological continues to be a commitment to a process of utter social immersion.

Kirsten Hastrup has argued that in the face of the mobility and displacement of peoples worldwide, anthropologists are being forced to relinquish the conflation of place with collective and cultural production (Hastrup and Olwig, 1997). Yet only a few years earlier, she and Peter Hervik were contending both that the anthropological tradition of fieldwork as participant observation is more relevant today than ever before, and that it requires the actual physical presence of the ethnographer as an absolute prerequisite (Hastrup and Hervik, 1994a: 3). It is as if in order to do something different, anthropologists have to reassure themselves and each other that it is not too different. Even such thoughtful critics appear unwilling to relinquish a long-standing epistemological tautology: that anthropology is validated as a separate discipline through a particular methodology which, while valued for its open-endedness, is in turn legitimated through spatial and social encapsulation. When am I doing anthropological fieldwork? When I am 'there' and doing nothing else. Given the persistence of conceptions of immersion and presence as archetypes for anthropological fieldwork and the continuing status of fieldwork as a virtual charter for anthropology as a discipline, it seems appropriate to examine these presumptions a little closer.

Autobiography, immersion and constructing the field

The conception of fieldwork as comprehensive immersion presumes a singularity of focus and engagement which flies in the face of the actual practices of many anthropologists whether working near or far from their usual place of residence. Many ethnographers are accompanied by or continue to live with their families (Flinn, 1998), visit or are visited by long-standing friends and associates, and maintain professional and personal communications, all while initiating relationships with and observing the activities of still other sets of people. These practices are hardly new. Indeed, one could argue that transgressions of the solitary fieldworker model of ethnographic fieldwork are as much an anthropological tradition as the model itself. If this model was unsustainable even during less reflexive phases of anthropological production, the effort to retain a version of it, however reformed, to take account of *fin-de-siècle* sensitivities, is puzzling, given nearly two decades of effort to bring the anthropologist's own positioning into focus. It is difficult to reconcile the contradiction between an emphasis on the importance of autobiography with the implicit insistence on an interregnum of the ethnographer's usual relationships, routines, commitments and preoccupations so that s/he can be utterly encapsulated in fieldwork. The notion of immersion implies that the 'field' which ethnographers enter exists as an independently bounded set of relationships and activities which is autonomous of the fieldwork through which it is discovered. Yet in a world of infinite interconnections and overlapping contexts, the ethnographic field cannot simply exist, awaiting discovery. It has to be laboriously constructed, prised apart from all the other possibilities for contextualization to which its constituent relationships and connections could also be referred. This process of construction is inescapably shaped by the conceptual, professional, financial and relational opportunities and resources accessible to the ethnographer. Seen from this perspective, an idea of fieldwork in which the ethnographer is expected to break from his/her usual involvements in order to immerse him/herself in the 'field' of others' involvements is an oxymoron. Instead, as the chapters in this volume illustrate, the construction of an ethnographic field involves efforts to accommodate and interweave sets of relationships and engagements developed in one context with those arising in another. Or perhaps to view ongoing relationships from altered perspectives as ethnographers ask different questions on 'entering' and 'leaving' the 'field'. As Nigel Rapport argues (Chapter 5, this volume), anthropologists have used the outward signs of transit entailed in travel from one site to another as the validation of what is much more crucially an experiential and cognitive rather than a physical movement.

While I studied the activities of a network of ethnic lobbyists in Montreal (Amit-Talai, 1996), I looked after my young son and also lectured and attended departmental meetings as I was required to do to earn my living. But my interest in this 'field', indeed my awareness that such an institutionalized round of minority representation even existed, arose from my previous involvement on this circuit as the paid employee of a community and lobbying organization. In this earlier role, I had spent most of my days immersed in the activities of the circuit. While this immersion contributed greatly to my knowledge and understanding of this set of activities and relationships, I was engaged in it as a participating lobbyist rather than as an ethnographer *per se*. Later, as a researcher, juggling other inescapable professional and personal commitments, I could not devote the same amount of time to the activities of the circuit yet I did feel that I was now seeing the circuit as an ethnographer rather than as a participant.

The melding of personal and professional roles in ethnographic fieldwork makes for a 'messy, qualitative experience' (Marcus and Fischer, 1986: 22) which cannot readily or usefully be compartmentalized from other experiences and periods in our lives. For a number of years, Noel Dyck was actively involved as a parent, coach and technical official in the sports programmes which occupy so many children in the Lower Mainland of British Columbia. This involvement had come to feature as his 'time out' from his professional roles. This welcome separation between domestic and professional activities unravelled, however, when Dyck started to recognize the rhetorical and ideological components of what had passed until that point as 'small talk'. Gradually, his analysis become more systematic, a shift finally formalized in an application for funding to study community sport. Yet the roles Dyck had previously performed as a less self-conscious participant, the relationships entailed in these roles and the knowledge they bequeathed did not end when he realized and formally acted upon the ethnographic potential of this field, nor did they end when this phase of fieldwork came to a close.

Helena Wulff's access to the backstage of the Royal Swedish Ballet Company, her ability to contextualize some of the dancers' biographical narratives, her understanding of the non-verbal bodily work entailed in ballet were made possible by experiences and relationships which she had shared as a dancer herself long before her re-entry into the 'field' of ballet as an ethnographer. Wulff argues that the stark dichotomy between native and anthropologist posited by Kirsten Hastrup has to give way to the more nuanced shifting multiple subjectivity experienced by many anthropologists. Wulff's perspective and relationships as an ex-ballet dancer and the new forms of nativeness she acquired in the course of her 'fieldwork' crucially informed but were not erased by the ethnographic lens she now trained on the ballet world.

It is important, however, to be clear that this interfusion of contexts, involvements, roles and perspectives is not peculiar to the circumstances affecting ethnographers working in close geographic proximity to their place of residence. After all, in studying professional ballet companies, given her previous experiences as a dancer, Wulff was in a sense coming 'home', but 'home' in this context was a transnational occupational field and her study of it involved multilocale fieldwork in a number of different countries.

The boundary between anthropological field and home which has so often been demarcated by the metaphor of travel has incorporated a presumption that 'home' is stationary while the field is a journey away. It is a presumption which is undone as much by the cognitive and emotional journeys which fieldworkers make in looking at familiar practices and sites with new ethnographic lenses as by the transnational organization of many academics' lives. Frequent migrants and travellers themselves, for many academics home is as peripatetic and multisited as fieldwork has increasingly come to be. As Sarah Strauss' and Caroline Knowles' chapters indicate, the two forms of journeys often converge. At first glance, Caroline Knowles' choice of research subject appears to establish a much sharper dichotomy between autobiography and fieldwork than is the case in Noel Dyck's and Helena Wulff's studies. As a white British professional, Knowles' own identity and history seem far removed from the black people diagnosed as 'schizophrenic' whose narratives she has collected both in London and Montreal. Yet as Knowles points out, her interest in the administrative and personal processes involved in racialization could equally be addressed in many other places. The specific choice of Montreal and London is 'frankly autobiographical: I once lived in one and now live in the other, and I am trying to devise a way of living in both'. Notions of home and belonging are key constitutive ideas of the transatlantic field inscribed by Knowles both personally and professionally.

Sarah Strauss' study of yoga as a 'community of practice' also involved multilocale research in India, Germany, Switzerland and the United States, but her ability to realize a project involving such dispersed locations was shaped by the interaction between the transnational connections of yoga adherents, her graduate training at the University of Pennsylvania and her subsequent peripatetic location as an 'academic migrant labourer'. After conducting her doctoral research in the Indian pilgrimage town of Rishikesh, Strauss accompanied her husband to Zurich where he had been hired as a post-doctoral researcher and used this base for a series of short ethnographic trips to other locales even while her possessions, bills and many personal associations remained anchored in the United States, her native country. As Strauss notes, her ability to imagine and act upon the research possibilities afforded by her husband's job in Switzerland was informed by an educational formation at the University of Pennsylvania that had featured an emphasis on transnational studies.

To the extent that the personal, professional and fieldwork involvements of ethnographers are mutually constitutive, the construction of ethnographic fields is not a one-way process of accommodation to the fieldworker's already existing associations and commitments, for these are also inevitably altered. However much ethnographers may seek to leave the field, whether through travel, changes in activity or shifts in perspective, they cannot help but take it with them because the 'field' has now become incorporated into their biographies, understandings and associations. I conducted fieldwork in Grand Cayman over the course of five visits between 1993 and 1996. Back in Montreal some time after the last of these visits, I was informed that a friend whom I had known in Grand Cayman was very ill and had returned to another province in Canada, her native country. In the weeks that followed I spoke on the telephone with her, with her friends in Canada and the Cayman Islands as we shared our anxieties and information about her condition. One of the people also seeking news of this situation was a colleague from Montreal who, while visiting me in Grand Cayman, had met my friend and was now concerned about her illness. In seeking and sharing news of my friend, I was surely not conducting research. But my friendship with her had arisen in the course of and had been crucially shaped by my research foci, just as the course of my fieldwork had been in no small measure affected by her incisive insights and thoughtful suggestions.

In the course of conducting fieldwork in Cordoba, Sarah Pink met and married her Spanish partner. Having arrived in Cordoba without local social networks, by the time she finished her fieldwork, she had developed local family and social responsibilities similar to those of her Spanish informants and friends. When she left Cordoba to return 'home' to Britain, she was accompanied by her partner and she remained in contact with Spanish friends through telephone calls, letters and visits. But Pink was not the only person from her Cordoban social circle to make the move from Spain to Britain. Her social life in Canterbury incorporated friends from her fieldwork now resident in Britain as well as new friendships with other Spanish migrants. Gradually, Pink came to realize that these personal relationships could be construed ethnographically as fieldwork, and she started to formalize her study of Spanish graduate migrants in Britain, but her key informants remained herself, her husband and friends.

How is it that so many of the contributors to this volume were able to sustain friendships that constituted but transcended their fieldwork engagements when other anthropologists have reported serious ruptures as a consequence of their effort to combine these professional and personal roles? Joy Hendry, reporting on the breach of a long-standing relationship when Sachiko, a Japanese friend, became a key informant and research assistant, wonders whether she needs to readjust her conception of friendship. In explaining the rift, Sachiko complained of being burdened by Hendry's constant presence and frequent enquiries about her private affairs as well as belittled by her new role as a waged subordinate (Hendry, 1992). One wonders why an intrusiveness which had not arisen during an association of many years should suddenly be introduced in the course of fieldwork. Perhaps what needed to be adjusted was not Hendry's notion of friendship which seems to have been quite effective at sustaining a relationship for many years, but the conception of immersion which she shares with many anthropologists.

One of the ironies of an a priori insistence on intensive immersion as the *sine qua non* of ethnographic fieldwork is the way in which it can, as in the case reported by Hendry, undermine the principal asset of this methodology: its malleability. The strength of this form of fieldwork is the leeway it allows for the ethnographer to respond and adapt flexibly to social circumstances as these arise, to be open to a wide variety of different types of relationships and interaction. Thus when Paul Stoller conducted fieldwork among West African street traders in Harlem, he realized that approaches which had been appropriate in his earlier study of Songhay religious practices in Niger would not be similarly effective or appropriate in this new situation.

> The precarious situation of the traders, of course made them suspicious of any newcomer even if he or she spoke an African language. Rather than plunging into the field with a barrage of demographic surveys or plans for intensive participant observation, I decided to periodically hang out at the 125th Street market . . . I am convinced, however, that had I adopted a less open-ended and more intensive field approach, the results would have been far more limited.

> (Stoller, 1997: 90)

There is, Virginia Caputo argues (Chapter 2, this volume), an instability to the ground that marks doing 'anthropology' at home because it requires a constant shifting of positionings between situations, people, identities and perspectives. But the range of experiences described in this volume suggests that fieldwork 'away' as well as at 'home' is similarly episodic and fluid. It is not a coincidence, I believe, that the willingness of these researchers to accept this level of indeterminacy has also been associated with a capacity to envision and pursue the ethnographic possibilities of a disparate range of situations: sporadic dialogues with a former resident of a small farming village in Northwest England; exploring children's narratives and songs in Toronto; multilocale research among black people diagnosed as 'schizophrenic', ballet dancers and yoga adherents; shifting from research among female bull-fighters in Spain to research among Spanish graduate migrants in a variety of locales in Britain, from tutelage relations in Indian administration to organized children's sports in the Lower Mainland of British Columbia, from ethnic lobbyists in Montreal to expatriate professionals in the Cayman Islands. To explore these 'fields', some of the contributors stayed put in one site for many months, others made short periodic visits to one or several sites, saw some informants daily, others very infrequently, still others balanced face-to-face interaction with email, letters and telephone calls. It is the circumstance which defined the method rather than the method defining the circumstance.

Place and fieldwork

So, what does this approach mean with regard to Hastrup and Hervik's call for the physical presence of the anthropologist as a *sine qua non* of anthropological fieldwork? In considering this question we need to step back for a moment and consider what anthropologists in general and Hastrup and Hervik in particular have been trying to achieve through participant observation. For Hastrup and Hervik, what the anthropologist is attempting to explore is 'the flow of intersubjective human experience' (1994a: 9), which is penetrated, however partially, through the ethnographer's own fieldwork experiences. They stress that the study of social experience concerns far more than just language or sterile cultural categories. With the shift in anthropological theoretical foci from a prescriptive view of culture to a focus on individual agency has come an interest in practice and motivation. And the practices through which cultural models are embodied involve values, emotions and motives as much as the words through which these are expressed. In this view, therefore, the strength of participant observation is the access it provides to lived experiences which incorporate but transcend language. The corollary to this approach is that more indirect interactions, for example, by telephone, are restricted again to the word, missing crucial dimensions of social performance which are non-verbal (Hastrup and Hervik, 1994a).

Yet the access of ethnographers to such social performances has always been limited, whether because some local arenas were restricted to long-standing intimates or to people of a certain gender, class, ethnicity, ritual status, etc. Even the most intense involvement in activities located at a specific site was unlikely, in and of itself, to provide direct information about influential but more distant processes and agents. The ethnographic 'field', therefore, has always been as much characterized by absences as by presences and hence necessitated a variety of corresponding methods – interviews, archival documents, census data, artefacts, media materials and more – to explore processes not immediately or appropriately accessible through participant observation.

This kind of methodological flexibility has become all the more crucial as the contexts in which anthropologists seek to conduct fieldwork have changed. Anthropologists have rarely been the only ones arriving and leaving their field sites. But today, the people whom they are trying to study are increasingly likely to be as mobile if not more so than the ethnographers trying to keep up with them. In the course of a year of fieldwork in north-west England, in the village of Wanet, Nigel Rapport amply fulfilled the methodological criteria of presence and immersion stressed by Hastrup and Hervik and Okely. 'I sat in my cottage and then my caravan, I visited local houses and drank in local pubs, I engaged in local relationships, I worked the land.' But during this period in which Rapport remained stationary, Greg, a former native of Wanet, journeyed in and out of the village. Nor was Greg a unique emigrant, for he was one of a large number of former Wanet residents who had settled elsewhere and now visited their former homes with variable frequency. As Greg came and went, he elaborated on a personal life narrative which suppressed the distances between his visits to Wanet and re-established his sense of belonging and groundedness in this locale. In echoes of Wulff's argument for a blurring of the distinction between native and anthropological perspectives, Rapport argues that the narrative form acts as a *modus vivendi* for fieldworker and ethnographic subject alike as both seek 'a place cognitively to reside and make sense, a place to continue to be'.

Karin Norman was already conducting fieldwork in Gruvbo, a small town in central Sweden, when the public housing area in which she had rented an apartment became the site of a reception centre for 'refugees' mainly from the former Yugoslavia. Norman's field site was changing as she stayed in her apartment, looking out of her kitchen window. She became close to several Kosovo Albanian families in particular, but in less than a year the whole situation changed again. The reception centre was closed down and the refugees were relocated to a variety of sites elsewhere. Norman felt abandoned, left behind. Gruvbo lost its meaning and she found herself also moving, trying to maintain her contact with those Kosovo Albanian families that were relatively nearby and struggling to maintain her connections with those further away. 'For several years then, everyone has been on the move, nothing seems predictable, and the field keeps changing boundaries, connecting several locations.'

The increasing mobility of the people whom anthropologists study has coincided with a period of critical introspection in anthropology resulting in a re-evaluation of a number of long-standing conventions and assumptions. Among these has been the deconstruction of 'a place-focused concept of culture' (Hastrup and Olwig, 1997: 4) and the allowance instead for a more contingent relationship between collective identity, place, social relations and culture. The shift away from locality as the boundary and site for cultural production has allowed anthropologists to take more cognizance of migrants and travellers whose social networks and frames of reference are likely to be dispersed and multilocale rather than conveniently fixed in one place (Hastrup and Olwig, 1997). Anthropologists have correspondingly redefined their ethnographic 'fields' to explore the multisited, transnational circulation of people, practices and objects (Marcus, 1995). As the chapters by Wulff and Strauss indicate, just in and of themselves the logistics of spreading one's attention over activities and individuals at several sites necessitates a methodological shift from older conceptions of an extended presence in one locale. Instead both Wulff and Strauss combined this kind of stay with a series of much shorter visits to other sites.

There is however much more to the shift from the study of small, localized communities featuring dense and multiplex networks to that of territorially dispersed and fragmented networks than a simple multiplication of the sites at which an anthropologist conducts fieldwork. Combined, the personal networks of the expatriate professionals and workers who make up a large segment of the workforce of the Cayman Islands are virtually global in their reach. Yet the amount of overlap between them is very small. They originate from a number of different countries and, unlike the circular migration which has featured in movements from and within the Caribbean, many of the temporary workers arriving in the Cayman Islands had no previous associations with this locale. Yet the nature of the extralocal relationships and attachments which expatriates maintain and form while living in Cayman is potentially crucial since, as unenfranchised contract workers, most will eventually leave this location (Amit-Talai, 1997, 1998). To try to track these networks or the movements of expatriates beyond the Cayman Islands I would have to find a means of defining the parameters of and moving through a diffuse and largely unintegrated field demarcated principally by a temporary biographical connection with one particular site and my own investigation. In other words, my 'field' would be defined in terms of a social category that I have singled out rather than a self-conscious social group, whose members are interacting with one another on an ongoing basis, independently of my intervention.

Such a shift renders the ethnographer an even more central agent in the construction of the 'field'. Thus the fulcrum of the network of Spanish migrants who formed the subject of Sarah Pink's fieldwork in Britain was Pink herself. This was not a collectivity that existed independently. Some of these individuals knew each other, others came into contact with each other partly through Pink's own efforts, but only Sarah Pink herself knew or was in touch with all these individuals. Ironically, given Hastrup and Hervik's call for the physical presence of the ethnographer, in such a scattered and sporadically connected 'field', the closest one may come to participant observation may be through the vehicles of indirect electronic communications joining together a number of dispersed associates, while face-to-face contact may be more reliant on dyadic encounters planned for and structured by the fieldworker's movements. Even in more self-aware and integrated fields such as the transnational yoga 'community of practice' studied by Sarah Strauss, Strauss' movements and contacts still served as the key articulation between all the individuals, events and sites she encountered.

In seeking to expand their research scope to include the study of mobile individuals, dispersed and/or fragmented social networks, anthropologists may no longer be able to rely on a concept that traditionally has been as, if not more crucial than place for locating their field: the habitus of collectivity. Episodic, occasional, partial and ephemeral social links pose particular challenges for ethnographic fieldwork. How do we observe interactions that happen sometimes but not necessarily when we are around? How do we participate in social relations that are not continuous, that are experienced most viscerally in their absence? How do we participate in or observe practices that are enacted here and there, by one or a few? How do we take into account unique events that may not be recurring but may still have irrevocable consequences: a demonstration, a battle, a sports event (Malkki, 1997)? Where do we 'hang out' when the processes which we are studying produce common social conditions or statuses (freelance workers, peripatetic entrepreneurs, consultants, tourists) but not necessarily coterminous collectivities? To cope with these conditions, it may not be sufficient or possible for anthropologists to simply join in. They may have to purposively create the occasions for contacts that might well be as mobile, diffuse and episodic as the processes they are studying. But what then of the 'total experience' (Okely, 1992: 8) of fieldwork?

Coming 'home' again

It is becoming a virtual truism to note that the distinction between 'home' and 'away' has become blurred by the transnational contexts in which anthropologists and their ethnographic subjects now move. Karin Norman started off her fieldwork 'at home' in a Swedish town and ended up in Kosovo; Sarah Pink started off in Cordoba and returned 'home' to Britain, only to find that her fieldwork friends and partner had followed. But are these and similar efforts by other anthropologists to achieve this kind of ethnographic mobility undermining the contextual depth they once achieved through intensive fieldwork in more contained and localized communities? And without that kind of fieldwork is anthropology still anthropology?

In 1982, when addressing a similar range of issues *vis-à-vis* ethnographic fieldwork in dense urban settings, Sandra Wallman cautioned against equating the discipline of anthropology with its principal technique of enquiry and confusing the perspectives facilitated by participant observation with the method itself (1982: 190–191). It is the perspectives highlighted by Wallman, the appreciation of context, meaning and social relationships that still shape anthropology, and thereby the crucial contributions it can make to an understanding of the coming century's ethnoscapes. Anthropology's strength is the ethnographic spotlight it focuses on particular lives, broadly contextualized. In this focus, anthropology, at best, collapses the distinction between micro and macro and challenges reifications of concepts such as diaspora, state, globalization and so on which, in their geographic, political and social reach, can easily appear distant and abstract. It allows us to penetrate even those institutions or structures whose size and influence threaten to overwhelm analysis through a focus on the actions, understandings, decisions and relationships of specific people whom they affect or incorporate. In turn, our efforts at contextualizing the actions and understandings of these specific actors always impart an open-ended quality to ethnographic investigation. Changes wrought by time, unfolding spatial configurations, the intricacies of even the most contained and continuous of relationships ensure that we are always chasing context but never squaring it off. This open-endedness is further heightened by the social nature of ethnography which makes it fundamentally *ad hoc*, sense-making as the poetics of the possible and negotiated, equal measures of serendipity and deliberate enterprise. Where, when, how and whom we encounter can never be subject to our firm control.

Paradoxically however, the old 'arrival' tales in exaggerating the social isolation of the 'field' also robbed it of much of its ethnographic context. More recent interpretations of ethnography as social experience have in turn tended to overstate the fieldworker's experiential envelopment in the field, a strangely persistent bubble of isolation in an otherwise earnestly contextualized (at least in principle) situation. We cannot disconnect ourselves from our lives to live our fieldwork, just as our subjects cannot disconnect themselves from the world and their pursuits to engage with or to be abandoned by us. They are as likely to leave us when we don't want them to or to follow us when we think we have left for good. Surely then in examining the role of the ethnographer, the defining questions are not how many senses we engage while conducting our research, whether we carry out long-term, full-time continuous fieldwork, make numerous brief visits or sustain ongoing but part-time contacts, or have face-to-face or electronically mediated communication. Surely the crucial issues that should concern us are the frameworks which anthropologists and the various people they encounter in their fieldwork use to site their activities, their sense of self, their homes, their work and relationships. Because in considering the structural, biographical, intellectual and political issues which enter into these efforts at siting fieldwork in our lives and ourselves in the lives of our informants, we are also considering the common dilemmas we and others face in trying to make sense of our passages through 'a world in motion' (Rapport, Chapter 5, this volume).

To overdetermine fieldwork practices is therefore to undermine the very strength of ethnography, the way in which it deliberately leaves openings for unanticipated discoveries and directions. If in cleaving to a methodological orthodoxy, anthropologists a priori limit rather than leave open the scope of circumstances to be studied, they will be operating at epistemological cross purposes with their own disciplinary objectives. Thus the answer to what happens to anthropology if its practitioners adapt their fieldwork practices to the exigencies of new circumstances is that it wouldn't remain as anthropology if they didn't.

References

Amit-Talai, Vered (1996) The Minority Circuit: The Professionalization of Ethnic Activism in Montreal. In Vered Amit-Talai and Caroline Knowles (eds) *Re-situating Identities: The Politics of Race, Ethnicity and Culture*. Peterborough, Ont: Broadview Press, pp. 89–114.

—— (1997) In Pursuit of Authenticity: Globalization and Nation Building in the Cayman Islands. *Anthropologica* XXXIX: 5–15.

—— (1998) Risky Hiatuses and the Limits of Social Imagination: Expatriacy in the Cayman Islands. In Nigel Rapport and Andrew Dawson (eds) *Migrants of Identity: Perceptions of Home in a World in Movement*. London and New Jersey: Berg Books, pp. 41–59.

Callaway, Helen (1992) Ethnography and Experience: Gender Implications in Fieldwork and Texts. In Judith Okely and Helen Callaway (eds) *Anthropology and Autobiography*. ASA Monographs 29. London and New York: Routledge, pp. 29–49.

Clifford, James (1992) Traveling Cultures. In Lawrence Grossberg, Cary Nelson and Paula A. Treichler (eds) *Cultural Studies*. New York and London: Routledge, pp. 96–116.

Flinn, Juliana (1998) Introduction: The Family Dimension in Anthropological Fieldwork. In Juliana Flinn, Leslie Marshall and Jocelyn Armstrong (eds) *Fieldwork and Families: Constructing New Models for Ethnographic Research*. Honolulu: University of Hawaii Press, pp. 1–21.

Flinn, Juliana, Leslie Marshall and Jocelyn Armstrong (eds) (1998) *Fieldwork and Families: Constructing New Models for Ethnographic Research*. Honolulu: University of Hawaii Press.

Gupta, Akhil and James Ferguson (1997) Discipline and Practice: 'The Field' as Site, Method, and Location in Anthropology. In Akhil Gupta and James Ferguson (eds) *Anthropological Locations. Boundaries and Grounds of a Field Science*. Berkeley, LA and London: University of California Press, pp. 1–46.

Hastrup, Kirsten and Peter Hervik (1994a) Introduction to (eds) *Social Experience and Anthropological Knowledge*. New York and London: Routledge, pp. 1–27.

Hastrup, Kirsten and Peter Hervik (eds) (1994b) *Social Experience and Anthropological Knowledge.* London and New York: Routledge.

Hastrup, Kirsten and Karen Fog Olwig (1997) Introduction to Karen Fog Olwig and Kirsten Hastrup (eds) *Siting Culture: The Shifting Anthropological Object.* London and New York: Routledge, pp. 1–14.

Hendry, Joy (1992) The Paradox of Friendship in the Field: Analysis of a Long-term Anglo–Japanese Relationship. In Judith Okely and Helen Callaway (eds) *Anthropology and Autobiography.* London and New York: Routledge, pp. 163–174.

Malkki, Liisa H. (1997) News and Culture: Transitory Phenomena and the Fieldwork Tradition. In Akhil Gupta and James Ferguson (eds) *Anthropological Locations. Boundaries and Grounds of a Field Science.* Berkeley, LA and London: University of California Press, pp. 86–101.

Marcus, George E. (1995) Ethnography In/Of the World System: The Emergence of Multi-Sited Ethnography. *Annual Review of Anthropology* 24: 95–117.

Marcus, George E. and Michael M.J. Fischer (1986) *Anthropology as Cultural Critique: An Experimental Moment in the Human Sciences.* Chicago, IL: University of Chicago Press.

Okely, Judith (1992) Anthropology and Autobiography: Participatory Experience and Embodied Knowledge. In Judith Okely and Helen Callaway (eds) *Anthropology and Autobiography.* ASA Monographs 29. London and New York: Routledge, pp. 1–28.

—— (1996) *Own or Other Culture.* London and New York: Routledge.

Okely, Judith and Callaway, Helen (eds) (1992) *Anthropology and Autobiography.* London and New York: Routledge.

Robbins, Joel and Sandra Bamford (eds) (1997) Special Issue: Fieldwork Revisited. *Anthropology and Humanism* 22(1).

Stoller, Paul (1997) Globalizing Method: The Problems of Doing Ethnography in Transnational Spaces. *Anthropology and Humanism* 22(1): 81–94.

Wallman, Sandra (1982) Appendix on the Survey: Fieldwork strategy. In Sandra Wallman and Associates, *Living in South London.* Aldershot, Hants: Gower Publishing, pp. 190–207.

Chapter 2

At 'home' and 'away'

Reconfiguring the field for late twentieth-century anthropology

Virginia Caputo

Introduction

This chapter explores the relationship between anthropological configurations of the 'field' and 'fieldwork', key orienting concepts of the
discipline on the one hand, and contemporary research practices on
the other.[1] I argue, following Clifford (1992) and Gupta and Ferguson
(1992, 1997), that a continued insistence on a spatialized notion of
a 'field', as a site of research involving physical displacement to a geographically distant place in order to pursue extended face-to-face
encounters with 'others', obscures many of the realities faced by
anthropologists working at the end of the twentieth century. Not only
does a spatialized sense of the field persist despite recent critical re-
evaluations of place and culture in anthropology that challenge a view
of the world made up of discrete places (Appadurai, 1988, 1990;
Kaplan, 1990; Scott, 1989), it continues to uphold an evaluative hierarchy regarding the kinds of fieldwork and subjects of research that are
deemed 'appropriate'. In turn, this has implications for the kinds of
anthropological knowledge that are produced.

These issues became particularly significant for me while pursuing my
doctoral research. As I attempted to design and carry out a field-based
study of gender in Canadian children's lives in the same city in which I
resided at the time, I was continually faced with negotiating with a
heavy-handed disciplinary legacy, especially in my own challenge of
the central symbol of 'the field'. What follows is an account of some
of the critical junctures and predicaments that I encountered in my
anthropological journey. I begin by considering the questions of
authenticity and value in the ways fields and fieldwork are determined
to be 'real', and hence more valuable than others. In doing so, I hope

to explore some of the issues that arise for those of us who work in anthropology in 'non-traditional' ways.

Beginnings

At the beginning of the doctoral programme, all graduate students were asked to complete the same form outlining the details of our research interests and intended research projects. There were three boxes to complete on the form. Of the three, it was the third – 'geographic area' – that caused me the most difficulty. In light of my interest to study children in a Canadian context, I considered several responses, yet none seemed adequate. Neither North America nor Canada represented my 'geographic area'. It was a predicament that I would encounter many times throughout my research.

When I began the comprehensive examination process, the situation arose again. With the guidance of my supervisory committee, I was asked to design three comprehensive questions: two around substantive areas pertinent to my research and one question on my 'geographic area'. Once again I found myself at a loss for a way to proceed. After much discussion, the impasse was resolved. I would design a question around the predicament itself – the question of 'bounded' fields, rethinking the culture concept, and contemporary research practice.

'Real' fields, 'real' fieldwork

Despite the move out of literal villages, the notion of fieldwork as a special kind of localized dwelling remains.

(Clifford, 1992: 98)

As a graduate student, there were two issues which puzzled me as I began my research. First was the recognition that the concept of 'traditional' fieldwork continued to enjoy prominent status in the discipline; second was the concept's tenacity. In designing a field-based project, 'fieldwork', marked by travel to a geographically distant place inhabited by 'exotic others', was the definition that I thought had been overturned by critics who had argued for a more critical conceptualization of the concept in terms of encounters and relationships rather than 'natural', 'taken-for-granted' geographic locations. Yet, despite the trenchant criticism expressed over the last thirty years of the concept of culture as a discrete self-contained entity and bounded location, along with the increasing attention paid to theorizing about the interconnectedness of the world (Bhabha, 1994; Said, 1989; Spivak, 1990), anthropology, I realized, continued to cling at a certain level, to a colonial view of the world.

Apart from my own efforts at interrogating anthropology's enduring relationship with bounded fields and traditional fieldwork, other researchers have critically considered these conceptualizations, reworking and undermining them in light of contemporary anthropological research practices (see this volume).[2] While scholars have articulated several reasons for the persistence of what appear to be outmoded definitions of the concepts of 'field' and 'fieldwork', it seems to me that one of the critical ideas regarding the weight which fieldwork has carried and continues to carry for the practice of anthropology has much to do with anthropology's very survival. Indeed, the move to consolidate borders around the discipline in the interests of keeping it intact seems a plausible argument. As anthropology increasingly works at broad interdisciplinary levels, it seems that ensuring a separate identity from other related disciplines has become increasingly important. That is, as disciplinary boundaries dissolve and more and more overlap occurs between disciplines, anthropology has responded in part by re-establishing its own borders and reasserting what makes it unique from other disciplines. Fieldwork, one of the central enduring symbols of that which defines anthropological work, seems to be the target of this effort.

Moreover, tightening the reins around the meaning of fieldwork and promoting a 'traditional' understanding of the concept, at a time when contemporary anthropologists are increasingly working in unconventional places, is important not only in terms of disciplinary identity but also in terms of power. The move to police borders is not unique to anthropology, as is evident and has been discussed in many other contexts, i.e. the geopolitical scene, for example, which offers many instances of an intensification and politicization of cultural identities due to a changing world system (Hall, 1987; Mercer, 1990). What is relevant is the powerful system of valuation it upholds in the discipline and the epistemological and methodological repercussions of the move to consolidate boundaries. By this I mean that holding past examples of 'exotic' fieldwork as norms against which to compare the authenticity and value of contemporary research efforts powerfully affords a way for the discipline to differentiate between what are 'real' fields, 'real' fieldwork and, in turn, 'real' anthropology. This comes at a curious time since, on the one hand, broader anthropological discourses have considerably opened up possibilities for study, while, on the other, the discipline sets up its borders in restrictive and exclusionary ways.

My research 'close to home' and with people who do not fit the category 'exotic' is one example of a study that is caught in this crossfire. Despite efforts to argue that children are a group of people who are vital to understanding the conditions of a rapidly changing world, as are adults, and my arguments that my field site 'close to home' had all the features of 'real' fieldwork, i.e. it was marked by travel, physical displacement, intensive dwelling in an unfamiliar setting away from home, an experience of initiation, and movement in and out of a field, my 'field' continues to lie outside the bounds of what is deemed to be acceptable.

In a recent collection, Gupta and Ferguson (1997: 13) discuss this differentiating process in the context of an evaluative hierarchy in place in the discipline. Specifically, they argue that there is a 'hierarchy of purity of field sites' operating in anthropology:

> After all, if 'the field' is most appropriately a place that is 'not home', then some places will necessarily be more 'not home' than others, and hence more appropriate, more 'fieldlike'. All ethnographic research is thus done 'in the field', but some 'fields' are more equal than others – specifically those that are understood to be distant, exotic, and strange.

This hierarchy of field sites manifested itself in a number of ways in my experience. First, the strength and appeal of the anthropological 'journey elsewhere', and the notion of 'rite of passage' were clear features of the rhetoric which surrounded me in graduate school. The contradiction I experienced was that on the one hand, my reworking of the concepts of 'field' and 'fieldwork' was encouraged while, on the other, there was an expectation that I would nevertheless attempt to fit my work into a framework of what constitutes 'real' anthropology. This became especially clear while writing my dissertation. In an effort to facilitate this 'fit' within the parameters of what constitutes 'real' anthropology, i.e. carrying out fieldwork in a 'real' field site, and, in turn, to bolster my claim for anthropological legitimacy for the study, I decided to provide a methodology chapter typically found in 'traditional' ethnographies. In the chapter, I described the ethnographic site and provided details regarding research methods. In order to point out the irony of such a chapter in view of my 'geographic area', I explicitly stated that the chapter appeared in part because of an overarching concern for anthropological legitimacy that continually informed and compelled the writing of the dissertation.

In a different context, the hierarchy of field sites persisted as I moved into academia after graduate school. Despite the positive encouragement that the research I was carrying out was innovative and that it offered both a challenge to the kinds of anthropological knowledge and subjects that are worthy of anthropological attention, outside of the confines of graduate school, I have found my efforts to be received quite unevenly. At a professional level, I have found options restricted because of my choices of 'field' and 'fieldwork'. The idea that the bounded 'field' continues to mark what is authentic anthropology, for example, becomes most obvious when one looks at how job searches proceed. When applying for academic positions, 'geographic area' continues to be a key marker of a desirable job candidate. As a graduate student, I was aware that the research that I had designed clearly challenged many of the conventional practices of fieldwork and set me on a collision course with proponents of a strict disciplinary history. However, what I have been unprepared for has been how slowly change has occurred and how stern the discipline.

Strategies

Providing a disclaimer for a chapter in the dissertation was one of the strategies I used to 'play with' disciplinary conventions. Another strategy, intended to assert the authenticity of my study, was to include a 'story' that would approximate the arrival stories I had read in countless other ethnographies. I wanted to ensure that there was a sense of coming and going to and from 'the field' in my research. The story, which I decided to include in my ethnography long before my fieldwork began, would, I thought, be a way to authenticate and authorize the material. By including it, I argued that I could point to the irony and constructedness of such a tale in light of the research with children in an urban Canadian context, while at the same time guaranteeing a certain degree of anthropological legitimacy for my research. Playing with the concepts of 'field' and 'geographic area' in my version of an 'arrival' story, however, proved to be more complicated than first envisaged.

At times, I was cautioned to rethink my ironic use of the arrival story, noting that this move only served to reinforce the idea of discrete and separate places. Some of my fellow graduate students thought that my preoccupation with asserting the authenticity of my study was unnecessary in light of how much more open and flexible the discipline had become. However, these colleagues also confidently called themselves 'Latin Americanists', 'Africanists' and so on. Others, who had designed fieldwork that would return them to their home countries, compared their 'fields' with mine by drawing on the similarities of experiencing fieldwork in urban or rural contexts despite different locations in the world. They too felt that my concerns that my work be viewed as 'real' were unfounded. I was encouraged to continue to challenge disciplinary boundaries set up by expectations of 'real' fieldwork.

Despite their reassurances, however, I included not only an arrival story in my ethnography but also one of departure. By including the arrival story, I believed I could argue that my research contained all of the necessary features that constituted 'real' fieldwork, only defined in different ways.

Arrivals and departures

At first, it looked to me like an ordinary shoe box. I listened as the friend who had prepared the package explained each of the items she had included in the box. I was to take it with me to 'the field'. Mystery novels, she said, would help me through the long hours of waiting for informants to arrive, or for days when interviews would be cancelled because of inclement weather. Her experience of fieldwork was filled with time to wait and read; she seemed certain I would experience the same. Along with the assortment of mystery novels, the box also contained treats that I might indulge in while 'away'.

The box was an important gift, an assurance from a trusted friend that my fieldwork would be like any other 'real' fieldwork. At least, this was my interpretation of the gesture. It signified for me that I would be put to the test, as had other fieldworkers, to endure the typical features of this endeavour – long hours waiting for something to happen, rained-off interviews, homesickness, deprivation and so on. The box sat on my bookshelf for the duration of my field research, a constant reminder of my continual departure and return from the field.

The field, home and back again

Enforcing 'traditional' fieldwork as an archetype against which other kinds of fieldwork are measured enables the discipline to wield a great deal of power regarding the kinds of sites and subjects that are deemed to be legitimate anthropological ones. It serves to uphold the notion that the 'field' remains separate from the 'home' in 'real' anthropological fieldwork. In turn, this conceptualization sets up other relationships between what is valued/devalued and what is considered work. Home, and work that takes place close to home, is made distinct from work that takes place 'away'. For feminist anthropologists, questions of valuation and epistemology that are linked to definitions of 'home' have been key to debates for some time. Specifically, the continued devaluation of fieldwork undertaken 'at home' and the effort to expose and disrupt systems of devaluation of certain kinds of knowledge and practice in the discipline has been a challenge for feminist anthropologists. My focus on children, a group of people whose voices have largely been devalued and ignored, was meant to echo the earlier attempts of feminist anthropologists who worked to reinsert the voices and experiences of women into the anthropological record by interrogating the link between power and the exclusion of certain kinds of knowledge, particular kinds of work, and different ways of 'knowing'.

With regard to undertaking fieldwork at home, the difficulty in differentiating between work 'at home' and 'away' became most apparent when comparisons were drawn between my field site and those of my graduate student cohort. In graduate school, I was one of several people who conducted fieldwork locally. Some international students made up this cohort of fieldworkers. For them, conducting fieldwork locally was, in fact, fieldwork 'abroad'. Other international students returned 'home' to carry out their research – to India and Indonesia, for example. Rarely was the distinction between 'home' and 'away' explicitly discussed. Yet in my case in particular, the inability to delimit a 'geographic area' became a predicament.

As I reflect on these diverse fieldwork experiences and the increasingly interdisciplinary interests of graduate students, as well as shrinking grants and financial support for research, I am concerned by the power that the concept of 'field' retains, especially in light of a 'place' like Canada. Most importantly, it is a term linked with the status and importance of research and its position in academia. It fuels my concern to query the source of the power to define the terms.[3]

My research experience was not marked solely by 'leaving for the field' for an extended period of time. Mine was the experience of continually coming and going to and from the field, to the point where, at times, the field became indistinguishable from home. While this posed several problems that needed to be resolved during the research process, it had never been addressed or discussed prior to leaving for the field. Blurring field/home boundaries was further enhanced by technologies that facilitated these crossings by linking my field with home, home with other fields and my home with other homes. For example, my fax machine connected me with a supervisor overseas, and telephone calls at home connected me with key informants after I had left the field. At times, I did not need to physically travel to the field to be able to reach my 'key' informants or for them to reach me. Furthermore, my subjects were not restricted by place either. Apart from the songs and stories I collected from the children with whom I worked, friends and colleagues would send their own tapes of children from their field sites in Tonga, Ecuador and from children living on the Navajo reserve for me to compare with my Canadian collection. My point is that while the concept of journey was evident in my fieldwork, it was certainly not a conventional one. Keeping the field and home conceptually separate and distinct in practice, a key marker of 'real' fieldwork, was impossible for me. At first, I attempted to overlook the difficulties I was experiencing in negotiating these different sites because I took it to be a sign of failure at some level. As my research progressed, however, I came to the understanding that in fact, the difficulties were an important part of the process of research itself. Indeed, the interruptions experienced in practice became part of the resulting ethnography.

Working in reconfigured fields: multiple roles in experiences of fieldwork

In discussing her research with youth in inner-city Montreal and the Outaouais region of western Quebec, Amit-Talai (1994: 191) writes about the challenges of fieldwork 'close to home':

> ethnographic research in one's home city is not easier than research far from home. It can be much harder, demanding a degree of self-consciousness that anthropologists may aspire to everywhere but find especially acute in the role conflicts generated by this kind of ethnographic fieldwork.

There can be no doubt that a juggling act is involved when conducting research in the same city where one lives. The situation necessitates continuous shifting according to whether one is at home, at work, in the field, or dealing with family circumstances. Unlike traditional fieldwork that operates from a space largely removed from everyday situations, relationships and routines, fieldwork undertaken 'at home' involves adding another dimension to the network of one's established social relationships and commitments once fieldwork begins. Recently, many researchers have commented on the complexities of this facet of research 'at home' and have offered ways to carry out studies in these complicated situations. Hoodfar (1994), for example, discusses the 'stressful and somewhat schizophrenic existence' she experienced while doing research in Montreal when compared with the field experiences she had in Cairo. She points to the difficulty of the situation, stating that (p. 221):

> I have often regretted not being engaged in research in a situation where my only contacts were my informants, where I could dissociate myself from my normal day-to-day role in order to negotiate a more effective role in my field research. . . . It is clear that doing research in the vicinity of where one lives ('anthropology at home') has important implications for one's research and for the researcher.

In my experience, the instability of the ground that marks doing 'anthropology at home' became a constant feature in carrying out fieldwork in an urban site. In turn, coherence in the role of fieldworker was not part of my experience. Rather, my fieldworker persona was made up of a series of partial identities that abruptly shifted according to changes in context. For example, while I worked in the field for several days of the week, I also kept in contact with my home department. At times, predicaments that arose in the field were discussed immediately with members of my advisory committee. I recall the meeting I requested with one adviser after spending one month in the field. The fieldwork was more stressful than I had imagined and I feared that I was not 'getting any data', i.e. children's songs and stories. Self-doubt and insecurity regarding ideas about 'children's cultural production' were put at ease as my adviser guided me through what, I learned later, was a typical stage of research. I had the luxury of the immediacy of the academic context for support. On the other hand, while this immediacy was beneficial in this instance, at other times it made the fieldwork more difficult because of the continuous monitoring of my progress that resulted from the contact.

Second, because of my presence at the university some of the time, colleagues who forgot that I was in the field expected me to remain actively involved in academic and social networks, something that would be impossible to expect from those conducting fieldwork 'away'.

Thus I would argue that one of the difficulties peculiar to research conducted close to home is that one is never able to be completely 'in the field', nor is one ever completely able to 'leave the field'. In my experience, it was precisely my presence in the midst of this swirl of sites, and the difficulty of sustaining the various positionings that doing fieldwork 'at home' entailed, that led me to directly question the veracity of traditional anthropological criteria to define 'the field' by geographic location, a language different from one's own and a clear separation of home from the field.

Third, the ethnographer is not the only one caught in the move to constantly negotiate this shifting ground. The people with whom we are working in these urban environments are involved in complex movements of their own. For example, even though the subjects of my recent research were children and young people, their lives were very complex. Each person was a member of various groups – families, community centre programme members, peer groups according to changing contexts including schools and neighbourhoods – that demanded of their time in different ways. The logistics, therefore, in carrying out research in this kind of dynamic urban landscape are considerable and challenging. Again, I have found that this facet of fieldwork 'at home' has been left largely unacknowledged.

Conclusions

Narrow definitions of the concepts of field and fieldwork have been used in the discipline to consolidate boundaries around anthropology as a way to distinguish it from other disciplines. Redrawing these sharp lines allows the discipline considerable authority against a landscape of changing political and cultural conditions to reassert what is 'real' anthropology. In turn, it also reinforces what is considered to be 'real' anthropological knowledge.

For contemporary anthropologists increasingly working 'close to home', at interdisciplinary levels, and with subjects who do not fit into the category 'exotic', these disciplinary moves are of concern because of the discriminatory and exclusionary power they hold. In this chapter,

I have argued that reconfiguring and critically reworking the concepts of 'field' and 'fieldwork' so that the naturalness of these categories is exposed is vital to the life of anthropology into the twenty-first century. In short, retaining a spatialized understanding of the field imposes limitations and biases that are unproductive in contemporary anthropological research contexts.

In focusing this discussion through my own research experiences with children in an urban Canadian location, I have argued that the urban field site is not only a setting for research but a research issue itself. The practice of conducting fieldwork in the vicinity of where one lives presents many unique challenges that have been left unacknowledged. In unsettling the boundaries around some of the concepts that have been central to the identity of the discipline, my intention has been to examine some of these challenges facing anthropology as it moves into the twenty-first century.

Furthermore, I have been interested in demonstrating that fieldwork carried out in a locality that is not geographically distant allows one to return, as Visweswaran notes, more 'profoundly' home just as an experience that is organized around a metaphor of travel affords this opportunity. The physical act of travel to another place does not guarantee cultural understanding or illumination on its own. Rather, the unique insights and experiences that are gained through fieldwork are apparent despite the actual physical distance travelled. In my research experiences, the field 'close to home' allows as unique an experience as one situated in a place far away. And, more importantly, once the restrictions of this metaphor of travel are lifted, 'home once interrogated is a place we have never before been' (ibid., 1994: 113).

For my part, I have attempted to reconceptualize the terms of 'home' and 'away' through my experience in a particular kind of 'field'. It is a field in which I am at once 'at home' and 'away'. In my understanding, these are not mutually exclusive terms; the lines between the two are not always distinct.

Thus I conclude that my fieldwork was often an 'exotic' experience. In undertaking this work, my understanding of cultural difference has not been as an essence that can only belong to people defined in terms of 'other' places and time. Rather, difference emerges from the movements and activities of individuals and groups in local situations who continuously draw from and negotiate their places in an increasingly interconnected world. As Clifford states (1988: 14), 'one no longer leaves home confident of finding something radically new, another

time or space. Difference is encountered in the adjoining neighbor-
hood, the familiar turns up at the ends of the earth.'

Notes

1 The author wishes to thank Vered Amit for her helpful insights and critical
  reading of drafts of this chapter.
2 The conference 'Anthropology and "the field": Boundaries, Areas, and
  Grounds in the Constitution of a Discipline', was organized by Stanford
  University and the University of California, Santa Cruz and held in February
  1994 to discuss issues about anthropological reconfigurations of the concept
  of 'the field'.
3 These issues are discussed by Margaret Rodman in 'Second Site', a paper
  presented at the American Anthropology Association Meeting, Atlanta,
  Georgia, 1994.

References

Amit-Talai, Vered (1994) Urban Pathways: The Logistics of Youth Peer
  Relations. In Vered Amit-Talai and Henri Lustiger-Thaler (eds) *Urban
  Lives. Fragmentation and Resistance*. Toronto: McClelland and Stewart Inc,
  pp. 183–205.
Appadurai, A. (1988) Introduction: Place and Voice in Anthropological
  Theory. *Cultural Anthropology* 3(1): 16–20.
—— (1990) Disjuncture and Difference in the Global Cultural Economy.
  Public Culture 2(2): 1–24.
Bhabha, Homi (1994) *The Location of Culture*. New York: Routledge.
Caputo, Virginia (1996) Musical Matters: Performativity, Gender and Culture
  in an Anthropology of Urban Canadian Childhoods. Ph.D. Dissertation,
  York University.
Clifford, James (1988) *The Predicament of Culture: Twentieth-century
  Ethnography, Literature and Art*. Cambridge, MA: Harvard University Press.
—— (1992) Traveling Cultures. In Lawrence Grossberg, Cary Nelson and
  Paula A. Treichler (eds) *Cultural Studies*. New York and London: Routledge,
  pp. 96–116.
Gupta, Akhil and James Ferguson (1992) Beyond 'Culture': Space, Identity,
  and the Politics of Difference. *Cultural Anthropology* 7(1): 6–23.
—— (eds) (1997) *Anthropological Locations. Boundaries and Grounds of a Field
  Science*. Berkeley: University of California Press.
Hall, Stuart (1987) Minimal Selves. In *The Real Me: Postmodernism and the
  Question of Identity*. London: ICA Documents, No. 6, pp. 44–46.
Hoodfar, Homa (1994) Situating the Anthropologist: A Personal Account of
  Ethnographic Fieldwork in Three Urban Settings: Tehran, Cairo, and
  Montreal. In Vered Amit-Talai and Henri Lustiger-Thaler (eds) *Urban*

Lives. Fragmentation and Resistance. Toronto: McClelland and Stewart Inc., pp. 206-226.

Kaplan, Caren (1990) Reconfigurations of Geography and Narrative: A Review Essay. *Public Culture* 3(1): 25.

Mercer, Kobena (1990) Welcome to the Jungle: Identity and Diversity in Post-modern Politics. In J. Rutherford (ed.) *Identity, Community, Culture and Difference*. London: Lawrence and Wishart, pp. 43–71.

Said, Edward (1989) Representing the Colonized: Anthropology's Interlocutors. *Critical Inquiry* 15: 205–225.

Scott, David (1989) Locating the Anthropological Subject: Post-Colonial Anthropologists in Other Places. *Inscriptions*: 27.

Spivak, Gayatri Chakravorty (1990) *The Post-Colonial Critic: Interviews, Strategies, Dialogues*. New York: Routledge.

Visweswaran, Kamala (1994) *Fictions of Feminist Ethnography*. Minneapolis: University of Minnesota Press.

Chapter 3

Home field advantage?

Exploring the social construction of children's sports

Noel Dyck

This chapter examines certain advantages and problems associated with conducting social anthropological research 'at home'. While this practice has become increasingly common during the past twenty years, a subtle ambivalence concerning its legitimacy continues to reside within the discipline.[1] My purpose here is not to rehearse the general arguments offered in favour of conducting anthropological research where one normally lives.[2] The cumulative case already presented in support of this type of anthropological undertaking has, to my mind, been compelling. Yet having acknowledged this, I must confess to having experienced diffuse and unanticipated feelings of concern when anthropology began to seep out of the confines of an academic career and spill over into what had become part of my home life.

Briefly, in the wake of completing a doctorate, obtaining an academic appointment and becoming a father, there developed a tension between the time available for academic work and that required to share the responsibilities of maintaining a home and rearing children. During the early years of this new way of life I would dutifully arm myself with unread ethnographies or student papers before setting off to spend my share of time in providing transportation and waiting while our children attended music lessons, swimming classes and gymnastic programmes. But attempts to optimize use of waiting time by catching up on reading or dabbling in other tasks were rarely satisfying, let alone productive. Eventually I resolved to separate the demands of home and work and to pass the hours spent watching children's soccer matches or attending athletics competitions amiably and paternally. I began to look forward to these weekly outings and casual conversations with other parents in attendance as a welcome 'time out' from the rigours of departmental meetings and the routine of writing about relations between aboriginal peoples and national governments (cf. Dyck,

1985, 1991, 1997; Dyck and Waldram, 1993). In the absence of other volunteers I even assisted with coaching in soccer and athletics.

This congenial division of paternal and professional labours began to unravel during a children's track meet held one sunny summer weekend. During such meets medals are typically awarded to first, second and third place winners in each age- and gender-differentiated event. The presentation of medals occurs routinely and continuously throughout the meet, and winners tend either to stuff medals and ribbons into carrying cases or to hand them over to parents or friends for safekeeping before trundling off to their next athletic event. What caught my attention that particular afternoon was a man of approximately my age who was dressed for the hot weather, as were many other parents and coaches, in a pair of shorts, sandals and sports shirt. What seemed remarkable to me was that he also wore two gold medals around his neck along with an enormous smile. I was struck with a powerful impression that here was the father of a successful athlete who was acting almost as though he had won the medals himself.[3]

In the following days I related this incident to several people, including a mother with whom I shared a waiting room while our daughters took their weekly piano lessons. Recounting the story of the man with the medals around his neck, I reached my verdict-cum-punch line: that 'it was almost as though he had won the medals himself.' After politely chuckling at my story, she paused for a moment, and then observed thoughtfully, 'Well, in a way he had.'

With that comment she deftly connected an incident that had initially seemed humorous and somewhat bizarre to an ongoing discourse on parenting that I had – without fully recognizing that I was doing so – been sharing with her and with other parents in serial fashion during the previous months. What I had viewed simply as friendly 'small talk' that made the time pass pleasantly was revealed to be a rhetoric centrally concerned with the aspirations, sacrifices and values of parenting. Once this became apparent, my carefully nurtured partition between anthropology and time spent attending and helping with community sport activities for children vanished.

I started to scribble down occasional notes, to cut out interesting articles from local community newspapers and to listen more carefully to parents' talk, albeit in ways that followed no particular plan beyond that of better understanding a field of personal interest and involvement. In due course this shifting posture led me to inflict my stories and tentative analyses upon those anthropological colleagues who exhibited even the slightest interest in sports or child rearing. Finally, after a protracted period of struggling with doubts about the merits of proceeding any further, I decided to apply for funding and to transform what had been an enjoyable personal pastime into the focus of professional enquiry. By steps and stages, I had become involved in conducting anthropological research at playing fields and other locales of community sport that had become more or less comfortable and taken-for-granted parts of my life.

This process of moving from the pursuit of a personal interest to embarking upon formal study took several years longer to accomplish than it ought to have done. The delay resulted from difficulties encountered in coming to terms with an inchoate set of misgivings raised by the prospect of doing 'serious' anthropological research 'at home'. If one agrees with Cohen (1994), Crick (1992), Okely (1992) and others that what goes on inside the researcher is an important form of anthropological data, it becomes significant to identify and understand sources of both attraction and ambivalence in doing anthropology, wherever it is conducted.

In this chapter I pose a set of general questions about the practice of anthropology at home. What might 'home' comprise in any given situation and which advantages and problems arise when one transforms home into a 'field' of study? How can anthropologists reconcile 'participation' with 'observation' while conducting ethnographic research in places and on issues with which they are personally involved? Which considerations should govern what, where and how we write about relationships and activities that may involve relatives, neighbours and consociates? Finally, how might contemporary social anthropology encourage and facilitate studies of 'home', wherever and whatever this may be, by individual anthropologists and by our students? These questions are examined in terms of an ongoing ethnographic study of the social construction of children's sports within adult organized community leagues for boys and girls in the metropolitan area of British Columbia. The broader concern, however, is with how social anthropologists can identify and resolve the doubts and difficulties that still stand in the way of our discipline becoming a means for comprehending a rapidly changing world made up of 'ourselves' as well as 'others'.

Finding the 'field'

Beyond discussions of the relative methodological merits of 'outsider' and 'insider' anthropology (Aguilar, 1981) and the contention that either can be conducted on a more or less equal footing (Segalen and

Zonabend, 1987), we encounter searching examinations of possible discontinuities between anthropological endeavour and the types of accounts that our subjects produce about their own lives and relationships. Strathern (1987: 16) argues that in order to ascertain whether or not an anthropologist is truly working at home it is necessary to determine if it is the case that investigator and the investigated are equally at home with the premises about social life that underpin anthropological enquiry. Identifying auto-anthropology as anthropology carried out in the social context that produced it, Strathern directs our attention to the crucial matter of the presence or absence of cultural continuity between the products of the anthropologist's labours and what people in the society being studied produce by way of accounts themselves (ibid.: 17). Balancing the claim that anthropology conducted at home might be said to be more reflexive and to provide greater understanding than 'outsider' anthropology with a less flattering possibility that such work may alternatively reveal anthropology to be merely mystifying the commonplace and revealing little more than what everyone already knew, Strathern concludes that auto-anthropology is likely to have a limited distribution (ibid.). Presumably, the unstated message is that ethnographers working on topics situated 'very near to home', who nonetheless wish to communicate with a broader anthropological readership, should be prepared to cast their studies in terms of ethnographic objectives and professional discourses that should be expected to be distinct from those employed locally.

Although not specifically addressing the practice of anthropology at home, Hastrup (1992) identifies a set of concerns central to such practice. Fieldwork in the postmodern condition, she notes, is no longer carried out 'from the door of one's tent' but instead ensues out of confrontation and dialogue between two parties engaged in a joint production of selfness and otherness (ibid.: 118). Arguing that 'othering' is an essential part of anthropological practice, Hastrup observes that subjects of anthropological enquiry have their own self-referential discourse and projects of self-realization that exist alongside ethnographic writing and the anthropological project of self-transcendence (ibid.: 121). While both subject and anthropologist are engaged through their dialogue and interaction in a joint creation of selfness and otherness, Hastrup contends that the ethnographic project systematically violates the 'other's' project:

> However much we replace the monologue with dialogue the discourse remains asymmetrical, like the languages involved. The

purpose of ethnography is to speak about something for some-
body. It implies contextualization and reframing. At the autobiographical level ethnographers and informants are equal; but at
the level of the anthropological discourse, their relationship is
hierarchical. It is our choice to encompass their stories in our
narratives. We select the quotations and edit the comments.

(ibid.: 122)

Strathern's reckoning of the limitations of auto-anthropology and
Hastrup's rendering of the conceptual violence inherent in fieldwork
offer serious cautions to an anthropologist contemplating ethnographic
research at home. Yet both seem to assume a necessary opposition
between the purposes and terms of home and anthropology as well as
a relatively clear delineation of the boundaries between the two. While
this may sometimes be the case, I am not persuaded that it must invariably be so. My experience of drifting into the practice of anthropology
at home suggests that a substantial territory exists wherein what is
home and what is anthropology and, furthermore, which inscribes or
instructs the other is by no means certain. While one's disciplinary
training will certainly shape the organization of fieldwork, so too will
the ethnographer's combined life experience enable or inhibit particular
kinds of insights (Hastrup, 1992: 119; Thorne, 1993: 111). Accord-
ingly, it would seem appropriate not only to leave open for examination
the nature of the relationship between anthropology and home in any
ethnographic project, but also to take note of the particular ways in
which an individual ethnographer may incorporate different aspects of
home and anthropology in his or her performance as a positioned subject. Between the ostensibly diverging objectives of self-realization and
self-transcendence lies a common prerequisite task of self-identification.

If the notion of 'field' in anthropology has tended to stand for that
which is at least initially unknown, unfamiliar, unusual and challenging,
then 'home' might be taken to represent that which is, conversely,
known, familiar, routine and more or less comfortable. Of course,
field and home also revolve around a spatial metaphor characterized
by externality and distance from one's own society, on the one hand,
and a sense of personal identification with a social setting, on the
other.[4] The people of the field are 'others' while, presumably, the
denizens of home are 'us'. According to this admittedly simplified
schema, the field constitutes a place for ethnographic enquiry while
home may perhaps be taken for granted, at least with regard to

establishing analytical and research priorities. In practice, however, where and what comprises 'home' and 'us' for an individual ethnographer may be less than obvious, and thus needs to be considered.

Born in Canada, I have lived in the Lower Mainland of British Columbia for over two decades. Sport has been a continuing interest since childhood, first as an athlete and player of team sports, later as a fan of professional and then amateur sport, intermittently as a sports official and finally as a coach. My ethnographic incursion into children's sport has drawn not only upon the memories that I, as an adult, carry of my own childhood experience, but also my subsequent transition into parenthood. Involvement in children's sports has accompanied personal participation in the realm of domesticity, family relations and the public organization of childhood, areas which for me were not initially matters of sociological interest but rather an intimate space that I and members of my family were sharing with neighbours, friends and consociates. By all of these measures my involvement in and understanding of children's sports in British Columbia could be readily classified as belonging to the personal and domestic part of my life.

Yet at the same time that I entered into these activities, I was also intellectually engaged with relationships of coercive tutelage and resistance in the field of Western liberal-democratic states' administration of aboriginal peoples and their lands. Specifically, this involved investigating and analysing paternalistic bureaucratic systems that were founded upon the presumed need to deliver aboriginal peoples from the stigma and vulnerability, poverty and misery associated with aboriginality in the European mind (Dyck, 1991). The ostensible goal of such systems of state tutelage has been to reshape aboriginal peoples 'for their own good'. In retrospect, it is not difficult to recognize how certain parallels in relations between federal Indian agents and Canadian aboriginal peoples served to direct my attention somewhat uncomfortably to the tutelary purposes of parents and other adults in shaping the form of children's sports in my own suburban community. While these insights may be readily linked to my anthropological training and experience, it is not apparent to me that the means by which I learned to make sense of aboriginal peoples' relations with national governments are fundamentally unlike those by which I have begun to identify the processes by which adults such as myself go about the business of constructing children's sports. Indeed, what was once strange and difficult to grasp concerning aboriginal peoples' dealings with national governments has in time become analytically explicable, publishable in anthropological outlets, and even of interest to some aboriginal readers and governmental officials. Why should it be otherwise when I turn my attention to the organization of children's sports in my own community?

Constructing children's sports

As I began to take a scholarly interest in children's sporting activities I was surprised to discover just how little studied and poorly understood were certain aspects of what was for me being transformed into an emerging field of enquiry. The greatest bulk of recent academic publications on sport appear to have been authored by sports psychologists and kinesiologists who seem driven to engineer new ways of enhancing athletic performance without much concern, beyond that dictated by considerations of bio-mechanics, for whether athletes might be children or adults. Within the sociological literature on sport in contemporary society there has long been a tendency to take for granted children's involvement in organized sporting activities. There are, of course, exceptions to this pattern, including Gary Alan Fine's study of pre-adolescent boys' involvement in little league baseball in the United States (1987). In Fine's study, however, attention is given primarily to interaction among the boys, their dealings with their coaches, and the athletic and social action that occurs on or immediately around the field of play. Left largely in the background in this study were the parents and other adults who more or less regularly attended ball games and supported little league baseball.

No less surprising was the discovery that various provincial and national sports organizations that oversee amateur sport in Canada have at best an anecdotal understanding of the nature and extent of adult involvement in organized sports for children. Although these organizations collect precise statistics concerning the number of child and youth athletes as well as coaches registered with their member clubs, they take little systematic account of the substantial forms of parental support and involvement upon which community sports clubs for children depend so heavily. A basic survey of local sports clubs that I mounted in order to obtain a better measure of various dimensions of organized community sports for children in one suburban area of the Greater Vancouver Regional District (Dyck and Wildi, 1993) revealed that almost 15,000 of the 40,500 children under the age of 19 in these communities took part in community sports activities organized outside of school programmes. They represented just under half of all children in the district between the ages of 5 and 18.

The minimum cost for personal sports equipment for these child and youth athletes amounted to some $1.6 million per season, and the forty-five clubs in the district (which together offered twenty different sports[5]) had operating budgets during the 1992 to 1993 season of $1.9 million. These clubs held an additional $1.2 million in accumulated capital equipment assets, not counting the extensive municipal sport facilities (in the form of playing fields, gymnasia, swimming pools, ice rinks and other facilities provided by local governments) used by these clubs for practices, competitions and tournaments.

In addition to these resources some 3,500 adults served as club officials, coaches, managers, referees and judges. Few received any form of payment for their efforts, let alone expenses to cover incidental costs for local travel. Although it was not possible to obtain detailed figures concerning the numbers of hours contributed by these volunteer officials, it is safe to conclude that a hundred hours per season per volunteer comprises a decidedly conservative estimate of the time donated to organized children's sports activities in this locality. Nor does this figure make any allowance for the support of parents who routinely drive their children to and from practices and competitions, who watch and cheer from poolside or sidelines, and who participate in fund-raising activities mounted by ambitious coaches. The extent of overall investment in children's sports, including not only actual financial expenditures but also the enormous amount of time volunteered by adult sports officials and parents, speaks to the significance invested in these activities by adults. While several sports bodies subsequently appended copies of the survey findings to their applications for further government resources, the extremely limited nature of their knowledge of the extent of support activities that occur beneath their jurisdictional 'umbrellas' was remarkable.

As Finnegan's (1989) study of music-making in an English city demonstrates, anthropology possesses a capacity to identify, survey and explore forms of social and cultural activity that tend to be overlooked or taken for granted within contemporary Western societies. Moving beyond the statistical findings reported above, ethnographic studies of community sports for children can take note of not merely the outer dimensions of the organizational apparatus created by adults but also the diverse and sometimes contradictory interests and rationales that typically proclaim that all of these activities are conducted 'for the kids'. The recent emergence of a vibrant anthropology of childhood has made signal contributions to interdisciplinary studies of childhood that have, in turn, worked to decentre the stifling paradigm of socialization that has long underpinned developmental psychology and much educational practice. Anthropologists studying children and young people have constructed an impressive corpus of ethnography and theory[6] that has been invaluable as I have laboured to obtain a comparative perspective on activities within which I was until recently involved almost exclusively as a participant.

Yet without prior personal involvement in the realm of children's sporting activities, I doubt that I would have been able to identify the pertinent social dimensions of parental involvement in this field of activity, let alone recognize the opportunities that these present for ethnographic research.[7] My biography as a parent participant in these activities had, among other things, afforded me a basic familiarity with the scale, complexity, intensity and contingency of community sports for children. These insights emerged out of personal experience that made visible and interesting a situation and set of relationships that would, in the absence of such non-professional involvement, likely have escaped my attention. The casual conversations that parents engage in while watching their sons or daughters take part in competitive matches or while waiting for them to emerge from practice sessions feature not only commentary upon the activities at hand but also discussions about other matters of common concern to parents. Moreover, aside from convening at scheduled practices, competitions and sporadically staged fund-raising events such as 'bottle drives', parents who become known to one another are sooner or later likely to meet each other in chance encounters while shopping for groceries or attending school events. In suburban communities where neighbours often know little about one another beyond first names, these kinds of child-centred relationships between adults can become the stuff of imagined forms of 'community'.[8] Relationships forged between parents who have endured a full season of cold and rainy afternoons standing on the sidelines while their children's soccer team has soared to victory or suffered repeated defeats can provoke a sense of camaraderie among otherwise diffuse collections of mothers and fathers. Community sports activities serve to foster friendships that may continue to operate away from athletic venues not only between children, but sometimes also between parents. Within these situationally specific contexts, imagined selves, identities and communities may be created, shared and enjoyed.[9]

Ethnographers are suitably prepared to map out such 'found' social fields and to tease out emerging analytical problems in ways that practitioners of other methodologies are not, in general, equipped to do. The frequently encountered serendipity of ethnographic fieldwork, where preliminary research plans are deftly adjusted to take account of phenomena unknown to or unappreciated by the ethnographer prior to commencing field research, has encouraged the development of such mapping abilities among anthropologists. This capacity to connect diverse and even contradictory discourses to patterned activities, institutional interests and personal relationships that span a variety of social realms is not widely distributed within the social sciences. Returning to my example, the significance of adults' involvement in constructing children's sports reaches beyond mere ethnographic endeavour. It is not just a matter of reporting that parents and other adults happen to spend a great deal of time in community sports for children. Indeed, recent global economic restructuring has led to a widespread reduction in the availability of resources to both formal and informal educational sectors (Persell, 1991). Thus the time and attention made available to child and youth athletes by adults who are neither their parents nor their schoolteachers occurs, so to speak, against the larger grain of relations between children and adults in contemporary societies. What is more, activities such as community sports provide the children who partake of these with a markedly different interactional repertoire than others who are reported to be spending less and less time with adults or even in unsupervised play with other children (Fine and Mechling, 1991). These patterns may have significant implications for the social skills and future life chances of children who have (and those who have not) been able to take part in community activities which feature substantial participation by a range of adults. By the same token, the manner in which the world given to children is formulated primarily by adults raises other important questions about how activities for children are designed and managed, and how children learn to renegotiate various aspects of these activities (ibid.: 59).

The sensitivity of anthropology to symbolic dimensions is fundamental if one seeks to connect the conceptually diverse but ethnographically overlapping concerns of sport and parenting. The structured competition and fantasy essential to sport is not only a vehicle that can be used for selling products to television viewers; it also provides a familiar idiom and unobtrusive medium to parents who may be quietly anxious to test and, if necessary, reshape the abilities of their progeny in order to prepare them for eventual full entry into an adult world that is said to be becoming increasingly competitive.

More could be said about the ethnographic and intellectual potential offered by the study of children's sport activities, but my underlying purpose is not to justify the significance of this particular field of research that I have happened into. Rather, I wish to suggest that a wide variety of research projects can be encountered at home, if one is so inclined. Moreover, these undertakings need not be considered as pallid replacements for more traditional and 'legitimate' field research that ought to be conducted by ourselves and our students 'overseas' except for the drying up of required financial support. Anthropology conducted at home can afford challenges and opportunities that sustain the practice of our discipline at a time when great uncertainty exists within universities concerning the future of the social sciences. Ethnographic research conducted in home fields can demonstrate the intellectual and practical contributions that anthropology can make to our own societies and communities at a juncture when the relevance of every discipline is being called into question. What is more, this can be done without remaking the discipline into a derivative form of qualitative sociology or popular culture precisely by retaining the comparative disposition, if not the empiricist illusions, that have long been central to the practice of social anthropology (Holy, 1987).

I do not, however, wish to suggest that only an insider could conduct field research in the particular setting that I have presented here, although the dispersed and intermittent nature of contact between parents would make it difficult to observe or take part in parental encounters without the investment of considerable time and effort. Nor would it be easy for an anonymous outsider to lurk on the margins of children's activities without attracting the attention of vigilant parents. It would be quite feasible for an ethnographer to arrange to interview parents, but even here I suspect that the advantage would go to one who was also a parent. Knowing what I now know about adults and the social construction of children's sports I would feel relatively confident of being able to mount a study of these relations in another community, and perhaps even another country, where I had no personal involvement or known history of participation that might hinder my investigations. Whether I would be able to achieve access to as broad a range of situations and conversations the second time around would remain to be seen. But why replicate an investigation that would demand substantial time in order to cover ground already traversed, however slowly, in the course of being a parent and a coach? While the possibility of conducting comparative work on the issues and relationships that I have been concerned with in recent years is attractive in many ways, any notion that such work would have to be carried out 'far away' and on 'others' to transform the original undertaking into legitimate anthropological endeavour would be little more than a continuation of an exoticist inclination within the discipline.

'Us' and 'Them'?

Along with the opportunities offered by the prospect of conducting anthropology at home rest a series of methodological challenges, many of which have already been identified and discussed within the literature. Frykman and Lofgren (1987: 3–4) have commented on the problem, not of getting into a new culture but of distancing oneself from far too familiar settings, while Callaway (1992) has noted the difficulties encountered when research information is derived through forming personal relationships. Finally, Young (1991: 26) has raised the troubling matter of whether studies of one's own community that seek to pursue an anthropology of the self constitute participant observation or espionage. These and other concerns delayed my decision to undertake a formal study of community sports activities for children.

The first and perhaps most challenging problem I wrestled with was how to manage the continuing transition from being just another parent to becoming anthropologically attentive to becoming an 'out' researcher. As I grew aware of the ethnographic salience and analytic interest attached to various forms of parental discourse, it became increasingly difficult for me to converse with parents and coaches about these matters in the normal course of events without feeling that I was, in some senses, acting like a spy. Short of wearing a cap with a label proclaiming 'anthropologist at work', I was initially unable to resolve this dilemma. In the short term I made it a rule not to initiate discussions or to steer instrumentally those started by others towards topics of anthropological interest. Instead I listened carefully and endeavoured to answer as non-committally as I could whenever parental talk traversed into areas of interest. I also resolved not to make any future reference in writing to any confidences or insights provided by the children with whom I worked unless this could be done without any chance of their identities being made known.

In the longer term, however, the only way to resolve these difficulties was to make it a formal study and to make my identity as a researcher known as widely as possible. Strategic distribution of copies of the survey of community sports clubs that I initiated (Dyck and Wildi, 1993) prompted a feature article (along with a photograph) in a community newspaper that not only revealed my interests but also invited children, parents and coaches who were willing to be interviewed to contact me at my university office.[10] Judging by the number of formal and informal responses that I received, I was assured that my announcement had been widely heard. Moreover, I learned that my previous participation in a series of educational television programmes on anthropology in contemporary life had long since alerted many parents and children to my employment as an anthropologist and my interest in the activities of everyday life. From this point on I was able to pursue various lines of enquiry more directly and vigorously through formally organized interviews.

Nevertheless, outside of these formal interviews the challenge remained of distinguishing between and balancing personal and professional interests in situations that involved individuals with whom I had formed long-standing relationships. My friends and family were certainly aware of my academic interest in the activities which we shared, yet what has often concerned me is that those who are not trained as ethnographers seldom have a fully informed appreciation of the manner in which ethnographers may inconspicuously monitor and mentally record conversations and casual interactions and link these to larger issues. In truth, I am not certain that it is either possible or desirable to 'turn off' my anthropological eye, ear or mind and still retain my integrity as an individual. But I have also been unwilling to use personal relationships surreptitiously for professional purposes. The resolution that I reached with myself was to exercise particular care and discretion in making any future ethnographic use of what I heard or saw in these personal situations. What this means is that there are particular stories that I have been told and incidents that I have seen that I have silently placed 'off the record' ethnographically. Nevertheless, my awareness of these matters enables me subsequently to openly investigate such practices in a manner that is professionally and personally appropriate.

A second set of concerns encountered in the course of formulating this research undertaking has involved the highly contested nature of the social territory that I am investigating. In the wake of the Ben Johnson 'doping' scandal at the 1988 Olympic Games in Seoul, the Canadian sports establishment was thrust into a series of long and laboured investigations into the premises and practices of Canadian sports. A task force on federal sports policy commissioned by the Minister of State for Fitness and Amateur Sport presented an astonishing report in 1992 which identified sport as the potential solution for virtually all of Canada's social, political and economic problems. For instance, the report claimed that:

> Sport helps Canadians face the reality of globalization by developing competitive skills and behaviours that are rapidly becoming essential to our economic survival. As well, on the economic side, sport is a multi-billion dollar industry providing jobs to thousands of Canadians. . . . For all these reasons, the Task Force concludes that sport – from recreational sport through organized competitive sport to high performance sport – must be promoted and accessible to all Canadians.[11]

Clearly, studies of the social organization of children's sports in Canada can expect to attract a highly interested and decidedly partisan audience of non-academic readers. The survey of community sports clubs that I conducted attracted considerable interest from a number of provincial sports organizations and netted me an invitation to address the annual conference of one of them. Municipal agencies charged with the responsibility of planning and operating leisure facilities have also been in touch. Their reading of that report seems to have identified me as being a supporter of organized sports. Their offers of logistical support so that I might conduct similar research in the field raises the possibility that any subsequent publications that feature what might be viewed as direct or indirect criticism of adults' involvement in organizing children's sports, not to mention of the Canadian sport bureaucracy, may evoke a similarly speedy but somewhat different type of response from these sources.

Aside from any connection to sport, studies of children, child rearing and parenting in contemporary Canadian society cannot remain untouched by the intense and complex debates currently raging on issues of children's rights, parental responsibilities and state monitoring of family relations. Although studies of children and child rearing are generally still not regarded as being especially important or prestigious within academic circles, children comprise a contested domain within North American society (Wolfe, 1991: 5). Parenting has become an increasingly self-conscious activity, as is witnessed by the broad range of parenting courses offered and attended within suburban communities. The caricatured figure of the sports parent who vicariously and instrumentally pursues athletic success through the achievements of his or her child is well known to Canadian parents, even by those who dispute the frequency with which such 'bad' sports parents actually appear in everyday life:

> Bad parents are such an extraordinary minority that hockey parents are a bit like heavy traffic, no one taking notice of the vast majority of cars that share the road and show courtesy, everyone fixating on the dramatic and unfortunately tragic. Sitting up in the stands, we also forget that most around us are well behaved, as embarrassed as we are by the boorish behaviour of some other parents.
>
> (MacGregor, 1995: 312)

Without pursuing these issues further, the existence of typologies featuring 'bad' and 'good' parents testifies to the highlighted moral dimensions seen to be underlying parenting activities. Ethnographers who choose to study what may initially be thought to be placid, quasi-domestic activities will be quickly apprised of the political concerns that permeate this sector. I suspect that on occasion my presence at certain sports events as a parent of participating athletes may have been complicated by the fact that I had already given a great deal more analytical attention to certain types of conflicting relationships than had many other parents. Sometimes, I suspect, it might have been easier for me and for my children had I been able to acknowledge only one way of looking at these situations and the larger issues that underpinned them.

A third area of concern appears for the anthropologist working at home when preparing research publications that may readily circulate as widely or even more widely outside of academia than within. The sensitivity with which reports, articles, books, or even public lectures or addresses may be met outside of social science circles has been referred to above. One way of protecting oneself from potential pitfalls may be to steadfastly avoid publishing in outlets or speaking in venues that can be readily penetrated by any but the keenest academic reader or listener. Presenting findings under the protective covering of abstract and densely thicketed theoretical sections offers one a strategy for discouraging outsiders from entering into or readily comprehending our discourses. Yet whatever safety is to be derived from this tactic, it amounts to a continuing denial of the eminently perceptive, useful and practical nature of social anthropological knowledge. This, of course, raises another debate that cannot be adequately entered into here, but suffice it to say that I believe social anthropology has much more to gain than it has to lose by experimenting with various means for sharing our insights and findings with diverse lay audiences.

Anthropologists working at home are typically faced with a range of options when seeking to publish their findings in academic journals, books and collected volumes. This is primarily a function of two factors. First, one's subjects are at or near the doorstep virtually year round, year in and year out. Moreover, the relative accessibility of anthropologists not only to research subjects but also to others who take an interest in one's findings increases the scale and number of requests that may be made of an ethnographer. For example, studies of children's sports activities are conducted within settings that are or might potentially be crowded by practitioners of a range of other disciplines including representatives from developmental psychology, education, cultural studies, leisure studies, the sociology of sport and of the family, and others. It is no more possible to master all the theoretical preferences, vast literatures and specific terminologies extant in each of these disciplines than it is to ignore pertinent works conducted by individual researchers in these different disciplines. Nevertheless, even limited participation in such emerging areas of interdisciplinary work creates reading demands but offers publication opportunities that create yet further demands. To prepare ethnographically based analyses for inclusion in non-anthropological social science publication sources is to take on the never-completed task of explaining the assumptions and justifying the legitimacy of anthropological methodology, theory and writing to non-anthropologists. Anthropologists working at home may even become tempted to steal away for longer or shorter periods into these interdisciplinary circles and discourses, particularly when recognition of the intrinsic interest of an area of research may be forthcoming there rather than within one's own discipline. Those working within the field of the anthropology of childhood are likely to be familiar with this experience.

The problem is not whether anthropologists working at home will be able to publish their works in academic outlets, for there is by now an impressive body of volumes, books and essays based upon such ethnographic research that have appeared both in anthropological and general social science journals or publication series. It is, instead, a question of whether the findings derived from anthropology practised at home will be accepted on their own merits and be permitted to make a substantial contribution to the discipline. Within another decade the vast majority of our students who go on to conduct independent ethnographic research are likely to do so close to home. Unless their teachers have given some thought to how this work can be facilitated and its findings incorporated back into the discipline, there will be a strong likelihood of slippage whereby talented and energetic young anthropologists take their interests and abilities to other more welcoming disciplinary homes.

This does not need to be the case. Of all the social sciences, anthropology is probably the best suited to foster and encourage a globally informed discourse not only of 'otherness' but also of widely varying yet by no means unique and incomparable 'usness'. Making any clear-cut distinction between 'us' and 'them' – just as between 'insider' and 'outsider' research – is, of course, a great deal more complex and problematic than any simple invocation of these categories may imply. The particularities of any given situation reveal subtly varying and sometimes overlapping degrees of 'insiderness' and 'outsiderness'. My point is not to draw greater attention to categorizations of 'us' and 'them', but rather to suggest that anthropologists, wherever they work, would do well to distinguish between activities and relationships of which they have a substantial understanding and those which they know primarily in terms of a reading knowledge. This approach tends to make 'home' far less a matter of birthplace or nationality than of continuing personal engagement in certain types of social aggregations, activities and relationships. Personal engagement of this sort may resemble fieldwork in many respects; where it differs is that it need not necessarily serve as a means to a professional end. It is an end in itself.

Indeed, maintaining a rationale for continued 'outsider' anthropology in the future will increasingly necessitate taking into account the kinds of anthropology that have been developed within the societies and communities into which overseas ethnographers seek to venture. The first step towards achieving this end will be to find ways of encouraging anthropologists to take on, write up, report and reflect on studies of diverse aspects of home. The comparative predispositions of the discipline offer an important means for beginning this task.

Conclusions

One final point remains: What costs will face the ethnographer who opts to study the ostensibly familiar and intimate settings of home? Will the real test of just how alienating anthropology at home may be and may even have to be to retain its disciplinary authenticity turn upon whether one can continue to inhabit the home space that has become the object of ethnographic inquiry? So far I can report that many, though not all of the activities that drew me to undertake formal study of adults' involvement in the social construction of children's sports have kept me involved as a coach, even after my children have graduated from these activities. What is more, I am less and less driven to record field observations, even though I continue to conduct associated types of research in this field. Thus I conclude not only that anthropology may be usefully informed by one's experience of home, but also that home can survive fieldwork, though not entirely unchanged. The broader implications of not only collecting fieldnotes in conjunction with living one's everyday life but also of organizing one's understanding and memory of larger and smaller parts of one's own life in explicitly analytical terms are not immediately transparent. The combining of the personal and the professional that inevitably occurs when we use our personal biographies and our pre-existing knowledge of our varying 'homes' as means for deciding what anthropologists might usefully investigate will create new and exciting opportunities for research and analysis. This course will also pose challenges and personal choices and costs that need to be recognized and reflected upon as essential components of such enterprise.

Doing fieldwork at home, around issues and through relationships in which one already had prior personal involvement, vividly underscores the role of biography in eliciting the research questions and fieldwork choices made by anthropologists. One's biography does not, however, simply invent these. What we select as issues to be investigated through ethnographic fieldwork and where we choose to conduct that fieldwork are choices that are shaped by an interaction between our personal life experiences, anthropological training and theoretical predilections. While a fair amount of attention has been given to the role of biography in shaping fieldwork interactions, too little attention has been paid to the role of biography in shaping our awareness of research possibilities.

These are important issues for anthropologists to address, whether working 'at home' or in areas and with peoples previously unknown to them. But it comprises an inescapable dilemma for an anthropologist working 'at home', for here the personal and the professional are inextricably intertwined at every step of the ethnographic and wider anthropological endeavour. The ongoing dynamic between them offers scope for detecting the possibilities for and merits of projects and issues that would otherwise be relatively hidden from the public and theoretical eye. But intertwining the personal and the professional also entails costs: the costs entailed in transforming friends and family into informants and, potentially, informants into friends and family.

Notes

1 See Ortner (1991: 185–186) for an example of such ambivalence.
2 See Jackson (1987) and Messerschmidt (1981) as just two examples for many such discussions.
3 This impression remained, even though I noted that he didn't have any pockets into which he might have put the medals. Since that time I have noticed other parents wearing their children's medals at athletics meetings.
4 A number of different approaches to and dimensions of 'home' have been analysed by feminist scholars. See e.g. Martin and Mohanty (1986); Rose (1993: 47–56), and Sarup (1994).
5 Each club offered one sport, with the exception of the local chapter of the Special Olympics which co-ordinated a number of sporting activities for its child and adult members.
6 See e.g. Amit-Talai and Wulff (1995); Clark (1995); James (1986, 1993); James and Prout (1990), and Thorne (1993).
7 I note also that Finnegan's (1989) interest in studying music-making in the city in which she worked and lived was based upon her own long-standing involvement in choral singing.
8 This is not the place to address the many problems posed by the slippery and diverse meanings attached to the notion of 'community' in anthropology as well as other social sciences. Suffice it to note here that what 'community' comprises, or is said to comprise, in any given situation reflects the definitional purposes of the definers rather than any general agreement inside or outside the discipline concerning the 'real' nature of 'community'.
9 I am referring here to Appadurai's (1991) provocative essay on the power of the imagined in social life.
10 I must acknowledge the good advice of Philip Moore at Curtin University for leading me in this direction.
11 Minister's Task Force on Federal Sport Policy, *Sport: The Way Ahead. An Overview of the Task Force Report*. Ottawa: Minister of State Fitness and Amateur Sport and Minister of Supply and Services Canada, 1992, pp. 9–11.

References

Aguilar, John L. (1981) Insider Research: An Ethnography of a Debate. In Donald A. Messerschmidt (ed.) *Anthropologists at Home in North America: Methods and Issues in the Study of One's Own Society*. Cambridge and New York: Cambridge University Press, pp. 15–26.

Amit-Talai, Vered and Helena Wulff (eds) (1995) *Youth Cultures: A Cross-cultural Perspective*. London and New York: Routledge.

Appadurai, Arjun (1991) Global Ethnoscapes. Notes and Queries for a Trans-national Anthropology. In Richard G. Fox (ed.) *Recapturing Anthropology: Working in the Present*. Santa Fe, New Mexico: School of American Research Press, pp. 191–210.

Callaway, Helen (1992) Ethnography and Experience: Gender Implications in Fieldwork and Texts. In Judith Okely and Helen Callaway (eds) *Anthropology and Autobiography*. ASA Monographs 29. London and New York: Routledge, pp. 29–49.

Clark, Cindy Dell (1995) *Flights of Fancy, Leaps of Faith: Children's Myths in Contemporary America*. Chicago and London: University of Chicago Press.

Cohen, Anthony P. (1994) *Self Consciousness: An Alternative Anthropology of Identity*. London and New York: Routledge.

Crick, Malcolm (1992) Ali and Me: An Essay in Street-Corner Anthropology. In Judith Okely and Helen Callaway (eds) *Anthropology and Autobiography*. ASA Monographs 29. London and New York: Routledge, pp. 174–192.

Dyck, Noel (ed.) (1985) *Indigenous Peoples and the Nation-State: Fourth World Politics in Canada, Australia and Norway*. St John's, Newfoundland: Institute of Social and Economic Research.

—— (1991) *What is the Indian 'Problem': Tutelage and Resistance in Canadian Indian Administration*. St John's, Newfoundland: Institute of Social and Economic Research, Memorial University of Newfoundland.

—— (1997) *Differing Visions: Administering Indian Residential Schooling in Prince Albert, 1867–1995*. Halifax: Fernwood Publishing.

Dyck, Noel and James B. Waldram (eds) (1993) *Anthropology, Public Policy and Native Peoples in Canada*. Montreal, Kingston, London and Buffalo: McGill-Queen's University Press.

Dyck, Noel and Grant Wildi (1993) *Creating Community Sport for Kids: A Survey of Community Sport Clubs and Associations for Children and Youth in Coquitlam, Port Coquitlam, and Port Moody British Columbia, During the 1992-3 Season*. Burnaby, British Columbia: Department of Sociology and Anthropology, Simon Fraser University.

Fine, Gary Alan (1987) *With the Boys: Little League Baseball and Preadolescent Culture*. Chicago, IL: University of Chicago Press.

Fine, Gary Alan and Jay Mechling (1991) Minor Difficulties: Changing Children in the Late Twentieth Century. In Alan Wolfe (ed.) *America at Century's End*. Berkeley, Los Angeles and London: University of California Press, pp. 58–78.

Finnegan, Ruth (1989) *The Hidden Musicians: Music Making in an English Town*. Cambridge: Cambridge University Press.

Frykman, Jonas and Orvar Lofgren (1987) *Culture Builders: A Historical Anthropology of Middle-Class Life*. New Brunswick, NJ and London: Rutgers University Press.

Hastrup, Kirsten (1992) Writing Ethnography: State of the Art. In Judith Okely and Helen Callaway (eds) *Anthropology and Autobiography*. ASA Monographs 29. London and New York: Routledge, pp. 118–133.

Holy, Ladislav (ed.) (1987) *Comparative Anthropology*. Oxford: Blackwell.

Jackson, Anthony (ed.) (1987) *Anthropology at Home*. ASA Monographs 25. London and New York: Routledge.

James, Allison (1986) Learning to Belong: The Boundaries of Adolescence. In Anthony P. Cohen (ed.) *Symbolising Boundaries: Identity and Diversity in British Cultures*. Manchester: Manchester University Press, pp. 155–170.

—— (1993) *Childhood Identities: Self and Social Relationships in the Experience of the Child*. Edinburgh: Edinburgh University Press.

James, Allison and and Allan Prout (1990) *Constructing and Reconstructing Childhood: Contemporary Issues in the Sociological Study of Childhood*. Basingstoke and New York: Falmer Press.

MacGregor, Roy (1995) *The Home Team: Fathers, Sons and Hockey*. Toronto: Viking Press.

Martin, Biddy and Chandra Talpade Mohanty (1986) Feminist Politics: What's Home Got to Do with It? In Teresa de Lauretis (ed.) *Feminist Studies, Critical Studies*. Bloomington: Indiana University Press, pp. 191–212.

Messerschmidt, Donald A. (ed.) (1981) *Anthropologists at Home in North America: Methods and Issues in the Study of One's Own Society*. Cambridge and New York: Cambridge University Press.

Okely, Judith (1992) Anthropology and Autobiography; Participatory Experience and Embodied Knowledge. In Judith Okely and Helen Callaway (eds) *Anthropology and Autobiography*. ASA Monographs 29. London and New York: Routledge, pp. 1–28.

Ortner, Sherry B. (1991) Reading America: Preliminary Notes on Class and Culture. In Richard G. Fox (ed.) *Recapturing Anthropology: Working in the Present*. Santa Fe, New Mexico: School of American Research Press, pp. 163–189.

Persell, Caroline Hodges (1991) Schools Under Pressure. In Alan Wolfe (ed.) *America at Century's End*. Berkeley, Los Angeles and London: University of California Press, pp. 283–297.

Rose, Gillian (1993) *Feminism and Geography: The Limits of Geographical Knowledge*. Minneapolis: University of Minnesota Press.

Sarup, Madan (1994) Home and Identity. In G. Robertson, M. Mash, J. Tickner, J. Bird, B. Curtis and T. Putnam (eds) *Travellers' Tales: Narratives of Home and Displacement*. London and New York: Routledge, pp. 93–104.

Segalen, Martine and Francoise Zonabend (1987) Social Anthropology and the Ethnology of France: The Field of Kinship and the Family. In Anthony Jackson (ed.) *Anthropology at Home*. ASA Monographs 25. London and New York: Routledge, pp. 109–119.

Strathern, Marilyn (1987) The Limits of Auto-anthropology. In Anthony Jackson (ed.) *Anthropology at Home*. ASA Monographs 25. London and New York: Routledge, pp. 16–37.

Thorne, Barrie (1993) *Gender Play: Girls and Boys in School*. New Brunswick, NJ: Rutgers University Press.

Wolfe, Alan (1991) Change From the Bottom Up. In Alan Wolfe (ed.) *America at Century's End*. Berkeley, Los Angeles and London: University of California Press, pp. 1–13.

Young, Malcolm (1991) *An Inside Job*. Oxford: Oxford University Press.

Chapter 4

Here and there

Doing transnational fieldwork[1]

Caroline Knowles

Introduction

In everyday discourse home and field assume and reinforce each other. Home is the life from which we venture forth and ply our trade, the interpretation of that which is not home – the field – a domain of work which in practice we distinguish from the rest of life by means of various devices. Home and field invoke the duality of belonging and alienation, familiarity and investigation, which implicitly function as fieldwork strategies. What home and field actually are, and how researchers organize the relationship between them, are issues worthy of further investigation. The positioning of home and field is particularly complicated in cases of multilocale lives and work, though as Marcus (1995) points out, fieldwork as it is traditionally practised is already multi-sited. What happens when the field is also home? While researchers have been quick to document the transnationalism of others (Basch *et al.*, 1994; Chamberlain, 1994; Garcia, 1994) they have been slow to reflect upon the impact of their own transnationalism on their research. What happens when here and there contain both home and field? What are the threads connecting life and work when researchers are themselves transnationals?

Fieldwork and the significance of here and there

Being there in the field is anthropology's central rite of passage (Gupta and Ferguson, 1992) and the field is traditionally conceptualized as a place in the anthropological imagination. An anthropological sense of place prioritizes the narratives of territory, imagined or otherwise, as points on the surface of the globe: most university anthropology departments still advertise their faculty requirements in precisely these terms. For this reason alone it is worth pointing out some of the implicit meanings of place in anthropological discourses. Places are, of course, peopled, and by far the most important and engaging dimension of place are the social relationships they support. Although it is an obvious point, we should not forget that social landscapes – the substance of anthropological enquiry – are often conflated with the physical spaces which serve as a shorthand way of referring to them. Traditionally, the romance of anthropology rests in the exploration of remote and exotic places (Gupta and Ferguson, 1992: 6) which are only remote and exotic in relation to the everyday world of the anthropologist and her audience here at home. The field as a domain of investigation is hence enlivened by the mundanity and knowability of home; and the researcher is the conduit by which they are connected, the 'link between an unproblematised "home" and "abroad"' (Gupta and Ferguson, 1992).

Here and there are part of the narrative conventions of anthropology: ways of speaking about movement to and from the field. But we know from those who work at home that the travel this involves is not about physical distance. Sociologists like myself routinely excavate their own backyards, yet effect a similar, though less dramatically spatialized distinction. Stumbling into my office at the university recently I was disturbed to find two of my research assistants interviewing one of the 'schizophrenics'[2] from our research project. A symbolic distinction had been violated although the distance – between my office and the day centre where we usually did our interviews – was less than a kilometre. When part of home is the field, the researcher strenuously works to differentiate that part of home by constructing a field by means of the narrative conventions of anthropology. Home and field are concepts used to distinguish the everyday life of the social investigator from the task of investigation, and from the lives of the objects of their narratives. Distinguishing the lives of the investigator and the investigated secures our right to speak authoritatively about them. Rendering the object of investigation in exotic terms – a narrative device used also by sociologists who investigate the exotic at home (Atkinson, 1991), my own research on schizophrenics[3] being a case in point – also serves as a distancing device. The separation between here and there/home and field is a spatialized symbolism in which place becomes a way of distinguishing work from non-work, us from them and social investigation from life itself. It is precisely this which rescues the investigator from the research frame, while simultaneously preserving the authenticity of the business of anthropology.

But what happens when we take a closer look at these distinctions between home and field?

This chapter revisits home and field and tentatively draws some connections between the two. It argues that when homes contain fields, as may well be the case when researchers are themselves transnationals, conceptions of home (which are always necessarily partial and selective) are highly significant in defining the field and the researcher's position within it. In order to understand the relationship between home and field, we thus need to examine the researcher's intellectual, political and transnational autobiography. Although this kind of reflexivity has been dismissed as 'navel gazing', it is, as Okely (1992: 2) argues, a critical scrutiny of the self and the fieldworker's relationship to the field. 'Ethnography requires a personal lens' (Okely and Callaway, 1992: xiii) and the ethnographer self (and, as I shall argue its sense of home) is a resource in making sense of others. What follows is a discussion of my own fieldwork and its relationship to my own sense of home, a discussion which I hope contributes to our collective understanding of what is a perplexing and intriguing issue in contemporary social theory – the nature of home.

Positioning anthropologists in the field

Understanding the relationship between home and field requires a reflexivity about what we do and why we do it: an exercise which places the social investigator back in the research frame. The field has many dimensions. It pinpoints a set of intellectual pursuits which may not have an obvious relationship to the researcher's life. My own fieldwork, for example, involves collecting life-story narratives from black people diagnosed schizophrenic which I analyse for clues about the racialization of identities and notions of belonging as well as for an insider commentary about the workings of the community mental healthcare systems through which these lives are organized. The material I collect allows the identification of some of the micro-elements of race formation, a set of processes discussed by Winant (1994: 270–271), in the dialogues which occur between the administration of blackness by mental health agencies, and the existential narratives of the self through which the administrative is processed in the living of (schizophrenic black) lives.

The field is far more than a set of intellectual pursuits; it also has a political context. In this case it forms part of an intensely political debate about the ways in which black people are treated by mental healthcare agencies, debates which are closely connected to the broader racial politics of the locales in which the research is situated. It would be impossible for a white researcher to investigate this without establishing some credentials as an anti-racist. Being white carries an enormous burden of representation which is bound up with a history of racial oppression. No researcher could collect information which contains painful personal accounts of black schizophrenic lives without making it clear where she stands on the issue of racism. There is no neutral position in which we can stand in the field.

The field also describes some specific networks of social relationships which, on the face of it, may also have no obvious relationship to the researcher. British, but not Canadian, community mental health facilities, for example, construct their own forms of racialized belonging, consciously manipulating the meaning of blackness.[4] In both countries the mentally distressed live nomadic lives by virtue of the ways in which the community system works. In common with other black populations, these are lives marked by more global movements – between the Caribbean, Africa, Britain and North America – between different versions of lives and family relationships. Resituating race in a global framework as some sociologists insist we should (Rattansi, 1994: 48–56), is tricky precisely because racialized myths of belonging and exclusion are calibrated in national terms. On the face of it my choice of a field of intellectual enquiry seems far removed from my own experience as a white researcher; I am not black and neither are any of my family or friends suffering from schizophrenia. But it is, in fact, closer to home than it seems, as will become clear in the section dealing with the meaning of home (p. 63).

More obviously autobiographical is the fact that the field also involves choices of locale. Most of the domains of intellectual enquiry covered by anthropology – kinship, ethnicity, religion, symbolism, work, creolization, transnationalism – could actually be studied anywhere. So why, if my colleagues will forgive me for running through the field sites in our department, the Solomon Islands, the Yukon, the Cayman Islands, Iran, Brazil, India, China, Cameroon or Quebec? Insofar as choices of locale are discussed at all, they are shrouded in academic rationale as the narrative traditions of anthropology-in-search-of-travel-funding and the development of expertise in an area demand. This tends to obscure the links between field site(s) and home(s), issues which are evidently cast around the researchers' autobiography.

Our choice of field site allows us to go away or remain at home, it allows us to live other lives in other places. Careful choice allows us to escape cold Canadian winters, live temporarily in exotic places, participate in other social relationships, stay close to home while children are young, and take breaks from the routines of family life and friendship networks. Fieldwork, like theory, is disguised autobiography (Cohen, 1993); the field offers another place in which the shortcomings of our regular life can be, at least temporarily, adjusted.

My own case is no exception. I could actually study racialization almost anywhere, although it would always take different forms in different places. In fact I work between two field sites: one in Britain, the other in Quebec.[5] The rationale for this dual locale is regularly set out in applications for funding, increasingly the yardstick by which academics are measured on both sides of the Atlantic, in which the benefits of 'comparison' are hopefully foregrounded by the applicant. Multi- or dual locale fieldwork, research which crosses national boundaries in its attempts to discuss the quintessential issues of the postmodern condition, is beset by problems of a theoretical as well as practical nature. The problems of the field are compounded when multi-field sites are involved.

First the theoretical. Framing research in terms appropriate to two or more field sites is a tricky business. This is not just a matter of the lexicon used to represent the research. In the case of my own research there are crucial differences in what is being compared – for example, two radically different psychiatric systems – which make the framing of comparison a rather hazardous business. Blackness and race, two of the key terms problematized by my research, connect with the political landscapes of Britain, but squarely miss those of Quebec where language, the distribution of ethnicity, assimilation and the terms in which the nation-in-waiting will be constituted are key features of the political landscape. Montreal contains most of Quebec's besieged and numerically small black population; a population which lacks the critical mass necessary to effectively launch a counter-attack on the terms of its political exclusion in the ways in which black British people have. Blackness as a focus for social exclusion and counter-assertion is well established terrain in British psychiatry (Littlewood, 1993), but it is uncharted territory in Quebec where a fear of ethnic monitoring and a benign but ineffective rhetoric of multiculturalism hinder the calculation of racial inequality. My project is hence cast in terms which make sense in Britain but not in Quebec, and it raises serious questions about whether we can generate analytic categories which are suited to conducting socially and politically relevant research across national boundaries. Or is the transnational researcher simply in the business of imposing the conceptual apparatus of one locale on another in researching across the administrative and political boundaries of nation states?

The second problem is more practical. Funding agencies have their own agendas. Currently these favour what Hammersley (1992: 135) calls 'practitioner ethnography' and it is difficult at a time of public funding cuts to contest the need for research to have practical, social policy-oriented outcomes. Such research tends to be local rather than multilocal, and coincides with the other agenda of funding agencies: the defence of the beleaguered Canadian taxpayer who will not directly benefit from research conducted in other countries. When it comes to funding, and for that matter the organization of research, multi-field site projects need to negotiate the very boundaries across which they are conducted.

Third is the problem of concealing the autobiographical nature of field site choices. The autobiographical framing of research projects contradicts the narrative traditions of anthropology and casts doubt on the authenticity of the research. This is rather odd, given the current importance placed on reflexivity throughout the social sciences. Edmund Leach's command that ethnographers must admit to the reflexivity of their activities and become autobiographical seems not to have been heeded, and there is a paucity of published examples of this kind of reflexivity in anthropology (Okely and Callaway, 1992: xi). The link between my two field sites of London and Montreal is frankly autobiographical: I once lived in one and now live in the other, and I am trying to devise a way of living in both. Like many other immigrant transnationals, I build and live in 'social fields' (Basch *et al.*, 1994: 7) which span national boundaries connecting my societies of origin and settlement. Not being eligible to vote in Canada, I vote in Britain, file two sets of income tax returns, maintain a house in North London, earn my living teaching Canadian students, publish in both places and go back to Britain two or three times a year to service professional, family and friendship networks. But unlike other immigrants, my research is one of the mechanisms through which I sustain my multi-stranded life. Quite clearly in this case, the field is about the researcher's autobiography, a story in which notions of home and belonging (to which I will return) occupy central positions.

The fieldwork mechanism

Fieldwork and autobiography are evidently closely connected but they are not the same thing. A clarification of their differences deepens our understanding of the relationship between them. Fieldwork is described as a mechanism because it is a set of mutually adapted parts or processes focused, as I will argue, on the project of the researcher's autobiography or account of the self.

How does this mechanism work? Fieldwork offers the transnational researcher the prospect of reconnection with a former life or the prospect of escape; it sustains the possibility of alternate senses of belonging and self, deftly buried in conceptions of work and intellectual enterprise. The self is not a thing but a selective and imaginary interpretation of the words and actions used to speak about lives (Freeman, 1993: 6–8) and an ongoing project.[6] In my own case Britain could as easily be a draw as a no-go area. So it is not that we can simply read the researcher's autobiography in their fieldwork or predict their fieldwork from their autobiography. One does not have a predictive relationship with the other, but they are connected around the anchoring of the self in a version of home, a theme to which I will return. Fieldwork is thus an adjunct to autobiography, but the connection is not a straightforward one.

Paradoxically, as well as facilitating movement back and forth between alternate versions of a life, fieldwork can also anchor the self in a moving landscape. During my professional life I have moved my household, body and possessions to Nigeria, back to London, and then to Toronto, Vancouver and Montreal. While in each place I have set about investigating the configuration of local race politics. This has not entirely distracted me from my interests in a very specific part of (East) London and its racial landscape which has intrigued me over the last twenty or more years. Fieldwork thus provides (intellectual) continuity, allowing the researcher to both move and stay put, and raises some interesting questions about the sense in which we move when we migrate. A Czech refugee who fled following the Soviet invasion of 1968 recently described to me how she repositioned herself in Montreal over a twenty-year period. She did not actually move inside her own escape story, or with the progressive loss of family in Prague. She did not move as her two Canadian-born children grew, or as her ability to communicate in French improved. Neither did she move in situating herself within a distinctively European sector of Quebecois society which is how she sees herself. Rather, she confesses, it took fifteen years of psychotherapy to really move her from Prague. The emotional and intellectual domains of our lives, it seems, are not easily relocated.

While fieldwork appears to be a means of achieving broader, more biographical projects for the transnational researcher, it quickly becomes the mechanism which organizes the terms of movement back and forth. As well as allowing me to pursue my sense of home in Britain, fieldwork provides a rationale which circumvents further accounting for my absence from my other life in Montreal. Mindful of the fact that research grants use public funds and their commissions must therefore be seen as work (fieldwork is just that, work), fieldwork structures the working day and week during my visits to London, with personal commitments crammed into evenings and weekends. Fieldwork simultaneously takes me home and limits my exposure to home: I am able to visit and maintain the distance which comes with other (work) commitments. It has become the device by which I manage a transnational life.

Finally, fieldwork is a mechanism which creates the other (Gupta and Ferguson, 1992: 14) as a distinct form of peoplehood in a dialogue with the self (Hastrup, 1992: 120; Okely and Callaway, 1992: xiii), a separation sustained through the distinctions the researcher construes between her life and the research process itself, each with its own field of social relationships. The process of revealing the other also brings the self clearly into view as not the other; and so it can be argued that fieldwork, in its outcome if not its intent, is as much about the autobiography of the researcher as it is an investigation of the other. The people I interview are black, a fact which foregrounds for me the whiteness of myself, of which I am otherwise unconscious. We are British in markedly different ways. We live in Montreal on quite different terms. They are diagnosed and administered (differently in the two cities) as mad. Their lives are inscribed by the administrative actions of community psychiatric agencies and the social relationships of psychiatric care. My life is circumscribed by different bureaucratic purposes at the university and through the schools which my children attend. They hear voices and see things which they relate to me. Their pain is my data. They live in homeless hostels, spending their days in day centres where I interview them. They are managed by the pharmacological regimes of psychotropic medication. My own life is managed by quite different constraints. The local politics of race and mental health set us firmly apart in calibrating forms of social recognition, lives and social relationships. The self – the object of autobiography – comes clearly into focus in its distinctiveness from the other – the object of fieldwork – and fieldwork is the means by which this conceptual distinction in peoplehood is organized. The distance between self (reconstructed in the tasks of fieldwork (Hastrup, 1992: 120)) and other also raises important questions about the nature of home and the extent to which belonging is a shared activity,[7] questions to which we will return.

Autobiography and fieldwork then are not the same thing. Fieldwork is a mechanism facilitating a selective and analytical recounting of the lives of others. It negotiates, in no predictable way, the researcher's account of the self. Autobiography, on the other hand, is a selective narrative reconstruction of the life of the researcher, an account of the self. Fieldwork is woven around the life of the researcher in a complex, unpredictable web. It can take the researcher home and organize her exposure to home. It can precipitate movement and fix in place. It is a firmly separated set of social relationships in which the self and the other are staked out in their respective projects of autobiography and fieldwork.

Autobiography

Autobiography is not the same as life: it is the telling of stories about life, a selective recounting of memories and experiences which position the self in the world. It is evident from the above discussion that the researcher's autobiography is an intellectual tool of some sort[8] which interacts with the field to produce the narratives of anthropology. More obviously, the autobiography of the transnational researcher contains many insights into the lived interior of transnational mobility. Autobiographical stories of mobility counter what Clifford (1994: 313) refers to as 'abstract nomadologies' by filling in the details which allow us to think of transnationalism as taking quite different forms. In the 'power geometry' of transnational migration, those who write about it – journalists and academics like myself – are on what Massey (1991: 25–26) calls the 'prosaic fringes'. Neither the technocrats controlling the information superhighway nor the refugees forced to escape political persecution and death, we are volunteers. But volunteers come in many varieties, as my own migration story shows. Not part of the exodus of British 'lifestyle migrants' in search of improvements in the quality of urban life (Findlay, 1988; Ongley and Pearson, 1995; Zodgekar, 1990), but part of a relationship in which we have agreed to take it in turns to live at home to enable us both to service our kinship obligations; our movements back and forth across the

Atlantic are in fact the outcome of earlier movements embedded in our respective genealogies.

My maternal and paternal grandfathers (one Protestant and one Catholic) left Ireland in the early years of this century for different reasons, married English women, stayed to fight wars in British uniform but never applied for British citizenship. My maternal grandfather, marginalized through his Irishness in a Devonshire village by retired colonels and civil servants, returned to a veranda-ed existence which they represented as the home from whence they had been dispatched in the service of Empire. My partner washed up in Toronto as a child in the flood of 1950s migrants from the Caribbean to which his ancestors, British political dissidents in the eighteenth century, had been shipped as plantation supervisors of transported African slaves. This is a family in which the elders are resolutely 'Canadian' in their national allegiances and in their use of the Caribbean as a playground rather than an ancestral home, and their racialized versions of themselves as 'pure Anglo Saxon' are maintained only by carefully editing versions of the family. Autobiography thus fleshes out the bare analytic bones of transnationalism, clarifying distinctions between different kinds of movement and belonging as well as the personal/public histories around which they were created.

Home

Home is central to fieldwork. It is the here, the rest of life, from which there is cast. Home is also central in casting the project of the self, the object of autobiography, and it is the implicit object of the fieldwork mechanism. It is no straightforward matter in multilocale lives and research – where and what is home in the late twentieth century? (Robertson, 1995: 39). Home, its defence and the calculation of membership are central themes in popular cultures (Cohen, 1996a, 1996b), but it is also a feeling or sense experienced by individuals (Rapport, 1995: 269) which focuses on belonging. These are not separate dimensions of home but dimensions which, as I will argue, encounter and negotiate each other. Belonging may be a central part of home but it is no less problematic. We do not know whether belonging is problematic in a practical or everyday sense. Many people calibrate their lives in terms of multiple belonging and have strategies for dealing with mobility which involve the routinization of movement back and forth (Rapport, 1995: 268–269), or the kind of emotional/intellectual fixing I described earlier. But belonging is certainly analytically problematic, raising as it does fundamental questions about the significance of locality (Robertson, 1995: 39); about the place of memory (Nora, 1989: 7); about the tracing of genealogies and ancestry; and about the images of place and the construction of symbolic landscapes (Cohen, 1996b: 170–172). But as the narration of life is the material of social analysis, and, because a reflexiveness about the nature of home devolves on the geographically mobile – 'the senses of home and locality are contingent upon alienation from home and or locale' (Robertson, 1995: 39) – I will delve once more into my own story to discuss notions of belonging and to more specifically establish some of the connection between home and field alluded to earlier.

My own sense of belonging is cast between two homes. My home in Quebec is the home in which the activities of my life and work are conducted. This is a belonging of habitus and familiarity with friends, neighbours and colleagues. But my sense of belonging here is not one that is publicly validated in the rhetoric of ethnic nationalism which counts as Quebecois only those with ancestors who came from France in the seventeenth century. The public sense of belonging available to me is that of a comfortable, privileged and rapidly disappearing Anglophone minority which also has historical roots in the province, roots which I do not, as a recent immigrant, share. Quebec is a place in which I will only ever have a partial sense of belonging, but perhaps that is true of all the places to which one might belong. London, my other home, is also the site of a (rather differently constituted) partial sense of belonging. This is the place where I feel a sense of belonging, but also a kind of political disconnection which is in part to do with the popular narratives through which Britishness is expressed. Belonging, and hence the casting of home it seems to me, is both an emotional and a political activity. Of course it is also much more than this – but it is the emotional and the political I want to focus on for the purposes of this discussion of fieldwork.

London (not Britain) captures the emotional sense of belonging which I don't feel in relation to Quebec or Montreal. As an emotional activity, belonging is a liminal feeling or sense which erupts around the loss and nostalgic longing created by transnational migration. The irony of this sense of belonging is that it is always a mirage which disappears in the act of travelling to it. It is *de facto* not a lived belonging but a belonging of displacement remembered with nostalgia – the theatre of the past constituted by memory (Bachelard, 1994: 8). Hanif Kureishi (1995: 112–115) best captures this sense of home for me:

The rinsed streets were busy. Some of the chaos had cleared; once more crowds gathered around the tube station, waiting for friends. People were magnetized by the pubs or the French-style brasseries which were becoming popular; or they queued for the late-nighter, Truffaut's *Fahrenheit 451*. It was rare to see anyone over forty, as if there were a curfew for older people. . . . At university [Deedee said] I turned dour. Rather like, you know, I had hard political purpose. From the middle of the 1970s there was always the Party. If I wasn't studying, I was at meetings, or selling papers or standing on the picket line.

Emotional belonging is a belonging reinvented in memory, the most plastic, the most negotiable and the most open to 'imagineering' (Cohen, 1996b: 170) and irony. This nostalgic sense of home lives in and around the other home in which my daily life is conducted, containing as it does the prospect of another life, a dichotomy which closely mirrors the exotic/mundane distinctions of field and home.

The irony of using Kureishi's description of London to pinpoint an emotional sense of belonging leads us to the political dimensions of home. London is Kureishi's adopted home, a home in which his sense of belonging (whatever that may be) has to negotiate that sense of Britishness generated in popular culture and operationalized in the politics of racial exclusion. Being identified and identifying oneself as British is a political act. For myself (and many others) this is a source of deep ambivalence, the result of which is a highly qualified sense of belonging. While my own ambivalence focuses on racial politics, this has a broader social context which is interestingly summarized in this vignette from Patrick Wright's excellent anatomy of postmodern Britain, *A Journey Through Ruins* (1993: 14–15):

Among the underestimated attractions of Dalston Junction is a street corner full of forgotten municipal services. The public lavatories are of the attended Victorian variety with wrought iron railings . . . unlike many of their equivalents in more right-thinking and fortunately placed London boroughs that have been sold into private use as wine bars, pool halls and design consultancies. . . . The 'Town Guide Cabinet' is an example of the kind of street furniture that might more commonly be expected to grace seaside resorts and historical towns, but the one at Dalston Junction has been confidently adjusted to its inner city setting. . . . In most places a town guide like this would long since have been adjusted or disposed of as a broken relic, but at Dalston Junction it can stand unnoticed for forty years and then find new life as the map of a world on which the lights have gone down. . . . [The sudden arrival of a dark blue Bentley] deposited two gentlemen of advanced years on the pavement. . . . The man in front was Sir Alfred Sherman, former resident of Hackney, former Marxist and volunteer of the International Brigade, former adviser to Margaret Thatcher. . . . After glancing around uneasily at the nearby council estates, Lord Joseph [the other man] unrolled a banner on which were printed the words 'How Hackney Went to Hell', shook it out and then hung it up, with a little help from Sir Alfred, on the ornate iron railings of the Gentlemen's Lavatory. He then handed Sir Alfred an extended lecturer's baton – the sort preferred by true think-tankers that folds like a telescopic car aerial and can be fitted into a Saville Row breast pocket – and stood back to survey the unmarried mothers, while his companion mounted his soap box just next to the Town Guide Cabinet and launched into a speech that would inaugurate this unsuspecting visual aid into its new function as a guide to the abyss.

Here is the social backdrop of the ambivalence of belonging which makes Britain an easy place to leave: the tangle of the Victorian (and, we might add, relics of the feudal) and the postmodern; the rightward slide of politics into the abyss; the visible relics of a bygone age when there were local public services; the vibrant collective despair; and the coexistence of those trapped in post-war council housing and the gentrifying users of wine bars and design consultancies like myself. There is a perversity in casting belonging in a place most people would leave, given a chance, even if life is more comfortable at the privileged end of the social spectrum. Any act of belonging has to negotiate this social context, its political climate and its historical antecedents.

How difficult it is to be British! Or at least how difficult it is for those whose political allegiances incorporate a version of social justice in which blackness is not a major dimension of social disadvantage and exclusion to be British. Any belonging I might claim has to negotiate conceptions of homeland and Englishness and their narratives of racial exclusion in British popular culture which underwrite the social marginalization of black and Asian British people (Cohen, 1996a, 1996b). Heritage and ancestors, Renan's (1990) reusable past, are similarly mobilized to serve the project of constructing Britishness in racially exclusionary terms which celebrate the bloody plundering of colonial conquest. British expatriates in any of the former colonies live on the wrong side of a history of racial and colonial oppression and this is an uncomfortable position to be in. Clifford's (1994: 310–312) discussion of diasporic discourse[9] in which he points out that the British diaspora is black, makes the point that diasporality is a feature of racial oppression and not just dispersal or maintaining the memory of an origin. How then should the global dispersal of white Britons be interpreted?[10] As a contemporary form of colonialism? When home in popular culture is about territory and the myths of nation states and these are cast in racialized terms, this renders Britishness an unattractive form of belonging. Those who cast their political allegiance in terms of social justice and anti-racist struggle have somehow to negotiate these racist dimensions of Britishness.

Fieldwork provides the mechanism by which I manage this negotiation. My own modest attempts at unravelling racialization and its attendant forms of inequality of access and exclusion are closer to home than they at first appear. The field for me is a way of being British, selectively, so as to distance myself from the racism and gross social inequalities which come with casting belonging in these terms.

Home, then, is both political and emotional, and inevitably it is partial. Home is a selective positioning of the self around one's political allegiances. In the work of the transnational researcher, home and the positioning of the self in terms of home through the stories that are constructed about the self occupy a central position in defining the field in its broadest sense of a choice of locale as well as the choice of a domain of social relationships and objects of intellectual enquiry. The field is about us as researchers in ways that we need to reflect upon and subject to critical analysis. This is not a matter of simply putting the researcher back into the research frame but of noting the ways in which the researcher generates the research frame.

Notes

1 My thanks to the Conseil Quebecois de la Recherche Sociale for funding, and to Vered Amit for insisting that I reflect upon these issues.
2 Schizophrenia is in single quotation marks (the first time it appears only) to acknowledge that whether or not the people to whom this label is applied are schizophrenic is an issue which is fiercely debated.
3 See Knowles, 1994, 1997.
4 See Knowles (1997) for a discussion of this.

5 I actually live in Montreal which is politically and demographically distinct from the rest of Quebec, not least because it contains most of the immigrant population. Whether Quebec should or should not be considered part of Canada is, of course, a political debate which affects the lives of all who live in the province.

6 Freeman's (1993) excellent book provides an impressive account of the ways in which the self is invented in biographical and autobiographical narrative.

7 I do not intend to suggest that belonging is an individual activity, though to some extent it is, but to suggest that the terms in which it is a collective activity are calibrated by differences in social position, social recognition, race, ethnicity, gender and so on.

8 See Erben (1993) and Stanley (1993) for a more detailed discussion of how the autobiographical contains the social and can be used as a tool of social analysis.

9 Clifford (1994: 304, 310) points out that the term 'diaspora' is used to refer to those who think about themselves in terms of dispersal from an original centre, maintaining a collective memory, being marginal and eventually planning to return to that homeland. He notes that it also gives weight to claims by minorities against oppressive national hegemonies and that this element is a central one.

10 Turner's (1994: 145) discussion of the part which English intellectuals play in global culture is described as parasitic rather than diasporic.

References

Atkinson, Paul (1991) *The Ethnographic Imagination*. London: Routledge.

Bachelard, Gaston (1994) *The Poetics of Space*. Boston, MA: Beacon Books.

Basch, Linda, Nina Glick Schiller and Cristina Szanton Blanc (1994) *Nations Unbound*. Basel, Switzerland: Gordon and Breach.

Chamberlain, Mary (1994) Family and Identity. Barbadian Migrants to Britain. In Rina Benmayor and Andor Skotnes (eds) *Migration and Identity. International Yearbook of Oral History and Life Stories*, Vol. III. Oxford: Oxford University Press, pp. 119–135.

Clifford, James (1994) Diasporas. *Cultural Anthropology* 9(3): 302–338.

Cohen, Phil (1993) *Home Rules. Some Reflections on Racism and Nationalism in Everyday Life*. London: New Ethnicities Unit, University of East London.

—— (1996a) Homing Devices. In Vered Amit-Talai and Caroline Knowles (eds) *Resituating Identities. The Politics of Race, Ethnicity and Culture*. Peterborough: Broadview, pp. 68–82.

—— (1996b) All White on the Night? Narratives of Nativism on the Isle of Dogs. In Tim Butler and Michael Rustin (eds) *Rising In the East. The Regeneration of East London*. London: Lawrence and Wishart, pp. 170–196.

Erben, Michael (1993) The Problem of Other Lives: Social Perspectives on Written Biography. *Sociology* 27(1): 15–27.

Findlay, A.M. (1988) From Settlers to Skilled Transients: The Changing Structure of British International Migration. *Geoforum* 19(4): 401–410.

Freeman, Mark (1993) *Rewriting the Self. History, Memory, Narrative*. London: Routledge.

Garcia, Mario T. (1994) Identity and Gender in the Mexican-American Testimonio: The Life and Narrative of Frances Esquivel Tywoniak. In Rina Benmayor and Andor Skotnes (eds) *Migration and Identity. International Yearbook of Oral History and Life Stories*, Vol. III. Oxford: Oxford University Press, pp. 151–166.

Gupta, Akhi and James Ferguson (1992) Beyond 'Culture': Space, Identity, and the Politics of Difference. *Cultural Anthropology* 7(1): 6–23.

Hammersley, Martyn (1992) *What's Wrong with Ethnography? Methodological Explorations*. London: Routledge.

Hastrup, Kirsten (1992) Writing Ethnography: State of the Art. In Judith Okely and Helen Callaway (eds) *Anthropology and Autobiography*. ASA Monographs 29. London: Routledge, pp. 118–133.

Knowles, Caroline (1994) Biographical Explorations of Blackness and Schizophrenia. *Auto/Biography* 3 (1 and 2): 83–92.

—— (1997) Race and Place in 'Schizophrenic' Narratives. *Rising East* 1 (1): 78–96.

Kureishi, Hanif (1995) *The Black Album*. London: Faber & Faber.

Littlewood, Roland (1993) Ideology, Camouflage or Contingency? Racism in British Psychiatry. *Transcultural Psychiatric Research Review* XXX (3): 83–92.

Marcus, George E. (1995) Ethnography In/Of the World System: The Emergence of Multi-Sited Ethnography. *Annual Review of Anthropology* 24: 95–117.

Massey, Doreen (1991) A Global Sense of Place. *Marxism Today* 21: 24–29.

Nora, Pierre (1989) Between Memory and History: Les Lieux de Mémoire. *Representations* 26: 7-25.

Okely, Judith (1992) Anthropology and Autobiography. Participatory Experience and Embodied Knowledge. In Judith Okely and Helen Callaway (eds) *Anthropology and Autobiography*. ASA Monographs 29. London: Routledge, pp. 1–28.

Okely, Judith and Helen Callaway (eds) (1992) Preface to *Anthropology and Autobiography*. ASA Monographs 29. London: Routledge.

Ongley, Patrick and David Pearson (1995) Post-1945 International Migration: New Zealand, Australia and Canada Compared. *International Migration Review* XXIX (3): 765–793.

Rapport, Nigel (1995) Migrant Selves and Stereotypes. Personal Context in a Postmodern World. In Steve Pile and Nigel Thrift *Mapping the Subject*. London: Routledge, pp. 267–282.

Rattansi, Ali (1994) 'Western' Racisms, Ethnicities and Identities in a 'Postmodern' Frame. In Ali Rattansi and Sallie Westwood (eds) *Racism, Modernity and Identity*. Cambridge: Polity, pp. 15–86.

Renan, Ernest (1990) What is a Nation? In Homi Bhabha (ed.) *Nation and Narration*. London: Routledge, pp. 8–22.

Robertson, Roland (1995) Glocalization: Time–Space and Homogeneity–Heterogeneity. In Mike Featherstone, Scott Lash and Roland Robertson (eds) *Global Modernities*. London: Sage, pp. 25–44.

Stanley, Liz (1993) On Auto/Biography in Sociology. *Sociology* 27 (1): 41–53.

Turner, Bryan (1994) *Orientalism, Postmodernism and Globalization*. London: Routledge.

Winant, Howard (1994) Racial Formation and Hegemony: Global and Local Developments. In Ali Rattansi and Sallie Westwood (eds) *Racism, Modernity and Identity on the Western Front*. Cambridge: Polity, pp. 266–290.

Wright, Patrick (1993) *A Journey Through Ruins*. London: Flamingo.

Zodgekar, A.V. (1990) British Emigrants to New Zealand: Their Motives and Expectations. *International Migration* XXVII (4): 427–441.

Chapter 5

The narrative as fieldwork technique

Processual ethnography for a world in motion

Nigel Rapport

> The issue of the day is how to address the fieldwork enterprise in a post-structuralist period, how to understand the fieldwork time as a moment in a sequence . . . how to look at part-structures being built and torn down.
>
> (Moore, 1987)

Part-structure A[1]

Greg, 26 November in Wanet:

It's nice: the longer I'm here the more people recognize me again and even say 'hello' in the streets. They know me, and I find that very nice. Because I've left Wanet permanently for years, so I can't remember people and I can't expect them to remember me; a whole new generation has grown up in my absence. I don't even know what my peers are doing. . . . I went to boarding-school in Hogart when most Wanet children went there. Except a few girls who went to the all-girl school in Skipton. My school was part-boarding, part-not, and the girls were in a separate hostel to the boys. The boarding was paid for by the Department of Education, because there wasn't a school near Wanet where we could do A-levels, and the Willen road was then just two tracks of concrete with grass in between, and it used to get snowed in in winter and wasn't too good at some points; so it wasn't possible to coach people in and out like now. I went away to school at 11, and I hated it all. Because although the Wanet boys used to stick together more, they used to get picked on by the others who would gang up around corners and as soon as a Wanet man came they'd say 'there's one' and chase after him to beat him up. 'Hunt the Wanet Man' was a favourite sport. My school made Tom Brown's Rugby seem idyllic. . . . Now of course you can get to Hogart via Willendale or Riggdale, though I'm not sure how the present kids get there. Maybe via Leyton, with the Comprehensive kids. You see, Nigel: I've lost touch. Because I've not really lived here, except for holidays, since I was 11. And at one stage I was away for years at a time. And, in a place like this, it's easy to lose touch of events and of people, and for people not to know you when you come back. Of course, it's only really valid to stay in Wanet or to come back if you have a farm to go to. You stay if there's something worthwhile to inherit; so you learn all the necessary techniques because you have something to own to use them on. I used to notice in school how all the farm kids soon grew to look like their parents and grandparents – I mean their clothes, their looks, their mannerisms. Like in adolescence, when we need adults to copy and we pretend to be adults ourselves. Well, I used to see the Wanet farm children becoming just like their mothers and fathers. Like I can see Doris Harvey very much in her daughter Karen; they're exactly the same. And do you know Wendy Dover? They live in one of the new council houses. Well she looks so much like her daughter, Sarah, that sometimes I can't tell which one it is. I used to watch amazed in school as this transformation happened each time.

Part-structure B

The displacement upon which anthropological science is based Geertz has recently reiterated as entailing a 'being there', being in another form of life (1988: 4–5). This is what makes for the anthropological experience, and this is what makes its writing-up persuasive: anthropologists convincing readers of a movement between 'here' and 'there'. The movement is a cognitive one. Little or no physical movement is actually required in order to encounter another form of life – and probably never has been. Forms of life are forms of inventing the world through language, as Wittgenstein has shown us. What we can mean by a 'form of life' is the way we routinely interact one with another and with ourselves, through languages of various kinds, in the world. To encounter another form of life, therefore, is to change languages: to that of one's spouse, one's child, one's neighbour, one's political opponent, one's status inferior, one's alien religionist, one's cultural primitive – oneself in another consciousness. None of this necessarily entails physical movement; an experiential and cognitive shift is required. However, in the history of anthropology, this experiential shift has been generally glossed as a physical one. The physical and the experiential have been elided so that physical movement was the outward sign, the validation, of having been 'there'; proper, pukka anthropology entailed outward movement from the disciplinary to the global periphery.[2]

Furthermore, anthropological movement to another form of life has traditionally been posited upon a counterbalancing stasis concerning that form of life. The personal shock of the anthropologist's experience of otherness and displacement of identity is balanced, overcome and transformed into a matter for celebration, by claiming, as its opposite, the essential identity, fixity and impersonal inexperience of his objects of study.[3] As we suffer the 'culture shock' of movement, so they must enjoy the complaisance of immobility (cognitive and physical).[4]

But this no longer convinces. The literary turn which the social sciences have taken since the 1980s has ushered in new scientific-cum-fictional styles. What is now called for is an explicit admission in the text of the processes by which otherness is apprehended.[5] What is also called for is representation of 'being there' in another form of life in ways which do not presume the latter's stasis or coherency, longevity or collectivity: in ways which do not confuse the consequences of the cognitive movement of the anthropologist with the experiences (or lack of them) of others.[6]

Part-structure C

What is sought after in this chapter, more precisely, is an accounting for anthropological fieldwork which does not foreclose on notions of universal movement by 'informants': which takes account of social and cultural boundaries in continuous flux and of distance between people continually foreshortened by technologies of communication. A growing body of literature emphasizes the global mobility of contemporary life: its synchronicity (Tambiah), compression (Paine), massification (Riesman), creolization (Hannerz), deterritorialization (Appadurai), inter-referencing (Clifford), hybridization (Bhabha). Here is a world no longer divided into a mosaic of cultural-territorial segments but conjoined by a complex flow of people, goods, money and information, including even the most isolated areas in a cosmopolitan framework of interaction.[7] So: what of the practice of anthropological fieldwork in a world in motion? when 'there' is not a place?[8]

In 1987, Sally Moore described making the fieldwork enterprise more sensitive to situations which were constantly transitional as 'the issue of the day'.[9] Since no overarching ideological totalism could any longer be said to characterize an ethnographic setting – if it ever truly could – anthropologists in the field ought to recognize themselves as witness to events which instantiated not a priori social structures or symbolic systems but structural and symbolic orderings continually in the process of being created and dismantled. Hence, what anthropologists might endeavour to offer out of the field was a 'processual ethnography' of 'parts and pluralities in time' (Moore, 1987: 736).[10] Normative indeterminacy, she concluded, called for a new thematic emphasis. What I offer here is an argument on behalf of *the narrative* as both a fieldwork and an ethnographic technique which provides such a new thematic.

Narratives may be understood as stories people tell about themselves and their worlds. The medium of their narrational telling may vary (from words to images to gestures to routine behaviours), but what is invariant is the characteristic of narratives to propagate a meaningful sequence across time and space. Narratives embody a perceived order, and in their telling they maintain this order despite seeming temporal, spatial, experiential disjunctures. In a world in motion, narratives provide for the world-traveller – whether anthropologist or informant – a place cognitively to reside and make sense, a place to continue to be. Here, in short, is narrative as a *modus vivendi* for fieldworker and subject of study alike.

I hope to substantiate these ideas in an ethnographic analysis of an individual narrative from my fieldwork in the English village and valley of Wanet. As Greg journeys in and out of Wanet, his family home, periodically meeting up with Nigel, the domiciled anthropologist, so he continues a narrative account of his life in which his departures and returns are encompassed within an orderly version of his life course.

Part-structure D

For a year in the early 1980s I lived in the rural hill-farming valley and village of Wanet, in north-west England (cf. Rapport, 1993, 1994a). I sat in my cottage and then in my caravan, I visited local houses and drank in local pubs, I engaged in local relationships, I worked the land. And during this time, Greg came and went. I would hear about him, his latest news and doings, from his parents and sister who lived in Wanet and with whom I was friendly, and periodically I would see him.[11] He would return to Wanet for a day or two or a week or two, and we would run into each other and chat. But basically, I was resident in Wanet in the hope of coming to know something of local life, while he, a local, born into a long-lived local family, was one of a relatively large number of Wanet people who now resided outside their 'home' – with variable expectations of the permanency of this state of affairs – and returned with variable frequency and for variable periods of time.[12]

Greg's story, as I encountered it, seems an apposite one to recount here. He, 'my' informant, travelled around England and also abroad while I, 'his' anthropologist, stayed put. But he was far more grounded in Wanet than I – and felt that he should be. What I try to sketch here is how he managed to maintain that sense of groundedness and home, and how he came to express those feelings when we met. Moreover, in his method of accruing a sense of groundedness can be discovered an anthropological method, I argue. The way Greg coped with dislocation, overcoming it sufficiently to arrive at an expectation of finding himself 'at home' in Wanet, is at the same time a way for the anthropologist to situate himself in a 'field' locale which does not translate into a single time or place, and to interact with people who do not constitute a closed community. Greg's method was to recount a narrative of his life to me on each of his periodic returns. My method of representing Greg below is to describe-analyse the narrative he told.

Part-structure E

'Narrative can be conceived', Kerby opines, 'as the telling (in whatever medium, though especially language) of a series of temporal events so that a meaningful sequence is portrayed – the story or plot of the narrative' (1991: 39). Furthermore, narratives represented a 'privileged medium for understanding human experience', because there appears to be a human 'readiness or predisposition to organize experience into a narrative form' (Bruner, 1990: 45); it is 'in and through various forms of narrative emplotment that our lives – . . . our very selves – attain meaning' (Kerby, 1991: 3). As Barthes concludes: 'narrative is international, transhistorical, transcultural: it is simply there, like life itself' (1982: 252).

To elaborate somewhat on the above, human beings are narrating animals. Narratives represent a primary embodiment of our understanding of the world, of experience, and ultimately of ourselves: the typical way in which experience is framed and schematized and orderly worlds constructed. Narrative is the form of human consciousness, the form of our conscious experiencing. Carried variously in languages of words, images, gestures, behavioural routines, buildings, therefore, human narratives are ubiquitous. They are found in myths, fables, epics, novellas, histories, tragedies, dramas, comedies, litigations, dreams, mimes, memories, paintings, films, photographs, stained-glass windows, comics, newspapers and conversations. Rendering experience in terms of narrative is an instrument for making meaning which dominates much of life.

Narratives are inherently sequential. They articulate events, experiences, sensations and interpretations into a series, emplotting, relating and contextualizing them, so that a story, a history, an evolution takes shape – and progresses as new happenings are added. Hence, narratives posit an ongoing order, and meaningfulness, between distinct moments or sites of experience.

One of the most important stories to emerge is that of the individual's own self. The self comes to know itself through its own narrational acts. In narrative constructions of past, present and future, of relations of sameness and difference, the self is given content, is delineated and embodied. Moreover, while the self is an 'unfinished project', continually subject to being rewritten, never conscious of its story's end, and while consciousness at any moment may be fragmentary, narrative still holds together. Narrative transforms the inchoate sense of form in our experience, transforms the temporal and spatial fragmentariness of our lives, offering coherence: a sense that our lives may be, at every moment, at least partially integrated into an ongoing story. Narrative counteracts a sense of fragmentation, contingency, randomness, dislocation (both temporal and spatial); even anomic happenings can be interpreted in terms of established patterns, and to that extent rendered meaningful as routinized departures from norms.

Levi-Strauss famously hypothesized that myths should be understood as machines for the suppression of the sense of passing time and space (1975: 14–30), and while there is much in his conclusion which appears tendentious, nonetheless, it may be used to illuminate the method of Greg's narrative of self. For Greg maintained and rehearsed a personal myth which served to suppress the temporal and spatial distances between his visits to Wanet and so to engender a permanency to his life.

Following Propp, Levi-Strauss further identified certain 'mythemes' from which he said myths were composed: elements of plot, of characterization, of symbolization and symbolic opposition, which recurred in partial, complete or variant form throughout the text; myths were interweavings of mythemes culminating in some sort of resolution of a symbolic opposition concerning how precisely the social world was constructed and what social life might mean. In lieu of Levi-Straussian mythemes I would offer a description-analysis of Greg's narrative in terms of certain 'nar-themes' (narrative themes) or 'con-themes' (conversation themes). Here is 'myth' operating on the level of the individual self. And here too is a myth, a fiction, a way of writing, by which the anthropologist can gain and convey a sense of sequence, repetition and structure, on an individual level, amidst a world in motion. Let me briefly explain.

In analysing the play of conversation and the progression of 'talking-relationships' between individuals meeting in the city, in a further field-work (e.g. Rapport, 1987, 1994b), I felt one might identify 'nodes of communication' – words and phrases of greater and lesser length and complexity – around which conversational scripts were built up, developed and maintained by partners to the interaction. In their simpler forms, these nodes, like mythemes, were widely recognized and shared within the social milieu. However, in opposition to a structuralist interpretation, I was keen to maintain that those individuals who used the nodes to weave together the texts of their conversations were conscious of so doing, and that the routine resolutions, the ongoing talking-relationships that derived from their interweaving were original and personal to them. The common conversational nodes (my 'con-themes'), however seemingly conventional (even clichéd), were invested with and animated by personal and possibly private meanings. Furthermore, the construction of the social world they gave on to entailed no necessary collective complementarity, no significant semantic overlap, with that which derived from other conversational routines and other talking-relationships.

What I wish to argue here is that an individual can maintain comparable conversational nodes or con-themes in conversation with himself (or herself), and that it is from an interweaving and developing of these that his personal narrative or myth of self emerges and takes shape.[13] It is in this way that I would present and have understood Greg's story, below. In expressing himself before me (and others), Greg also acted as his own talking-partner, constructing and maintaining the worlds in which he lived. Through his narration, Greg provided for himself a cognitive and sentimental space, a place and a time in which to be – however seemingly familiar or banal, public, formulaic or inconsequential his utterings.[14] Moreover, his narrative contains personal con-themes or nar-themes which recur (à la mythemes) in partial, complete or variant form, as Greg seeks resolution of problems of meaning within that space.

Part-structure F

Over a year in Wanet, I met Greg in extended conversation on nine occasions. He came to my cottage for tea, I went to his parents' house to watch television and have dinner, we drank together in the village pub; largely he spoke and I listened.[15] In comparing Greg's different utterances I feel I can isolate at least sixteen regularly recurring themes. For convenient introduction, they might be labelled and listed as follows:

1 Greg's wish to renovate a Wanet building as a home for himself;
2 Greg's dislike of the twee way newcomers are renovating cottages in Wanet;
3 Greg's worry about Wanet land only being affordable by strangers;
4 Greg's one-time ownership of a café in the village;
5 Greg's sense of the logic of staying in Wanet to inherit a farm or land;
6 Greg's history of work in the Wanet area;
7 Greg's local roots in Wanet and links to family and peers;
8 Greg's knowing and forgetting of the names of local people and places;
9 Greg's recollections of his school-days;
10 Greg's pride concerning the presence and continuity of his family in Wanet;
11 Greg's relations with his father and his father's health;
12 Greg's feelings of claustrophobia in Wanet;
13 Greg's sister's marriage and her new in-laws;
14 Greg's knowledge of local geography;
15 Greg's account of rich and successful people migrating to and from Wanet;
16 Greg's sense of how Wanet can be variously related to the outside world.

Not all of these themes would appear in every conversation, and the appearance of each, as I say, would be variable in terms of length and complexity of treatment. In sum, my interactions with Greg and the themes he interwove took the form given in Table 1.

Table 1: My interactions with Greg and the themes he interwove

	Date								
Theme	20/10	22/10	21/11	26/11	28/11	29/11	30/11	24/5	27/7
1					*				*
2	*			*				*	*
3									*
4	*								*
5	*			*			*		
6	*	*	*	*					*
7				*				*	*
8	*			*			*		*
9				*					*
10				*				*	*
11				*					
12				*					*
13		*		*				*	*
14				*		*	*		
15				*					
16	*		*						

Let me exemplify with the following conversational extract from 26 November:

All the farming now has become really mechanized – even since I did my bit on Johnsland, where it was so labour intensive. Which means that all farmers now need education – which is why more are going to college or university. One of my school-friends, I remember, was brilliant at maths, and I think he came back here to farm on his dad's farm – or do the roads or something. I'd really like to trace some of my school-friends. After working for the County Council in Kendal, I worked for the Roads Department in Durham. I also used to work for Kendal Telephones, when it was done using electro-magnets, not done electronically, and operated by people. But my dad's not too pleased with me at the moment because I just broke our 10-inch chainsaw, trying to cut through a telegraph pole. So I'll have to repair that soon. Also my dad finds me too serious all the time: he misses some cheerful company. Once when I came home with *The Times*, I remember, dad thought that was really beyond the limits of proper seriousness – incredible!

In terms of the themes listed above, Greg begins here with number 5, concerning the logic of staying in Wanet if one expects to inherit a farm or land: 'All the farming now . . . going to college or university.' He continues with number 7, concerning his local roots and links to family and friends: 'One of my school-friends . . . trace some of my school-friends.' This is then followed by number 6, concerning his history of work in the Wanet area: 'After working for the County Council . . . operated by people.' And finally, Greg turns to number 11, concerning his relations with his father and his father's health: 'But my dad's not too pleased . . . the limits of proper seriousness – incredible!'

Let me continue, then, by focusing on two themes in particular: numbers 7 (Greg's local roots in Wanet and links to family and peers) and 8 (Greg's knowing and forgetting of the names of local people and places), and showing how they are reiterated in different conversations – and to what these reiterations might attest.

Theme 7

26 November: 'It's nice: the longer I'm here the more people recognize me again and even say 'hello' in the streets. They know me now, and I find that very nice. Because I've left Wanet permanently for years, so I can't remember people and I can't expect them to remember me; because a whole new generation has grown up in my absence. I don't even know what my peers are doing. Like Jim Tyne of Millwood Farm, or Kevin Black. Do you know him? He was back here at the weekend with the backward kids I think he teaches; I think it's Carlisle Rotary Club that sends them here. And then there's Ken and Brian and Will Brent – the three brothers from Larch Farm who you'll have met at badminton. They're the same age as my brother: 36; and I'm 34. Then there's quite a gap before Florence, who's 24 – I think. . . . One of my school-friends, I remember, was brilliant at maths, and I think he came back here to farm on his dad's farm – or do the roads or something. I'd really like to trace some of my school friends.'

24 May: 'I'd like to return here someday. Because I feel my roots are very deep here. I love local tradition and I care for every brick, so I'm keen to see any changes people make. . . . I don't like towns so much. I've rediscovered the countryside from York, and realized that that's what I'm used to and been brought up to, and love: to be near the changing seasons etc. I'd like to move back to Wanet one day; at least, it's very nice to know it's still here if I want to!'

27 July: 'I remember joining the village gangs of boys, and creeping along the other side of the hedge to grab dad's cooking apples. Although they weren't edible and I could have done it much easier from the garden!'

Theme 8

20 October: 'Shops around here are known by the names of their old owners, you know.'

26 November: 'I have a problem with names and nicknames in the village now. Everyone in Wanet simply uses Christian names for people, and often surnames aren't known at all. Like there was someone called Leslie Wright, and his son is called John Leslie not John Bloor. Eh?! Wait a minute. I'm really confused here!! I'm sure it was Leslie Wright, so how should his son come to be John Bloor? . . . Well, I don't understand, but you can see the difficulties we get into, Nigel, because mainly Christian names are used, and everyone knows him as John Leslie. Or again, people are called after the place they live or are associated with. Like "Josie at Cedar High". Do you know the chapel in Thurn? Well, they're converting it into a house, and the Wilburs now live there. And I was just explaining to dad about "Josie Wilbur in Thurn" and dad had no idea who she was until I said "Josie at Cedar High", because she used to be a living-in domestic there, and helped Doris. But then I suppose it's just a generation thing, because the next generation will grow up knowing her as "Josie Wilbur" or "Josie of Paddock House". Then again, some people are called after their spouse: like "Henry's Carol". Do you know the Jameses? . . . You see, Nigel: I've lost touch. Because I've not really lived here, except for holidays, since I was 11. And at one stage I was away for years at a time. And in a place like this, it's easy to lose touch of events and of people, and for people not to know you when you come back.'

30 November: 'The route that the annual Fell Race takes at Wanet Fair is up past Greenhill Farm, where Rosie Haines lives – Rosie does still live there, doesn't she? . . . She certainly used to; maybe she's moved now, I don't know.'

27 July: 'I'm disorientated when I return to Wanet – especially this time. I forget names, and people and places. Like I'm not sure which is Broad Farm, and who is Des Thwaite? and Will Thwaite who I heard just got married? . . . Peg and Bill had two children, Keith and Mary, who'd be about my age or older, so I suppose they could have had a son of marrying age.'

These two themes form a significant pair. They are so contrastive in tenor: 7 hopeful and upbeat, happy with the experience of return; 8 seemingly doubtful and confused, while 7 is confident of possibilities: of returning for good, of tracing peers. Indeed, it is to be expected that peers will need tracing, that while youth stays put, maturity gives on to a physical expansiveness. Greg is not alone in his transience, and any seeking out of traces would be mutual. In short, memories of life in Wanet are good and the possibility of an equally good future here is a matter of decision and intent. By contrast, if 8 is confident of anything, it is of ignorance and disorientation in Wanet. Yet this disorientation is balanced by an allusion of life lived elsewhere. If names, people and places are forgotten here, then it is because names, people and places elsewhere have replaced them. And in equal measure; there is a worried even expected ignorance here because of a knowledge of a depth of experience outside Wanet. Belonging in Wanet is a matter of owner-ship – whether of a shop or a farm (a matter Greg elaborates upon fully in Theme 5) – and having been away for years Greg's rights of this kind lie elsewhere. Nevertheless, Greg has not forgotten how to know in Wanet; the details might elude him, but he remembers the way of local knowing: shops and farms and marriages are known by the personal names, even the nicknames, of their incumbents, and con-versely, people are known by their 'properties'. In short, there is a logic and a propriety to Greg's present local ignorance and invisibility. And of course, paired together, not to mention interwoven with fourteen other such thematic strands, the fullness and complexity of the feelings and meanings Greg invests in his relationship with Wanet, in his narrative of his relationship with Wanet, begin to become apparent.

A final common feature of Themes 7 and 8 is their consistency over time. From my first encounter with Greg to my last, the distinct tenors of the two themes remain. As Greg returns to 7 and 8 in his utterances over time, notwithstanding the dislocations of time and space, so the constancy of their unchanging natures provides stability.

But the themes of Greg's narrative stand over and against dislocation in other ways too. For example, Theme 13 (Greg's sister's marriage and her new in-laws) presents a development of information and experience for Greg over time:

22 October: 'Bob and his family are something of a phenomenon in this dale. One son is an agricultural engineer in a town nearby, while two sons are farmers and are going to share the parents' farmhouse – if Bob's brother marries and Bob's own marriage to Florence really goes through.'

26 November: 'Has Florence told you about the Thomases? It's an enormous farm and probably owns more than any other set-up in the dale – even more than the Tynes of Millwood. Because Thomases Farm has two extensions updale and one more by Leyton. There are many small farmers in the dale who can't live on their farm income alone and so in off-seasons they farm the extensions for the Thomases.'

24 May: 'Florence left okay on her honeymoon! She went in a banger, with the Master of Ceremonies, to Lancaster, and there I think they're hiring a car; they're touring Wales or something: driving between places. . . . I'm pleased my parents have had a marriage in the family – and I'm equally pleased it wasn't mine! But Florence always wanted to come back to Wanet; the shop was just an excuse. I think she always fancied farm life. She was friendly with lots of farm people and spent time at different farms – like Scar Fell – looking after children and what have you. So she was just like a farmer's wife then, and I think she'll like the life of a farmer's wife. . . . But I also think she'll be more than simply a housewife. She'll keep up her other activities. She really likes people: that's her great love, her main interest. So she'll keep up as many activities meeting people as she can. . . . Not that she won't be kept busy on the farm all the time. It's a disciplined existence at Thomases, a traditional Methodist way of life – you know, hard work and no days off. But Florence will enjoy the religious aspect anyway and be used to that. And farming is a more fulfilling, valid activity than being involved with tourists all the time in a shop.'

July 27: 'I may be leading hay at Florence's tomorrow evening; if they do it I said I'd help. They're a bit worried about all the high ground they have to do. Florence is in thralls of marital bliss – I've not seen her so quiet before – though there's some tension at the farm, because they don't think she does a full day's work: coffee mornings and good works don't count as work for them! . . . Farming is a business to them, and the woman's job is to keep the men out at work by doing everything in the house. Her mother-in-law bakes all day, as well as doing her part on the farm, so they think that any time Florence has she should be helping her. . . . All bills are shared and paid by her parents-in-law. Bob has £20 a week for himself, and was meant to get a rise at marriage, but instead they decided to wait a while; eggs and milk they get from the farm, meat is in the freezer, so they say £20 a week is enough. £15 a week goes on other purchases, Florence says, which just leaves £5 for spending. Which leaves no room for initiative; nor is there meant to be any in a strict, old-fashioned set-up like theirs. Everything is reinvested. . . . Her mother-in-law came from Bedgedale: very old-fashioned and religious. And she's very much the central figure, the power figure, in the regime – even though she's ill with heart trouble these days and often incapacitated. While Florence has been a 'kept woman' for a long time!'

There is a change in tone from the first of these utterances to the last. What was a possibility – Florence's marriage – has become an actuality, and a family which was to some extent a distant even awe-inspiring 'phenomenon' has become, vicariously, Greg's own. Greg speaks excitedly throughout, but there is a confidence and an assurance of local knowledge at the end which has replaced the more superficial details of genealogy and land-ownership enumerated at the beginning. More precisely, Greg has re-acquired access to the more 'valid' local activity of farming. Through Florence, Greg is re-attached to living and farming in Wanet. Florence's return to Wanet and to the farming activities of their childhood models a possible future for Greg himself and serves as a stand-in until he decides for himself; Florence has led the way to marriage, residency and work in Wanet, but has also removed the pressure on Greg to make any such decision.

Furthermore, through the vitality of this abiding family connection with Wanet, Greg now finds himself attached to possibly the dale's largest landowner and agricultural employer – he even finds that the Thomases appreciate his help in coping with the farm's difficult high ground. In many ways, the Thomases represent something of an ideal family situation to Greg. For here is a thoroughly local Wanet family which nevertheless combines members' residency inside and outside the dale, juggles farm work with other occupations, and farms at a diversity of locations around the dale. And in the honeymoon period of her attachment to the Thomas family, what does his sister Florence do with their eldest son Bob but drive around the country, on tour in a hired car – something Greg can wholeheartedly appreciate. Finally, through the Thomas connection, Greg now has access to much prized local gossip: to knowledge of local developments and tensions in Wanet at an early stage of distribution.

But then, Florence is not him. In many ways she is the opposite of Greg: religious, married, an erstwhile 'kept woman' now validated by farm work as distinct from having to deal with tourists. These distinctions, then, justify Greg's continuing absence from Wanet. He is both 'of Wanet' in a newly ramified fashion and yet has renewed justification for not being 'in Wanet'.

Themes develop; themes interweave with one another, relating together in terms of similarity and contrast; themes are called up on different occasions as Greg deems apposite. The last substantive point I should like to make concerning the narrative Greg constructs is the homology which may be drawn between the cognitive manoeuvring Greg accomplishes within and with regard to the 'space' of his narrative and that which he thereby also achieves with regard to the space of Wanet and beyond. The cognitive realm of Greg's narrative, I have argued, amounts to an orderly, continuous, and entire personal world which offsets the spatial and temporal dislocations of which his experience, in Wanet and elsewhere, might seem to be composed. More particularly, the cognitive transitions between themes which Greg decides upon offset the experiential transitions to which, from the outside, his life might appear willy-nilly to be subjected. While his relation to Wanet, for example, might seem to attest to a kind of homelessness, in fact Wanet becomes an area of control in Greg's life, subject to his decisions concerning its nature as well as his ongoing relations with it. Greg decides about Wanet, decides 'Wanet', in short, in homologous fashion to him deciding about the nature, relations and transitions between, and expression of, the themes of his narrative. The narrative affords him experiential control.

Two themes in particular demonstrate the practice of Greg evaluating Wanet: numbers 15 (Greg's account of rich and successful people migrating to and from Wanet) and 12 (Greg's feelings of claustrophobia in Wanet).

Theme 15

26 November: 'Charles began as a road man, you know, when his dad owned a small house up past Mrs Blythe and farmed over the road. Then Charles expanded into tile-making and even set up a small business on his dad's farm – what's now Wanet Pottery: he built that building. And then, of course, he 'made it', and moved to Carlisle and began Lakeland Tile Company. Then finally, Charles came back here – the successful business man – to retire, and bought up Uncle Des's old warehouse – because it needed someone with money to make something out of that. . . . First there were plans to make a hostel for walkers out of it – rather crude accommodation – but then Charles built his mansion instead. The land used to be my grandpa's wood-yard. Then, on my dad's marriage, grandpa gave him part of it as a plot to build a house on. And then Des married the other child – Jane – and so got a plot to build a warehouse on, which he designed himself. . . . Des is quite a character. Did you hear about him? He came here because his father was a farmer here, straight from the town, in suit and shiny shoes. And he found it very hard at first. Then he found his feet, and opened a grocer's shop. Then he expanded and opened a warehouse – in what is now Dale Leather-goods – and moved into animal feeds. Finally he opened up the big warehouse, and that flourished until there was competition from a large Leyton firm and he was only selling to a few Methodists but had lost the rest of his custom. So he finally retired and sold out to Charles who also bought the rest of the wood-yard to make into a garden.'

Theme 12

26 November: 'It's nice to escape the hothouse at home for a bit. I'm already fed up with mum's routine: get up at 7:00, light the fires, make breakfast, take Florence to the shop, wash up, look after dad and make his meals – no wonder she gets fed up and is always anxious for a vacation break.'

27 July: 'I'm certainly not going to watch the Royal Wedding on TV all day! I might borrow a car and get away. . . . I feel claustrophobic here after a few hours of parental bickering. I like the anonymity of York and my independence. I can sit in a field and think and do nothing. But if you sit and do nothing here – without a fishing rod in your hands – for more than ten minutes, people think you're mad – certifiable! . . . I also find I lead too many lives here: what Hattie's plans are, or Jenny's; what dad does and whether he will sell; what Charles does – I know all about them, everything, because they are relatives, or friends and neighbours, and so I'm involved in everyone and everything around me. I prefer York where there's time to be alone and to think. Where they don't know me from others and I don't know them. Wanet is too much for me for too long.'

27 July: 'I'm getting away from Wanet tomorrow. A trip Kendal way. Mum wants to go to this place near Borrowdale: Scar House. She's not been there since she was a little girl, with her grandma, and she wants to see if it's the same.'

In Charles, the local man made good – from road worker to millionaire, from a small Wanet house to Carlisle tile works to a Wanet mansion – Greg has a model of his own possible trajectory. A return to Wanet in style, at least in security, is no mere dream; and Greg has worked for the roads department – besides the County Council, a telephone company, in a hostel for wayward children, a conservation project and art school – to make the comparison even closer. And if Greg now finds himself (categorized as) citified, then there is also the model of his Uncle Des who came to Wanet straight from town, in citified garb, who also made good, financially and socially. In short, Theme 15 tells of role-models whom Greg can summon up to evidence the way that successful dealings with Wanet are matters of personal initiative; individuals such as Charles, Des – and Greg himself – are able to decide their movements relative to the dale, its impingement upon their life course and lifestyle. In Theme 12, meanwhile, Greg accounts for his present decision to remain living in York. The family home, the dale as such, is too much of a hothouse for him; he finds its routines too constricting, its life too public and social. So he decides periodically to escape the house, family and social network, the dale, the area, and 'get away'.

Finally, the two themes play off each other in interesting ways. For while Theme 15 tells of those who have, as returnee or newcomer, made their own way in Wanet and physically formed Wanet through their businesses and homes into their kind of place, Theme 12 speaks of making one's own way by escaping Wanet's straits. In both cases, however, Greg narrates the story of individuals who lead independent lives, who map out their relations to a place and its people but are not tied to or by them.

Part-structure G

Let me restate the main points of my thesis. The 'writing' of an ongoing narrative allows an individual, such as Greg, to overcome what may seem to the outside observer to be the many temporal and spatial disjunctions of living in the 'non-places' of 'a world in motion'. For a narrative offers a cognitive construction of continuing symbolic order and experiential meaning. At the same time, apprehending narratives affords the anthropologist a means of understanding and describing-analysing individual informants who move in and out of his field of interaction and might never come together in the 'places' traditionally construed as being synonymous with communities: with those fixed locations deemed necessary for socio-cultural process. Here is narrative as 'personal myth'.

It is for this reason, moreover, that I have emphasized the individual and personal nature of the above utterances by Greg rather than other contextual features of the conversations and physical settings which formed the backdrop to their expression. In line with my earlier conclusions, I have stressed the 'hegemony' and integrity of the individual and his perspective over and against the different particular conversations and overt circumstances in which that individuality finds voice.[16] In short, I have contextualized Greg's words in terms of the personal document of his ongoing narrative of self rather than let the more superficial differences of talking-partner and setting hold sway. The overriding talking-relationship Greg was conducting in and through this narrative, I argued, was with himself.

Following Allport (1942), I would describe narratives as part of the generic category of 'personal documents' of expression which includes diaries, autobiographies, life histories and letters. An awareness of such expressive genres in anthropology is, of course, nothing new. But there is the question of emphasis and evaluation. For some, such as Abu-Lughod, 'ethnographies of the particular' – narratives of people contesting, strategizing, feeling pain, making choices, struggling, arguing, contradicting themselves, facing new pressures, failing in their predictions – can be used as instruments of a tactical humanism 'against culture': against that which would incarcerate 'others' in a bounded, homogeneous, coherent and discrete time and place (1990: 147). Telling stories of the lives and works of actual individuals, taking account of the centrality of meaning in human experience, evidences the fact that 'we all live in the particular'; it grants us a human similarity over and against cultural differences (1990: 157).[17] For others, in contrast, such as Weiner (1995), the value of personal narratives in anthropology is low and their use to be disparaged; at best, 'narrated memoirs' serve to mark out the rather feeble methodology of the oral historian.[18]

The important point, it seems to me, is that while it is true to say there is more to observe than 'stories about social life', it is not true that these other things are any less personal, any more collective, any more objectively accessible. As Crites admits (1971), besides narratives which propagate a meaningful sequence across time, we might also posit 'meditations, theories and abstractions' which remove human beings from time, and 'sensations and feelings' which stress the fullness of the moment. But such meditations and sensations are no less matters of interpretation by the individual, and no more properly or hegemonically determinable by the narrations of others. Other narrations may lie beyond an individual's particular narrations, and the anthropologist can collect and juxtapose these in his description-analysis – as may the oral historian – but one narrative does not necessarily 'situate' another, does not give on to a superior awareness. The narratives of words, looks and actions which an individual constructs enables the anthropologist to attempt access to his world but not to fix or contextualize the latter. The individual's life is in motion between narrative moments, and any acts of true contextualization are his. Hence I would agree with the conclusion of Watson and Watson-Franke (1985: 97), that through such 'personal documentation', the anthropologist is able to access the individual in the act of managing his self-defined transactions with reality, and so do justice to 'the flow of subjective experience': to those existential excursions into 'freedom' which individuals may take from out of the routine representations of their collective life-worlds.

This is not to say that such narrative excursions are necessarily successful, however much they are part-and-parcel of individual consciousness and the construction of that ongoing cognitive space in which individual lives are led. Individual lives can still feel dislocated, badly and painfully put together; individual narratives can still be fabricated in clichéd form to the point where their content also feels clichéd; individuals can still fail to exercise the potential which narrative construction affords them to gain self-awareness, to extend their consciousness of their own somatic processes (meditations and sentiments); and individual consciousness still need not equate with control over the life course. Nevertheless, narrative awareness, by the anthropologist as by the individual, does provide the potential means of, and the route to, existential freedom. Individual lives are not over-determined by so-called essential features of setting which lie beyond narratives as such – conventions, categories, genres, discourses, roles, statuses, structures, organizations and so on. Lives are within narrative control, even if the individual exercises his own badly or falls under the sway of others'.

In conclusion, then, I argue that the individual remains the 'anthropological concrete' (Auge 1995: 20) even when motion and process call the temporality and spaciality of the socio-cultural into question. Furthermore, it is in their narratives that individuals' sense of orders-within-change are located, and to the extent that the anthropologist can learn the individual's language, through a 'processual ethnography' of those narratives he has a technique of recounting individual transitions.[19]

Notes

1   In the spirit of Sally Falk Moore's (epigrammatic) exhortation, I have given the ensuing sections of this chapter no more distinct designations than 'Part-structure A', 'Part-structure B', 'Part-structure C' and so on. I mean to imply that particular anthropological orderings and sequencings (such as sectionalizing a paper) might be 'built up and torn down' – and ought to be so treated – in order to remain cognizant of all the competing possible readings of the 'same' ethnographic material.

2   The happy coincidence between this gloss and the history of Western colonialism has lately been well rehearsed: the consequences of *pukka* (Hindu: 'cooked', 'ripe') anthropology as deriving from disquisitions, in the language of civil servants, on forms of life in the colonies.

3 Hence one invents a 'culture' so that one can have informants who are 'culture members' (cf. Wagner, 1975), who are removed from the passage of time (cf. Fabian, 1983), who are habitually and unconsciously immured in the *habitus* of a life course so that their actions replicate a social structure (cf. Rapport, 1996).

4 Leach, for one, was well aware of this conceit. Nonetheless, he justified the use by anthropologists of what he termed 'scientific fictions', because he felt that one could not describe social processes directly from observation; description was almost impossible unless one treated society and culture as if they were 'naturally stable' and equilibrated systems. Borrowing Vaihinger's 'philosophy of "As if"', therefore, Leach argued that it was pukka to replace the confusion of reality with an abstract model based on the interpenetration of ideal types, so long as one remembered it was, after all, a fiction (1964: 285).

5 Only in this way, it is claimed, can anthropology hope to avoid the 'terroristic alienation' and 'monologic rape' of placing others within the 'disciplinary detail' of social and cultural systemics (Tyler, 1986: 128, 139). To posit total systems for other ways of life – physically distant, holistic, unconscious, static – is an unnecessary and even totalitarian procedure.

6 'Settled arrangements' in the field were always a story, Geertz admits (1995: 15–16). Actually, things were always multiform. But only now do we recognize our traditional categories of comparison – 'parts', 'norms', 'practices' and 'wholes' – and the master-plots and grand pictures of culture they gave on to – causal forces shaping belief and behaviour to a generalizable, abstractable pattern – as impossibly ill made. What is necessary, he concludes, is representation more attuned to 'hints, uncertainties, incompletions and contingencies: swirls, confluxions and inconstant connections'.

7 In Appadurai's terms, the loosening of bonds between people, wealth and territory, whereby money, commodities and persons now endlessly chase one another round the world, also impacts upon the imaginative resources of lived, local experiences, on localism as such (1990: 193–196). In Hart's words: 'everyone is caught between local origins and a cosmopolitan society in which all humanity participates' (1990: 6).

8 Cf. Auge's notion of the 'non-place' (1995). For Auge, the Durkheim–Mauss orthodoxy – of societies identified with cultures conceived as complete wholes; of localized universes of meaning, of which componential individuals and groups are transparent and representative expressions – is an ideological conception which needs updating; traditional Durkheimian conceptions of society and Maussian conceptions of the person have led the anthropology of identity and otherness up a blind alley. Of course, no one has ever been unaware of the relativity of socio-cultural 'places'; the image of a closed and self-sufficient world (of relations, identity and history) was never more than a useful semi-fantasy, a provisional myth, even for those who worked (in the academy and out) towards its collective materialization. Nevertheless, the ideology rests on an organization of space and time which modern life overwhelms and relativizes. Above all, modern life entails population movements, globalism and non-places: individuals entering and leaving spaces, alone but one of many. Modern life

produces a proliferation of non-places: transit points and temporary abodes; wastelands, yards, building sites, waiting rooms, refugee camps, stations, hostels and hotels, malls, where travellers break their journeys and thousands of individual itineraries (of unmediated individual engagements with the global economy) momentarily converge. Of course, this too is an ideology, no more pure than traditional 'places'. Fixity, social relations and cultural routine (groups, gods and economies) continue to reconstitute themselves so that place and non-place represent contrastive modalities, the first never completely erased, the second never totally completed. However, non-places remain the real measure of our time, for the possibility and experience of non-place is never absent from any place: no place is completely itself and separate, and no place is completely other.

9 Cf. Paul Carter (1992: 8, 101):

> We need to disarm the genealogical rhetoric of blood, property and frontiers and substitute it for a lateral account of social relations. . . . An authentically migrant perspective would, perhaps, be based on an intuition that the opposition between here and there is itself a cultural construction, a consequence of thinking in terms of fixed entities and defining them oppositionally.

10 In her ethnography of Chagga interaction in particular, Moore (1987) offered 'chopped-off anecdotes' which 'led in all directions' so as to evidence the plurality of epistemes in terms of which the world was locally understood and the plurality of symbolic orderings which the anthropologist might adduce.

11 Greg's parents were retired shopkeepers. His mother had had a shop in the nearby town of Leyton. That had now been sold. His father's shop, in the middle of Wanet village, and selling drapery and household goods, had been recently run by Florence, Greg's 25-year-old sister. But Florence was now to marry a local farmer, and Greg's father had decided to sell and to live on the proceeds through their retirement. Florence was a similar age to me but Greg was nearly ten years older; (a brother, Dick, living in Huddersfield, was two years older again). An artist by vocation, Greg was currently involved in the multimillion pound conservation project surrounding York Minster, refurbishing its sculptings and stonework by painstaking mason-work, and on a fixed-term contract.

12 I use the term 'home' advisedly insofar as Greg was concerned. He lived in York but Wanet was his home. I may have been in Wanet for the year but I was not of it; Greg was able to maintain a sense, however ambiguous, of still being of Wanet even though he was rarely (and the story had been the same for most of his life) in Wanet.

13 Virginia Woolf once contended (1980: 192–196) that we speak primarily in order to establish communication with ourselves. We communicate between those different and diverse selves which we create for ourselves and inhabit, cognitively, emotionally and physically, at different moments. Thus our primary talking-relationships may be described as being 'with ourselves' (cf. Rapport, 1993).

14 Cf. Shelley: '[A] single word even may be a spark of inextinguishable thought' (1954: 281).

15 The fieldwork identity of a taciturn listener was how I generally preferred to make routine and legitimate a local persona for myself (cf. Rapport, 1993: 55ff.).

16 Subjective processes, meanings and understandings undergird social practices and animate cultural forms, I have argued (Rapport, 1990), and it is through details of such particulars that any more general notions derive. (Cf. Rapport (1993) for an argument concerning the personal definition and importation of context in expression, and the diversity of possibly incompatible interpretations of meaning from which conversations between people are constituted and to which they give rise.)

17 Watson and Watson-Franke concur. They urge a greater appreciation in anthropology of the importance of personal narratives as means to restore to the individual a measure of his lost integrity, dignity and significance: 'expressive production[s] of the individual . . . can be used to throw light on his view of himself, his life situation, or the state of the world as he understands it, at some particular point in time or over the passage of time' (1985: 2). For while social science has tended to come to grips with experience by robbing it of its unique richness and fluidity, privileging models, quantities and the experimental testing of hypotheses, and translating experience into static and essential abstractions ('culture', 'social structure', '*habitus*', etc.), a narrative account gives on to that subjective, phenomenal consciousness through which the individual articulates, constitutes, his world. They conclude:

> Much ethnographic research lacks a true feeling for human life as it is subjectively experienced by individuals. We know the richness and complexity of our own inner life, and when we compare this to the many tedious, dehumanizing accounts of life in other cultures . . . we may feel an acute sense of disinterest and even outright alienation. . . . All too often the real things seem to get lost in the obfuscation of the investigator playing God with his constructs. . . . To understand the individual in his human fullness we must therefore suspend total commitment to our scientific preconceptions and enter into a dialogue with the life history.
>
> (1985: 96–97, 133)

Cf. Rapport (1994a) for a corresponding argument.

18 In a focus on such narratives Weiner sees, firstly, a narrowing of culture. Cultural knowledge is unevenly and restrictedly distributed, he claims; therefore, an isolating of any one person's narrative will represent a partial account of the total cultural repertoire of what is known. Secondly, to focus on narrative is to reduce social life to a text, whereas social life is significantly more than stories one tells: to wit, the contrast between what is said and what is done, between 'what language avers and what behaviour reveals' (1995: 5). The anthropologist, Weiner concludes, unlike the oral historian (and more like the psychoanalyst) must socially

situate the individual narrator so as to reveal influences and constraints upon his speech and action of which he may himself be unaware.

Weiner's view, however, appears to me outmoded: an enclosed view of culture and a closed view of anthropology. It is not 'a culture' which possesses a total repertoire of things known, but rather individuals who create and possess an ongoing multitude of diverse and discrepant knowledges in their animation and use of the thoroughly malleable matter of cultural symbols and discourses. Individual narratives are ongoing individual attempts to make the world orderly and meaningful, and while the means of doing this is a bricolage of largely inherited cultural forms – words, images, behaviours – it is not these which 'influence and constrain' so much as the sense he makes of them; it is not 'culture' which 'resides' within them but individual agency and consciousness, individuality.

19 I am very grateful to Vered Amit-Talai, in particular, and also to Allison James, Tamara Kohn, Evie Plaice, Thomas Schippers, John Gray, Noel Dyck, Caroline Knowles, Karin Norman and Karen Fog Olwig for their constructive comments on this chapter.

References

Abu-Lughod, L. (1990) Writing Against Culture. In R.G. Fox (ed.) *Recapturing Anthropology*. Santa Fe: School of American Research Press, pp. 137–62.

Allport, G. (1942) *The Use of Personal Documents in Psychological Science*. New York: Social Science Research Council.

Appadurai, A. (1991) Global Ethnoscapes. Notes and Queries for a Transnational Anthropology. In R.G. Fox (ed.) *Recapturing Anthropology*. Santa Fe: School of American Research Press, pp. 191–210.

Auge, M. (1995) *Non-Places: Introduction to an Anthropology of Supermodernity*, trans. John Howe. London: Verso.

Barthes, R. (1982) Introduction to the Structural Analysis of Narratives. In S. Sontag (ed.) *A Barthes Reader*. London: Cape.

Bruner, J. (1990) *Acts of Meaning*. Cambridge, MA: Harvard University Press.

Crites, S. (1971) The Narrative Quality of Experience. *Journal of the American Academy of Religion* XXXIX: 291–311.

Fabian, J. (1983) *Time and the Other: How Anthropology Makes its Object*. New York: Columbia University Press.

Geertz, C. (1988) *Works and Lives*. Cambridge: Polity Press.

—— (1995) *After the Fact*. Cambridge, MA: Harvard University Press.

Hart, K. (1990) Swimming into the Human Current. *Cambridge Anthropology* 14 (3): 3–10.

Kerby, A. (1991) *Narrative and the Self*. Bloomington: Indiana University Press.

Leach, E. (1964) *Political Systems of Highland Burma*. London: Bell.

—— (1976) *Culture and Communication*. Cambridge: Cambridge University Press.

Levi-Strauss, C. (1975) *The Raw and the Cooked*. New York: Harper Colophon.

Lloyd, G. (1993) *Being in Time*. London: Routledge.

Moore, S.F. (1987) Explaining the Present: Theoretical Dilemmas in Processual Ethnography. *American Ethnologist* 14(4).

Rapport, N.J. (1987) *Talking Violence. An Anthropological Interpretation of Conversation in the City*. St John's: ISER Press, Memorial University.

—— (1990) Ritual Conversation in a Canadian Suburb. Anthropology and the Problem of Generalization. *Human Relations* 43(9): 849–864.

—— (1993) *Diverse World-Views in an English Village*. Edinburgh: Edinburgh University Press.

—— (1994a) *The Prose and the Passion. Anthropology, Literature and the Writing of E.M. Forster*. Manchester: Manchester University Press.

—— (1994b) 'Busted for Hash': Common Catchwords and Individual Identities in a Canadian City. In V. Amit-Talai and H. Lustiger-Thaler (eds) *Urban Lives. Fragmentation and Resistance*. Toronto: McClelland and Stewart, pp. 129–157.

—— (1996) Cultural Forms and Individual Meanings. A Polemic against the Maltreatment of Individual Diversity in Anthropological Analysis. In J. van Bremen, V. Godina and J. Platenkamp (eds) *Horizons of Understanding. An Anthology of Theoretical Anthropology in Europe*. Leiden: CNWS, pp. 224–243.

Shelley, P.B. (1954) *Shelley's Prose*. Albuquerque: University of New Mexico Press.

Tyler, S. (1986) Post-modern Ethnography: From Document of the Occult to Occult Document. In G. Marcus and J. Clifford (eds) *Writing Culture*. Berkeley: University of California Press, pp. 122–140.

Wagner, R. (1975) *The Invention of Culture*. Englewood Cliffs, NJ: Prentice-Hall.

Watson, L. and M.B. Watson-Franke (1985) *Interpreting Life-Histories*. New Brunswick: Rutgers University Press.

Weiner, J. (1995) Anthropologists, Historians and the Secret of Social Knowledge. *Anthropology Today* 11(5): 3–7.

Woolf, V. (1980) *Orlando*. London: Granada.

Chapter 6

'Informants' who come 'home'

Sarah Pink

Introduction

Anthropological fieldwork 'at home' can be conducted in a multiplicity of different styles, each of which raises different sets of issues. In this chapter I discuss face-to-face and electronic fieldwork amongst Spanish graduate migrants in England to address questions of self-identity and the definition of 'research' when it is carried out 'at home'. This project, to which new technologies became central, was characterized by an unconventional ethnographic narrative and a deconstruction of personal/professional boundaries. It promoted a particular consciousness of the arbitrary nature of definitions of both self and research.

Since many of my informants were also my friends, my personal and professional lives were inextricably interwoven into the research. I was usually unable to dedicate time exclusively to research, therefore my contact with informants was necessarily intermingled with other professional or social activities. The project's structure varied significantly from the more conventional narratives of my previous and subsequent anthropological work[1] that had been framed by preparation 'at home', fieldwork overseas and my return with the data. Instead, the research in question developed from a set of social relationships that were originally identified as part of my personal (rather than professional) life: the study of migration through exploring representations of self that reflected aspects of my own experience; and the technologies of the research, email and mail groups that were part of my professional and social practices. The research is therefore inextricable from these other narratives. Keeping this in mind I have structured this chapter to discuss: first, aspects of the 'research context' and the definition of research; second, the broader academic and institutional context of research about graduate migration; third, representations of self and the production of knowledge on a face-to-face basis; finally, I relate issues raised in these earlier sections to the electronic context of the research.

Creating a project

It is difficult to pinpoint precisely when the 'fieldwork' began. The research developed in a context of friendship and shared lifestyle with different Spanish people in England. Initially I did not situate the practices of my social life as research, but rather as a way of locating myself in a social world, communicating with people with whom I sensed a 'common ground'. At an indeterminable point I began to imagine how these experiences might be written up as anthropology. Since the focus is on Spanish people who have moved to England, I take as a starting point my own (re)arrival; in 1994 after two and a half years of fieldwork in Cordoba (Southern Spain) I returned to Canterbury (Southern England). My research in Cordoba (see Pink 1997b) had focused on local and media discourses about women and bullfighting. My return corresponded with the presupposed structure of my Ph.D.: having 'completed' my fieldwork I reached the 'writing up' stage. However, I did not feel detached from the social world I had 'left behind'. My Spanish partner from Cordoba had accompanied me 'home' and I remained in contact with Spanish friends and events through a series of telephone calls, letters and visits (for weddings and holidays). Moreover I had not been the only person in my social circle who was planning to leave. There were few prospects for graduates in Cordoba in 1994 where, during the economic crisis of the mid-1990s the unemployment rate was at over 30 per cent. For my women friends who had studied English, the prospect of au-pair work in Britain became an increasingly viable and attractive option as they tired of part-time shop jobs or giving private tuition to schoolchildren (often earning less than £2.50 per hour).[2] Their motives were not solely economic however. Amongst others was their desire to travel and live abroad – an interest that we shared and nurtured in our conversations.

By early 1995 my partner and I had established a social life in Canterbury; several of our new friends were Spanish – mainly au pairs or language students who worked part-time to support themselves. Later, a close woman friend, a history graduate from Cordoba, moved to London through an au-pair agency that I had put her in contact with. One Cordoban friend was already with a family in North London, and another who had recently completed her English degree was working, again as an au pair, in Brighton. Thus my social life 'at home' was interwoven with the presence of friends from my fieldwork 'away'. The interconnections between 'the field' and 'home' were also continuously reconfigured in my research as my friends brought with them 'fresh data' in the form of newspaper cuttings about female bull-fighters. Until I left for Guinea Bissau in late 1996 family and friends continued to supply a flow of videos, press cuttings and commentaries for my bullfighting research.

A year later I moved on again to take up a lectureship at the University of Derby. In January 1996, with a week free from teaching and meetings, I took the two-hour train ride down to London to meet the friend who had moved there as an au pair the previous year. Although we were both living in England we had not met for six months but had maintained contact by letter and phone. A large number of things had changed in both our lives: I had married and begun a new job, she had moved from her au-pair position to work as a care assistant in a residential home for old ladies. It was a relief to spend an afternoon chatting with a good friend after living in a new town for five months. We spoke about our lives, hopes, concerns, friends and families, there was plenty of news to catch up on from our respective trips to Cordoba. We also discussed the new research project; my friend had a particular interest as she (like my husband) was a key informant. In our conversations we were representing our 'shared' understandings of reality.[3] Moreover, this 'shared' social domain that my Spanish friend and I spoke in and about spanned Europe. It was not located in any one fixed geographical place, nor did it pertain to 'a culture'. Rather, regarding cultures as 'provisional' (Okely 1996: 4) it is not appropriate to construct a Spanish graduate migrant 'culture' as distinct from other 'cultures'. There was not a culture 'out there' to do research on.

The 'research context'?

As I moved through time and space, across Europe, through my career from Ph.D. student to lecturer and through the two research projects, distinctions between domains such as field/home, personal/professional, informants/colleagues became blurred. Technology (in the form of email, fax, telephone, budget air flights, video and photography) allowed particular styles of communication to develop between researcher, informant, work, home. In this second research project I understood my position to be rather different from that which I occupied during fieldwork in Spain. I regarded the ethnographic narrative as altered and myself repositioned (both spatially and subjectively). Since my 'field' was not located in any one physical space I could not 'go to' the field any more than I could leave it.

Such a relation to 'the field' can be understood in terms of a notion of 'retrospective fieldwork' (see Okely, 1996: 10[4]). If the field is simultaneously 'everywhere and nowhere', 'the research' may be defined in terms of the researcher's decision to engage in the act of producing anthropological knowledge; that is (re)classifying interaction as research. For example, a conversation with a friend may retrospectively become an interview and a fieldwork 'event' may simultaneously be many other (maybe contradictory) events. In this sense, fieldwork can be seen as an activity that is intermingled with other aspects of life and distinguishable only when drawn out of this web of interconnected narratives. Such retrospective definitions of fieldwork raise issues connected to recent debates about anthropological writing, in particular, the question of tense.[5] If fieldwork is to be defined only after the event, the 'informants' located in this field are thus situated in the past. Similarly, the label of friend tends to be conceded or withdrawn (and replaced by 'informant') in an attempt to separate, for example, past and present, fieldwork and social life. Therefore while simultaneity, intermingling and continuity between experience and knowledge was an underlying feature of the genesis of this project, literary uses of tense and time in anthropological writing construct distinctions and categories which potentially deny these complexities of the 'fieldwork context'.

In a project that depends significantly on autobiography, this definition of fieldwork as only arbitrarily defined, and of research as retrospective demands a consideration of 'selfhood'. The use of 'self to study others' (Cohen, 1992: 224) is a fundamental principle of this fieldwork. I describe below how the 'fieldwork' consisted in discussing and sharing my own experiences with my 'informants'. In this sense the research often centred on my experience of constructing and representing experiences to a friend/acquaintance/informant, in a situation where she/he would be compiling similar interpretations and expressions of her/himself in relation to mine. I distinguish between face-to-face and electronic domains of the research in order to discuss continuities and differences between them, stressing how the self is experienced and represented differently in different contexts of the research. Different theories of self offer different explanations regarding how electronic communications are experienced and therefore what type of knowledge they may produce. Cohen stresses the significance of the experiential. He sees the individual as self-driven and argues that 'selfhood, the sense of personal identity, is not merely contingent or relative, but has a certain absoluteness, or a self-driven element' (1992: 226). Cohen's point is convincing because he grounds his argument in the *experience* of self. Poster (1995) has developed a concept of the individual that he specifically relates to electronic communication. In contrast to Cohen he presents a more abstract concept of the individual based in the *theory* of the self. Poster argues that the autonomous rational individual of modernity is destabilized (1995: 57) and identity fragmented through the 'postmodern' electronic communications enabled by what he labels 'the new media age'. Poster points out some interesting and important differences between electronic and face-to-face communication that I discuss in the final sections of this chapter. However, Cohen's insistence on the centrality of a sense of irreducible selfhood to the production of anthropological knowledge serves as a crucial reminder that understandings of culture and society are (more) usefully developed from experience. As Rapport points out: 'to understand the maintenance of cultural relations is to appreciate the specificity of the individual meanings that live through them' (1992: 203). It is in these terms that I consider the experiential dimension of on-line research to argue that the communication it entails is not essentially different from other 'fieldwork'.

'Migrants' and 'Europe': economic crisis, personal crises and 'Europe'

While my informants could be defined as migrants, my research does not fit easily into the mould of more conventional studies of migration. Migration studies may be understood to have developed in relation to the histories of population movements and developments in social theory (see Eades, 1987). Thus migration research has largely focused on the mass migration of unskilled labourers, stressing the interface between political economy and migrants' social relationships (both with one another and with 'home') (e.g. Angotti, 1993; Eades, 1987; King, 1993). More recently studies of how these migrants' urban lifestyles and experiences have changed add continuity to the subject (e.g. Anwar, 1995; Werbner, 1995), sometimes signifying the continuation of the same theme throughout the researcher's own biography (e.g. Werbner, 1987, 1995). In the 1990s a restructuring of the labour market and decrease in mass migration has allowed the movement of qualified migrants to become a focus for some contemporary (quantitative) research (Salt and Ford, 1993; Shuttleworth, 1993). However, while the existing literature suggests that graduate and middle-class migration is established as a category, it is little documented.[6]

Graduate migration does not yield willingly to research designs that demand a 'visible' unit of analysis; indeed, the category of 'graduate' is problematically vast and diverse. In my experience graduate 'migrants' from Spain tended not to live in concentration in particular geographical spaces nor to be linked by dense social networks. Thus participant observation under such circumstances varied from fieldwork strategies outlined in 'conventional' guides to conducting ethnography (e.g. Ellen, 1984). It corresponded more with a call to explore 'new' versions of an ethnographic narrative which reposition anthropologist and informant (see e.g. Kulick and Willson, 1995). Funded research with a dedicated allocation of time may tend to a more conventional structure and organization. In contrast, scarcity of funding, limited study leave and pressure to publish may encourage anthropologists to explore aspects of their everyday lives 'at home' as their research material, thus feeding professional profiles with autobiographical experience. Economic crisis affects both researchers and informants. The crisis of the mid-1990s was a significant backdrop both to my account of how the project developed and my informants' descriptions of their experiences, expectations, actions and geographical movements throughout that period. Political economy was also significant for the 'European' context in which the project was situated. Through the research I sought to address a series of social science concerns about post-1992 Europe. I intended to use my informants' accounts of their experiences as ethnographic data that would explore questions such as the extent to which European citizenship permits 'freedom of movement' and employment within Europe and the transferability of Spanish educational qualifications to a British employment market. More generally I was interested in how redefinitions of European political, social and economic boundaries, set at an institutional level, may be constructed, articulated and experienced at a personal level through individual practices.

Personal/professional selves in a friendly field

As 'informants' I sought recent 'migrants' who defined their priorities as including speaking English, making non-Spanish friends and integrating with a 'British' culture. The 'key informants' were myself, my husband and a number of my friends. Thus friendship was both a theme of the research and a vehicle for its implementation. Hendry's (1992) account reveals how the overlap of friendships with professional relationships can result in an unhappy union that damages personal feelings and the research process. While I set out to formalize my 'study' of my friends, they also regarded their situations with reflective and comparative interest. In this sense both informants and anthropologist were performing like Giddens' (1991; see also Shilling, 1993) model of the reflective individual of late modernity. My intention was to work 'with' rather than on my 'informants'/friends/colleagues and to interpret our discussions as the sites of the production of knowledge. In doing so I would not pretend to avoid what Hastrup calls 'the inherent process of "othering" in anthropology' (1995: 159). Through our self-reflection both my 'informants' and I 'othered' ourselves by attempting to stand 'outside' of and consider our situations and experiences 'anthropologically'. Some of my 'informants' were social anthropologists, some lectured in other subjects, and my husband joined the project as a researcher.

'Othering' is a practice not exclusive to the anthropologist, but also practised by her informants. It is part of the process of self-representation. Constructions of sameness and difference are also fundamental to attempts to define groups as marginal, but defining a group as 'other' is not, as the Spanish anthropologist Garcia implies, necessarily tantamount to marginalizing that group: 'I suspect that foreign anthropologists who studied or study Spain chose us because they considered us "marginal" in some way' (Garcia, 1991: 111). The assumption that anthropologists study 'the marginalized' seems co-terminous with the idea that to study is to marginalize. The alterity and distancing of anthropology from its object that is constructed through the 'conventional' ethnographic narrative does little to deny Garcia's point. However, by understanding individuals' positions as less fixed and deconstructing the distance between anthropologist and informant, the balance may be redressed to some extent. Sometimes my informants felt they were disadvantaged in ways that they directly related to their 'Spanish' identities (for example, in the job market). Our discussions of feelings of marginality, disadvantage or disempowerment often centred on comparisons of their frustrations with my own experiences as an English person in Spain. Marginality is contextual (see e.g. Shire, 1993) and can be experienced or perceived in certain social and geographical spaces but not in others. Marginalization is not simply rigidly inherent in a system, but contextual, experienced and perceived. It is a category identified with and constructed by those for whose lives it seems relevant at the time. The process of studying people, and the construction of continuities and differences that this entails, inevitably involves 'othering', but does not necessarily define one's informants as inferior or marginal.

Fieldwork in and about one's social life thus raises issues concerning the processes of categorization and the drawing of arbitrary boundaries. As the project unfolded, my self-conscious and retrospective placing of boundaries at anthropologically informed sites created the structure of the 'ethnographic narrative'. For instance, my fieldwork in Spain about gender and bullfighting was accompanied by a process of change in my personal and professional identities. Initially speaking no Spanish, I eventually spoke fluently, published articles locally, and met and married my Spanish partner. Professionally, I arrived as a student and became a researcher, 'photographer' and writer (see Pink, 1996). Personally, I arrived with no roots in local social networks and left with valued friendships and a Spanish family; I eventually lived in Cordoba as a person with family and social responsibilities similar to those of my Spanish friends and informants. These professional and personal narratives were of course intertwined; their separation is an anthropological construction. The first phase of the research focused on investigating the public world of bullfighting culture, the second phase dealt with the everyday concerns of Andalusian men and women as regards work relationships and family life. The first phase of my personal life was one in which Spanish domestic life was 'other'. In the second phase I lived with my Spanish family.

I employed other strategies to circumscribe this second phase of the research. For instance, before I left Spain I attempted some cut-off points to try and make the research 'end'. On one occasion my husband's cousin suggested that he introduce me to another female bullfight photographer. Two weeks remained before we were due to leave for England. I was already 'writing up' and enjoying 'social' (i.e. non-research) time with my friends and family. I declined the offer, telling him the research had ended for the time being. My informant-seeking quest had ended. I resolved to distance myself from the project, and from the active research of seeking 'data' and writing 'field-notes'.

Before leaving Spain I regarded myself as having moved into a professional stage of 'writing-up' and had no intention of embarking on related research in Britain. Nevertheless, in England I became aware of some interesting patterns in my conversations with the Spanish people whom I met socially. Largely recent graduate 'migrants', they were concerned with common themes such as language learning, seeking part-time work, travel and tourism in England, and meeting English people. Our one-to-one discussions often covered our hopes and aspirations, career plans, relationships, problems in and with England, reasons for 'migrating' and the question of whether or not to return home. Our conversations were not just about 'them' but simultaneously about me and my partner: how did we/I/he deal with similar problems? How did we feel about living in England?

These personal exchanges (parallel to interviews?) were mixed with group encounters (parallel to participant observation?); we organized parties, dinners, walks in the countryside, visited each other's houses, and spoke on the phone, not only in all-Spanish groups but more often in mixed groups of English and Spanish. In group conversations amongst the Spanish and with English we often covered themes of migrant identities abroad, of job hunting in England, attitudes of employers, the au pair experience, contact with home, and the prices and availability of tickets home. Friends from different parts of 'Spain' negotiated their national identities to reconcile a sense of who one is in Spain with a definition of self-identity in Britain. Particular discourses on Spanishness/Englishness developed during the course of our contact with one another and we established conventions as regards which language was to be spoken, on what occasions and with whom. In a sense we were constructing a 'hybrid' and temporary culture, a set of norms and conventions and a sense of history. In another context my partner and I found ourselves speaking 'Spanglish' with another Spanish-English couple: inventing the hybrid language through our own conversations.

Retrospectively I began to consider how we positioned ourselves in these discourses. Kulick emphasizes (following Probyn) that 'the self is a politically situated discursive arrangement', thus arguing that it is problematic to see the self as autonomous or independent (1995: 16). My anthropological understanding is based on the idea that neither myself, my partner nor our friends were autonomously placed in these discussions and friendships.[7] I do not suggest that the sense of self, or what Cohen calls the 'self-driven' element should be forsaken. Rather I stress the importance of recognizing how the social self becomes connected and completed in different interactions, and how both anthropologists and informants articulate themselves in different representations.

Negotiating common ground ('homes'?) with a stranger

After the meeting with my Cordoban friend described at the beginning of this chapter (see p. 98), I caught a train to Greenwich where I had an appointment to meet a new informant. I was seeking a Spanish-looking woman wearing a leather jacket; she was to look out for a tall English woman in a sheepskin coat. We found a lot to talk about in the one-and-a-half hours before my departure. I felt that we had covered 'common ground'. We discussed and compared our experiences of living with our foreign partners in one another's countries, the price of tickets between Spain and England, the reactions of our parents to our partners, our plans for the future, our hopes, relationships, food and cookery. Had my 'informant' been doing research about British women married to Spanish men she would have gone home with plenty of data. Her English partner is a Ph.D. student in anthropology and I passed on to her the names of anthropologists I had recently met whom I thought he might be interested in contacting. I had met him at a conference where I presented a paper on the first phase of my 'Spanish migrant' research (see below).

I also learned from my answers to her questions: Why had my hus-band decided to come to England with me? she asked. I found myself telling her one of several versions of the story of 'why' he came to England. Later, studying myself, I wondered why I had chosen to tell her that particular story; I reflected on several other variations that I could have selected. I had given an account which I felt represented 'the truth' (in this instance believing in my own truth) and which I hoped my husband would consider fair. It had a different emphasis from the stories he would tell his best friends and from the version he would write into a job application. I wondered how my informants in turn constructed the stories they related to me, and reflected on how I had assisted my friends in adapting their stories for job applications and CVs. Another Spanish friend spoke to me about story-telling: she described how she had discussed reasons for coming to England with three Spanish women friends. Each had told of how she had left Spain after a personal/emotional 'crisis', each had wanted to 'escape' to 'change my life', or had fled from a disastrous or painful relationship with a boyfriend. These shared realities and common pasts appeared important to my informants. I have had the opportunity to share with them other realities of, for example, living in and learning another language and culture, thus sealing our contact with one another through our constructions of sameness. Our 'stories' were constructed and told in a range of different situations and with different intentions: for instance, as self-reflective personal narratives, or as strategic public representations of self. Each different telling may reference different discourses, shaped to the objectives of the situation.

From life into a paper. But where is the 'data'?

The transition from experience to anthropological knowledge and later to written text was at times uncomfortable. My first paper was based on the stories of my informants/friends discussed above. Since the research process had felt 'unstructured' I was concerned that it did not represent real systematic research. I presented the paper at a conference on migration in December 1995. One participant felt my research and that of others who were not working with (constructed as) vulnerable, marginalized immigrants who must be helped by the knowing anthropologist[8] was worthless: she argued that there was no point in doing research unless it is about people who are suffering and need help. We don't need to understand the middle classes. Another conference participant, a Spanish Ph.D. student, had come to England originally as an au pair to learn English several years before returning to do her fieldwork in London (for me a potential informant). Do au pairs really have positive experiences? From my own experience and that of others I met in London, au pairs are very exploited – she questioned my data. I pointed out that there is no singular 'au pair experience' and that in my paper I had covered a range of different women's experiences, some good, some terrible. Doing anthropology 'at home' about people who have made my home their home, and in whose home I also have a home, raises issues concerning authenticity and authorship and questions the identities and securities of both anthropologist and informant. The Ph.D. student observed that when an English woman had attempted to conduct research with the Spanish women's migrant association she worked in, they just wouldn't talk to her!

When in early 1996 the research was funded,[9] I was able to re-formulate my understanding of the project. I employed a research assistant and began to take more copious field-notes. I regarded it as a more formal commitment and as legitimate work: my confidence in my 'data' grew. Professional recognition enabled me to resolve my concerns about the validity of mixing professional and personal narratives in the research. I was delighted to be able to afford to visit my

London-based 'informants' and both they and I, aware of the economic support that the research was being given, became conscious of setting aside time to 'work on the project'. A distinction was set up between being in the act of 'doing the research' and a more general state of 'doing research'. On other occasions the research had been less easy to distinguish. For example, I had financed my travel to Spain for Christmas, but had spent several days of this 'holiday' writing up field-notes. I was occupied during those 'holidays' talking to old friends and new acquaintances who were considering going to England to improve their English, to work for a few months in the summer or to stay for an indefinite period (and those who were not thinking of going anywhere). Most of my Spanish friends who had 'migrated' had returned for Christmas, we met and discussed our different experiences of being 'away' and when we would next be back. Not only did I spend time with 'returned migrants' but I also observed the reactions of their families and friends to their absence and presence. My previous fieldwork had set the context for my study of informants who had migrated from Cordoba. Similarly when I attended a conference in Madrid the following March I spent much time speaking with 'potential migrants' – under- and postgraduates who requested advice concerning further studies in England. However, neither of these journeys to Spain had been 'field trips'. The question of whether or when I was doing research was only superficially resolved by funding recognition. The definition of the research or separation of personal/professional activity usually occurred before or after the potential 'research act' rather than while it was being experienced.

Limited research time, the arbitrariness of the distinction between personal and professional, work and research, and home and field combined to produce a particular style of fieldwork 'at home', and a particular ethnographic narrative. These issues extended into the electronic technological domain of the research.

New communications technology and anthropological research practices

As part of fieldwork 'at home', an 'electronic ethnography' raises particular questions relating to the definition of research, the flexibility of identity, uncertainties of geographical/physical space and the 'ethnographic narrative'.

For my project, telephone communications were fundamental to both the social relationships explored and the fieldwork methodology employed. Few would argue with Hastrup and Hervik's comment that a telephone call cannot be substituted for fieldwork. But their argument that 'most of the relevant information is non-verbal and cannot be "called-up", but has to be experienced as performed' (1994: 3) should be qualified. Hastrup and Hervik fail to recognize that experience is frequently performed with and over the telephone: technology is part of the performance of everyday life, integral to social relationships and identities, and part of the research context; part of my 'field', and increasingly part of more distant fields. Many Spanish in Britain and their families and friends in Spain are going on-line at home and/or at work. In my experience new communications technologies, interwoven with telephone practices and discourses, become part of everyday experience. My electronic communications with Spain include text and digital images and are discussed in telephone calls.[10] Rather than simply 'enhancing' communications (cf. Poster, 1995, and see below), email introduces a dimension from which new points of reference emerge.

My use of new communications technologies in the research was a form of 'participant observation' with middle-class professional 'migrants'.[11] Some informants agreed that these forms of communication will become increasingly important in the future (for research as well as domestic and 'work' connections).[12] Multimedia communications offer new potentials that are being explored by technologically literate migrants with internet access and therefore research into middle-class migrants' lifestyles and identities spans face-to-face to cyberspace. Cyberspace thus represents a new domain that overlaps with other more 'conventional' fieldwork locales. It is another space, where migrant identities are represented in a variety of new textual and visual formats. Technology may become increasingly bound up with migrants' definitions of their self-identities as email (and voice mail) become interwoven with telephone use; as photographs are taken for the out-box (with digital cameras) rather than for the post-box, and edited on disk before being sent 'home' on-line. Part of material culture may become immaterial and artefacts virtual – at least at certain points in their life histories.[13] In this research context the meaning of location changes as social and geographical spaces diverge (and converge).

New communications technology played two interdependent roles in my fieldwork. First, technology may be defined as a professional and domestic commodity, consumed by both anthropologists and informants; it is not solely a 'research tool'. In my research, new technology became a talking point between anthropologist and informants, it was an aspect of our 'shared' experience and 'culture'. Through our practices we made the technology meaningful on our own terms and in contexts of particular sets of social relationships and ideologies. Second, technologies provided the media by which anthropologist and informants communicated. I consider some implications of electronic communication. Some 'migrants' were particularly conscious of the importance of the communication possibilities invited by these connections across otherwise vast geographical distances.

During a period of four months in 1996 I built up a frequent email correspondence with several Spanish people in Britain. These communications came about and were conducted in a variety of different ways. The interchanges were initiated in terms of my own dichotomy: some were cultivated specifically for 'research' while others were formed on the basis of friendship. For example, I 'met' one person by email; subsequently, since we lived in the same city we met several times for a drink or dinner. I did not conduct research 'on' this person, although she knew of my interest. Others I never met face to face: a mutual colleague gave me the email of a Spanish anthropologist working on a project similar to mine. We communicated about our common interests and she wrote her 'story' to me. I 'found' another informant in a mailbase list, a Spanish lecturer working in England. I noted his email address and contacted him, explaining my project and inviting him to participate. His positive response resulted in a flurry of emails, ideas, and answers to questions. For a time we collaborated to attempt to focus a mailbase group on our shared interest in Spanish people in England. I also communicated with Spanish postgraduate students who hope to study for a period in England, thus becoming involved in their 'migration' as I was with friends who came to England as au pairs.

My electronic ethnography was carried out amidst the busy activity of my everyday working life. During a day of teaching I would email a few questions to one person, chat on-line with another, initiate another email relationship with a Spanish person whom my husband met at a job interview, or send off some information to another who was trying to move to England. Curiously, these different aspects of the same research switched not only from my working day at the university to my research, but also between different aspects of my professional and personal identity. My electronic communications changed between friendship mode, to researcher, or to a range of different professional identities. As a researcher, one may also employ a multiplicity of different personal styles. On-line relationships and representations of self were carefully negotiated in both the more 'public' domain of an internet discussion group and the one-to-one communication directed between personal email addresses. One informant whom I had interviewed by email became curiously difficult to recognize in his contributions to a mail list.

Communications technologies as an academic project

The question of how new communications technologies impact on contemporary social, cultural and political forms, and simultaneously on the individual, the self, or the modern/postmodern 'subject' and his/her identity, has become the subject of some recent work in cultural studies (e.g. Poster, 1995; Mitchell, 1995). This literature thus attempts to theorize the context in which my ethnography was played out. For me to be a 'participant observer' it was vital that I chat on the phone or by email, watch television and play computer games with my informants/friends.[14] Since communications technologies (new and old) were part of my research context, part of the project entails understanding how these technologies are shaped, used and become meaningful on the terms of my informants (see Silverstone and Hirsch, 1992).

New communications technologies have already been appropriated by anthropology. Some have interpreted 'cyberspace' and 'virtual reality' from an anthropological perspective (e.g. Gray and Driscoll, 1992; Pinney, 1994). More notably, anthropologists use new technologies to develop didactic materials, databases, multimedia representation and the dissemination of anthropology on-line.[15] However, as a 'research context' new technologies present a new domain in which particular questions of the representation of self and certain opportunities for reflectivity in anthropological research emerge. In sum, new communications technologies may potentially take on various different identities within anthropology, for example: as a commodity pertaining to the material culture of anthropology – thus regarding anthropologists as 'consumers'; as a 'research tool'; as an object to be researched as an artefact; as an element of the practice of our informants; as the potential interface between 'us' and particular 'others'.

In the 1990s an extensive literature has begun to emerge in an attempt to define and theorize 'cyberspace' and the nature of the social, political and economic relations that it implies. A stress on subjectivity and notions of the self as partial, dividual and reconstituted in every new context are reflected in contemporary cultural studies and in recent discussions of anthropological fieldwork. A threat to the autonomy of the individual has been perceived by Kulick and Willson (1995) who argue that in anthropological fieldwork, the self as autonomous agent is put at risk in the context of sexual intimacy; Poster (1995) proposes that the modern individual's 'autonomous rationality' is challenged through his/her interaction with new communications technology.

Poster's work implies a model for reflective ethnographic research practices using new communications technologies. He focuses on 'the construction of the subject in relation to these technologies, the issue of the body and the question of postmodernity' in what he refers to as 'the second media age' (1995).[16] Poster draws together discourses surrounding (1) a new (postmodern) identity or subject position which departs from the notion of the rational, autonomous, modern individual, and (2) technological change and new systems of communication and the ways they will affect the individual/society (1995: 23). Poster argues that we should not treat new technologies as being simply 'enhancements for already formed individuals to deploy to their advantage or disadvantage' (1995: 24). Instead he proposes that electronically mediated communication:

> enacts a radical reconfiguration of language, one which constitutes subjects outside the pattern of the rational, autonomous individual. This familiar modern subject is displaced by the mode of information in favour of one that is multiplied, disseminated and decentred, continuously interpellated as an unstable identity.
>
> (1995: 57)

Poster emphasizes this by comparing print culture with electronic culture suggesting that print is 'often credited with shaping the autonomous rational individual, a condition of modern democracy' (1995: 70). As a more efficient storage system, electronic writing enhances this, but, he continues: 'electronic writing also subverts the culture of print' by collapsing the distinction between author and reader. In the case of electronic mail: 'As a form of writing, the message services foster not the autonomous, rational stable individual but the playful, imaginative multiple self' (1995: 71). Mitchell similarly locates (at least part of) his on-line activity in his daily life which he describes as follows:

The keyboard is my café. Each morning I turn to some nearby machine – my modest personal computer at home, a more powerful workstation in one of the offices or laboratories that I frequent, or a laptop in a hotel room – to log into electronic mail. I click on an icon to open an 'inbox' filled with messages from round the world – replies to technical questions, queries for me to answer, drafts of papers, submissions of student work, appointments, travel and meeting arrangements, bit of business, greetings, reminders, chit-chat, gossip, complaints, tips, jokes, flirtation. I type replies immediately and then drop them into an 'outbox'. . . . If I have time before I finish gulping my coffee, I also check the wire services and a couple of specialised news services to which I subscribe, then glance at the latest weather report. This ritual is repeated whenever I have a spare moment during the day.

(1995: 7)

I interpret Mitchell's 'I' that remains at the centre of his description as standing for the 'self-conscious' self of which Cohen writes. The 'multiple self' appears to be generated as multiple representations of self. If one locates Mitchell's experience in Poster's electronic context it would appear that the 'playful self' is in this sense autonomous, or at least in control, rather than 'multiple'. I would rather not refer to either Poster's theory or Mitchell's own email practices as constituting a postmodern lifestyle. Such communication should not be regarded as essentially different from other modes of communication. Instead, it seems more valuable to conceptualize electronic communications in terms of a series of continuities as well as differences from, for example, face-to-face or print communications. Poster observes that much of what goes on in cyberspace is shaped by existing aspects of culture and society, yet argues that contemporary society is made up of both modernist and postmodernist institutions: the former being those 'that support autonomous rationality and subordinate others (women, ethnic minorities etc.)'. The latter of which 'such as electronically mediated communications' he argues, 'support new configurations of the subject' (1995: 76).

While one can undoubtedly construct differences between 'face-to-face' and electronic communication, for ethnographic work a modern/postmodern dichotomy is less useful than a consideration of how electronic communications work in relation to other forms of communication. For my ethnographic work I found that email worked alongside face-to-face communication. My communications with different informants entailed a variety of combinations of email, letter, telephone and face-to-face exchanges. Moreover, the particular configurations of the subject that Poster identifies as being specifically related to new communications technology are also part and parcel of the everyday lives of 'modern' subjects. I refer back to one informant in Cordoba: 'Sometimes I don't know who I am: Maria the teacher, Maria the person with good qualifications, the young woman, . . . sometimes when I go out at night if I meet a man I like I don't tell him that I am highly qualified because that can put a man off.' If Maria was using email we could well see what she would be doing as simply an enhancement of the everyday practice by which she already switched between her different representations of self. When Maria has since emailed me I have considered the language she writes in and the stance she takes to understand her messages in terms of my interpretations of the way she had also conveyed her self-consciousness to me in the many conversations we had and letters we had exchanged. No doubt the other emails she sent on those days to different people were interpreted differently. In the hustle and bustle of a crowded café on a Saturday night one could socialize thorough a variety of different identities. I am not claiming that face-to-face and electronic communications are essentially the same. Rather I suggest that in both contexts my informants and I represented ourselves in terms of different categories at different times. Similarly the identities of the Spanish 'migrants' in my project were not 'fixed'. I have labelled them 'migrants' in order to fit my study into one anthropological category, they have equal potential to be middle-class students of English, marginalized workers, tourists, bourgeois travellers and more.

There are of course some significant differences in the ways in which we can 'manage' our 'selves' when communicating electronically. As Mitchell points out, whereas 'traditionally . . . one had to go somewhere to meet people, to dress in accordance with the occasion – to represent oneself through clothing, body language, speech, and behaviour' (1995: 7–8) these rules do not apply on the net. However, I suggest that individuals are no less 'autonomous' or 'partial' in electronic or face-to-face self-representations: while we may recognize and theorize about the ways in which individuals express their 'multiple selves' in either communication context, it appears that individuals (including anthropologists) attempt to maintain an expression of the stable self, of the autonomous rational individual when they are expressing themselves (even if they are actually talking about their unstable identities). Both myself and my informants strove to appear consistent as we communicated both electronically and face to face. This was crucial for the preservation of both our personal and professional reputations.

Internet, space and 'the field'

Mitchell's framework for understanding 'cyberspace' focuses on space and place. He highlights several aspects of this which are significant for an ethnography that incorporates new communications technologies.

> The net is ambient – nowhere in particular but everywhere at once. You do not go to it; you log in from wherever you physically happen to be. In doing this you are not making a visit in the usual sense; you are executing an electronically mediated speech act that provides access – an 'open sesame'.
>
> (Mitchell, 1995: 8–9)

In such a research context the 'field' can be seen as similarly being nowhere and everywhere. My ethnography allowed me to log on, work, socialize in both face-to-face and electronic contexts, go on holiday, or stay at home, but I did not move in and out of a geographical space that I could call 'the field'. I 'went away' to do fieldwork – to London, or to Spain. But this did not have to imply that 'the field' was somewhere that was 'away': it was, at the same time, in me and around me. As I moved, my immediate field was defined by my own interaction with it, be it spatial, telephonic[17] or electronic.

In the electronic context, I could make certain decisions concerning the extent to which I engaged with my field. I could switch in and out of different modes by doing fieldwork by email: I did not have to be a researcher in the field, I could switch from being a researcher – a migrant's wife, a lecturer, an academic, a book review editor, I could exchange news with a friend in Eastern Europe, or with a colleague/ friend 20 metres away in my university. This intermingling of fieldwork amongst other emails in my in- and out-boxes implies, as I indicated above, a novel version of fieldwork narrative. It also entails a recognition that similar processes occur in non-electronic research.

Fieldwork narratives

The ethnographic narrative has been a focus for some recent work on anthropological fieldwork. This has entailed an exploration of fieldwork narratives throughout reflections on experience in the field. Thus Kulick and Willson (1995) argue that ethnographers should situate themselves in their anthropological work in such a way that departs from a 'conventional' ethnographic narrative that has been described as one in which the feminine (feminized) field is penetrated by the male ethnographer in a colonial-like relationship. This perspective is particularly relevant to my fieldwork, first because it entails a dissolution of the distinction between the anthropologist's personal and professional biographies. Second, a linear narrative of anthropological fieldwork in which the anthropologist goes to the field, experiences culture shock, goes native and then goes home does not offer a framework for understanding the ethnographic fieldwork enacted in the project described in this chapter. Rather than travelling to and penetrating another place in a linear sense, an ethnographer may do his/her research 'at home' or 'at work' while simultaneously performing a multiplicity of other tasks and roles. In this sense the research and the anthropologist are defined both as project and as public self in terms of how they are situated in relation to, and as parts of, these other activities and identities.

The face-to-face, electronic, visual, written and telephonic representations of 'self' and 'other' that were woven into this research represent some of the various ways in which everyday life is performed and experienced in contemporary modern Western society. Anthropologists, academics, informants and friends use technology to mediate their relationships in various different ways. As we appropriate, shape and define technology it can become an aspect of fieldwork practice and may contribute to the production of anthropological knowledge along with our friendships, families, desires and other consumer goods with which we fill our shopping baskets.

Conclusion

In this chapter I have endeavoured to describe how anthropological fieldwork, social life, friendship and electronic communications are neither incompatible nor necessarily separate spheres of life. One's experience 'at home' may be translated or redefined as anthropology 'at home', and the artefacts, technologies and practices of anthropologists' everyday lives may be regarded as research tools and contexts. In the late 1990s anthropology 'at home' – when 'home' is a developed European country – needs to attend to the material and technological cultures in relation to which everyday lives are performed and selves are represented. Some of these technologies as well as the ways that fieldwork may be structured 'at home' imply a rethinking and deconstruction of the boundaries, narratives and assumptions underlying the 'conventional' anthropological research methods and narratives.

Notes

1 Ph.D. research in Southern Spain funded by the ESRC (1992–94) and fieldwork in Guinea Bissau (1996–97) made possible by sabbatical leave from the University of Derby.

2 The gender dimension of unemployment, au pair work and travel is not developed in this chapter but forms an important part of the project.

3 Here I mean 'shared' in the sense which Rudie (1994: 32) describes whereby communication takes place on 'a level' of intersubjective understanding.

4 Okely uses the term 'retrospective fieldwork' to refer to her anthropological writing about her autobiographical experiences of attending boarding-school as a teenager.

5 The issue of the use of tense in ethnographic writing is raised by Davis, who suggests that writing ethnography in the past rather than present tenses may 'invite new critique' (1992: 217). Davis, by deconstructing various uses of tense in anthropological writing, illustrates that it is important to use tense consciously in anthropological writing.

6 Some academics write of their own 'migrant identities', usually writing from the disciplinary perspective of cultural studies (e.g. Hall, 1987; Minh-ha, 1994).

7 Kulick develops this from the work of Strathern (1991), Probyn (1993) and Haraway (1991). His analysis represents a commitment to the idea of 'viewing the self as unbounded and connected' which 'entails a view of the self as inherently incomplete and partial' (Kulick and Willson, 1995: 17).

8 My construction of her subject position.

9 By the School of Education and Social Science, University of Derby.

10 This present practice will most probably adapt with the introduction of digital sound.

11 New communications technologies are often elitist tools. Access is an issue, and raises questions concerning marginalization and power. However, these issues are not developed here.

12 The concept of family 'home' pages may be realized representing whole families visually and in audio in 'cyberspace'. Thus a website may define a family which has a geographically disparate existence. In this context, the

term 'home', especially as it relates to 'home page', takes on different meanings.

13 The theme of the biographies of material artefacts, or the 'social life of things' (Appadurai, 1986), invites a fascinating area for discussion. An image may originate as a photograph, be scanned, digitized, electronically arrive in another country, be viewed on the net, printed, and later, for example, exhibited on the wall of a 'home'.

14 In March 1996, I switched on the television and witnessed two young Spanish men chatting up the local girls in the London soap opera *EastEnders*.

15 For example, the Centre for Computing and Social Anthropology at the University of Kent (UK) (and see Fischer, 1994).

16 Poster builds on the Baudrillard–Adorno debate over the effects of the media to develop a post-structuralist perspective which avoids 'technological determinism' (1995: 22).

17 Mitchell suggests that electronic mail is different from the telephone or fax because, while telephones link 'specific machines at identifiable locations (the telephone on your desk and the telephone on my desk, say), an exchange of electronic mail (email) links people at *indeterminate* locations' (Mitchell, 1995: 9). He does not, however, account for mobile phones.

References

Angotti, T. (1993) *Metropolis 2000*. London: Routledge.

Anwar, M. (1995) Social Networks of Pakistanis in the UK: A Re-evaluation. In A. Rogers and S. Vertovec (eds) *The Urban Context*. Oxford: Berg, pp. 237–258.

Appadurai, A. (ed.) (1986) Introduction. In *The Social Life of Things*. New York: Cambridge University Press.

Bell, D., P. Caplan and W.J. Karim (eds) (1991) *Gendered Fields*. London: Routledge.

Cohen, A. P. (1992) Self-conscious Ethnography. In J. Okely and H. Callaway (eds) *Anthropology and Autobiography*. London: Routledge, pp. 221–241.

Davis, J. (1992) Tense in Ethnography: Some Practical Considerations. In J. Okely and H. Callaway (eds) *Anthropology and Autobiography*. London: Routledge, pp. 205–220.

Eades, J. (ed.) (1987) *Migrants, Workers and the Social Order*. London: Tavistock Publications.

Ellen, R. F. (1984) *Ethnographic Research: A Guide to General Conduct*. London: Academic Press.

Fischer, M. (1994) *Applications in Computing for Social Anthropologists*. London: Routledge.

Garcia Garcia, J. (1991) Que tienen que ver los espanoles con lo que los antropologos saben de ellos? In M. Catedra (ed.) *Los Espanoles Vistos por los Antropologos* Jucar Universidad, pp. 109–126.

Giddens, A. (1991) *Modernity and Self Identity*. Cambridge: Polity Press.

Gray, C. and M. Driscoll (1992) What's Real About Virtual Reality?, *Visual Anthropology Review* 8(2): 39–49.

Hall, S. (1987) Minimal Selves. In *The Real Me. Postmodernism and the Question of Identity*. London: ICA Documents, No. 6, pp. 44–46.

Haraway, D. (1991) *Simians, Cyborgs and Women*. London: Routledge.

Hastrup, K. (1995) *A Passage to Anthropology: Between Experience and Theory*. London: Routledge.

Hastrup, K. and P. Hervik (eds) (1994) Introduction to *Social Experience and Anthropological Knowledge*. London: Routledge, pp. 1–27.

Hendry, J. (1992) The Paradox of Friendship in the Field: Analysis of a Long-term Anglo–Japanese Relationship. In J. Okely and H. Callaway (eds) *Anthropology and Autobiography*. London: Routledge, pp. 163–174.

King, R. (ed.) (1993) *Mass Migration in Europe. The Legacy of the Future*. London: Belhaven Press.

Kulick, D. and M. Willson (1995) *Taboo: Sex, Identity and Erotic Subjectivity in Anthropological Fieldwork*. London: Routledge.

Minh-ha, Trinh T. (1994) Other than myself/my other self. In G. Robertson, M. Mash, J. Tickner, J. Bird, Curtis and T. Putnam (eds) *Travellers' Tales: Narratives of Home and Displacement*. London: Routledge, pp. 9–26.

Mitchell, W. (1995) *City of Bits*. London: Routledge.

Okely, J. (1992) Anthropology and Autobiography: Participatory Experience and Embodied Knowledge. In J. Okely and H. Callaway (eds) *Anthropology and Autobiography*. ASA Monographs 29. London: Routledge, pp. 1–28.

—— (1996) *Own or Other Culture*. London and New York: Routledge.

Pink, S. (1996) Excursiones en la vida socio-visual del mundo de toro. In *Antropologia de los sentidos: la Vista*. Madrid: Celeste, pp. 125–138.

—— (1997a) Female Bullfighters, Festival Queens in the Dole Queue and Women who want to Fly: Gender, Tradition, Change and Work in Andalusia. *Self, Agency and Society* 1(2): 87–106.

—— (1997b) *Women and Bullfighting: Gender, Sex and the Consumption of Tradition*. Oxford: Berg.

Pinney, C. (1994) Future Travel. In L. Taylor (ed.) *Visualizing Theory*. London: Routledge.

Poster, M. (1995) *The Second Media Age*. Oxford: Polity Press, pp. 409–428.

Probyn, E. (1993) *Sexing the Self*. London: Routledge.

Rapport, N. (1992) From Affect to Analysis: The Biography of an Interaction in an English Village. In J. Okely and H. Callaway (eds) *Anthropology and Autobiography*. London: Routledge, pp. 193–204.

Rudie, I. (1994) Making Sense of a New Experience. In K. Hastrup and P. Hervik (eds) *Social Experience and Social Knowledge*. London and New York: Routledge, pp. 28–44.

Salt, J. and R. Ford (1993) Skilled International Migration in Europe: The Shape of Things to Come. In R. King (ed.) *Mass Migrations in Europe*. London: Belhaven Press, pp. 293–309.

Shilling, C. (1993) *The Body and Social Theory*. London: Sage.

Shire, C. (1993) Men Don't go to the Moon. In A. Cornwall and N. Lindisfarne (eds) *Dislocating Masculinity*. London: Routledge, pp. 147–158.

Shuttleworth, I. (1993) Irish Graduate Emigration: The Mobility of Qualified Manpower in the Context of Peripherality. In R. King (ed.) *Mass Migrations in Europe*. London: Belhaven Press, pp. 310–326.

Silverstone, R. and E. Hirsch (eds) (1992) *Consuming Technologies*. London: Routledge.

Strathern, M. (1991) *Partial Connections*. Savage, MD: Rowman and Littlefield.

Werbner, P. (1987) Enclave Economies and Family Firms: The Case of Manchester Pakistanis. In J. Eades (ed.) *Migrants, Workers and the Social Order*. London: Tavistock, pp. 213–233.

—— (1995) From Commodities to Gifts: Pakistani Migrant Workers in Manchester. In A. Rogers and S. Vertovec (eds) *The Urban Context*. Oxford: Berg, pp. 213–236.

Chapter 7

Phoning the field

Meanings of place and involvement in fieldwork 'at home'

Karin Norman

During the writing of this chapter,[1] telephone calls to and from the field have served as a reminder of the open-ended, somehow 'placeless' nature of much contemporary fieldwork. As usual I become engaged in listening, asking for information, enquiring about someone's well-being, consoling, giving advice, offering assistance, and presenting my views on various events and experiences. Emotionally, to some extent practically, I have continuously remained engaged in the lives of my 'informants',[2] partly through these phone calls. This is an ongoing fieldwork consisting of a great many short visits over several years, of always being accessible but often not 'there'. For both professional and personal reasons the possibility of carrying out prolonged, un-interrupted fieldwork as I have done before is restricted, so 'phoning the field' has at times been an important means of keeping fieldwork alive. In the context of this chapter, 'phoning' also stands meta-phorically for the seemingly limitless, hard-to-grasp yet intrusive aspects of fieldwork that many ethnographers probably experience, especially as now they more often conduct 'multi-local fieldwork' and turn to 'home' in search of 'a field'.

Quite generally, the study on which this chapter is based concerns the political and cultural situation of Kosova Albanian refugees in Sweden and their network of relations in Germany and Kosova.[3] How-ever, I will focus here on my experiences of carrying out fieldwork among some of these displaced persons and on how their experiences of exile reverberate in me. I attempt to explore how my own experi-ences and understandings of being 'at home' and 'away' direct my attention to specific problems and influence my fieldwork practice. This connects with experiences many anthropologists have of the problematic limits of participation and involvement and the changing boundaries of the 'field' over time: the difficulties inherent in being close, geographically and emotionally, and still maintaining a distance. In retrospect, I can see that at times my own experiences have conflated with the experiences and actions of the persons of my study and induced specific forms of involvement and intervention in their lives. This, in turn, pertains to the complexity of distinguishing the experiences of 'the other' from one's own, and of assessing the interpretive value of one's own feelings, thoughts and imaginings.

Meanings and whereabouts of 'home'

Anthropology 'at home' may have been, and perhaps sometimes still is used as an unreflexive equivalence for 'same (primarily Western) country' (or 'society') implying various similarities between anthropologist and informants such as language, culture, history. This is part of the territorialized conception of culture, society and nation. It used to be assumed, when anthropologists started studying in their European homelands, that they would be blinded by their cultural similitude with their informants and take too much for granted.[4] As Clifford notes, 'The fieldwork injunction to go elsewhere construes "home" as a site of origin, sameness' (1997: 213). Today, this has been inverted. Now it is primarily the 'native' anthropologist who is thought to have privileged access to the world of the other, who then is 'the same'. This native, however, is not a person native to the West but to a Third World country (cf. Yamba, 1985; Appadurai, 1988; Narayan, 1993; Motzafi-Haller, 1997). Exploring 'difference' therefore remains the prerogative of the Western anthropologist. However, for many anthropologists working 'at home', the issue is more complex, and it has developed into a particular commentary about the reflexive turn in anthropology, problematizing the implications of sameness and difference (cf. Jackson, 1987; Hastrup, 1995; Reed-Danahay, 1997). 'Home' is many things and conducting fieldwork is by definition not being 'at home', just like the 'field' is not a place but can be 'wherever you happen to be', wherever the subject of your study takes you (cf. Fog Olwig, 1997). Cohen and Rapport claim that '[U]nless contemplating their own navels, the very nature of their enquiry means that anthropologists are never "at home"' (1995: 10) – except among each other, as Strathern argued before them (1987).

Apart from such reflections on the problematic nature of various assumptions about 'home anthropology' (and by extension, ideas about being an 'insider'), there are some conditions and consequences of doing fieldwork 'at home' (I retain this concept, however diffuse its meanings) which are, I would suggest, specific, however different 'the field' is from one's everyday life. Such conditions have to do with, for example, nearness and accessibility, time-span, language and research costs. Depending on the specific field contexts, some have favourable consequences, others are more difficult to handle. For many anthropologists, conducting fieldwork 'at home' means that it can be practically and economically easy to come and go to the field. Such closeness makes it possible to keep fieldwork going over a long period of time, combining it with other work and family-related commitments. The termination of such fieldwork occurs not by leaving but by not visiting any more, which informants may have a hard time accepting or understanding. Doing fieldwork 'at home' can make it possible to work in one's own language (even if it differs more or less from that of one's informants), which in turn can make the field appear in some ways more accessible. Working at home can make the anthropologist appear (and feel) like 'one of us' who is expected to share certain cultural values and social experiences, to 'know'; or alternatively the anthropologist can be seen as different, a representative of the 'majority' and the powerful who might then be expected to have political or economic influence. These various images of who the anthropologist is may also coincide with how the anthropologist sees her- or himself. The 'field at home' loses many of its otherwise more specific boundaries (however constructed), which also means that 'the field' may spill over into one's everyday life, something that can be both emotionally and intellectually rewarding or quite difficult to manage, emotionally, and also practically.

If 'home' is a contested concept within anthropology, it is also a problematic experiential issue for many of us. In studies of migrants and refugees such conceptual and experiential issues seem all the more compelling (cf. Graham and Khosravi, 1997; Shami, 1999). The migratory processes and the complex, sometimes tragic, experiences of displacement which mark so many people's lives can come to resonate with certain experiences of doing fieldwork and pose a methodological challenge. Studying refugees living in Swedish exile sets the meaning of place and 'at home' in particular focus for me.[5] I am a citizen of Sweden, whose government has the power to bestow on or deny refugees the right of residence, of freedom of movement and of material well-being. This renders me an ambiguous person and resource *vis-à-vis* these refugees and raises many moral and methodological questions as to how I influence their situation through my form of participation in their lives. We are constantly confronted with the problem of trying to understand the thoughts and feelings of others, especially as we strive neither to reduce such subjective worlds to 'their culture' nor, on the other hand, to 'the individual' somehow 'outside' social life (Cohen and Rapport, 1995). No less important for my analytical attempts is the question of how I perceive their influence on me, since this has consequences for my interpretations. In other words, what is the nature of our mutual and fluctuating relations? What kind of knowledge does my emotional involvement generate?

Sweden has become a strange place through the refugees I have come to know, and together with them I feel strangely at home. No other fieldwork has, for me, revolved around such strong and contradictory feelings of closeness and estrangement as this. It evokes in me the ambivalent feelings I have towards 'being at home' and 'going away'. And reading my fieldnotes I see how preoccupied I am with the meaning of 'exile' and with my very strong emotional ties to some of the refugee families. I interpret this as related to certain experiences from my earlier life. All fieldwork enterprises have an autobiographical side to them that should not be ignored but analysed in relation to the questions we ask, and especially those we do not usually think of raising or avoid more consciously. As Okely succinctly puts it, if 'the personal is political', the 'personal is (also) theoretical' (1992: 9). During most of my childhood I followed my parents to new places or was left behind while they were on the move. As I remember it, I was for many years intensively concerned with determining my national identity and which language was really my own: Norwegian, Swedish or American; I was troubled whether I was to be religious like my very old-fashioned grandmother or an atheist like my internationalized parents. Other places, other houses, other people were, and to some extent still are, a source of hope and anxiety. Doing fieldwork has been one way of reliving and yet transforming this experience. The effort to understand the ideas and experiences of others by relating these to what it evokes in oneself makes fieldwork anthropology's most valuable asset in the creation of its specific form of knowledge. Even more than my earlier field experiences, studying the Kosova Albanian refugees has spurred me to reflect on this process. In my previous writings I have tended to avoid the issue of my 'own experience' however much, or just because, it has preoccupied and disturbed me.

Most anthropologists today will agree that the person, the self of the anthropologist, is significant for the choice of field and for his/her fieldwork practice. Yet the issue of what this implies for particular anthropologists may perhaps still remain open because often enough the anthropologist, the fieldworker, does not have an answer to this question. To feel is one thing; to understand what these feelings entail, how they may govern one's actions and reflections and theoretical preferences is quite another. Considering influences of 'cultural background' on one's work, or academic tradition, age, gender and such more typical 'traits' of the social person seems less problematic than trying to sort out how a particular anthropologist emotionally experiences, and mobilizes these elements, as well as more diffuse idiosyncrasies in relation to persons and events in the field. Anthropologists are divided as to the prominence they lend to these more complex dimensions of experience, some still dismissing them as more or less irrelevant self-indulgences or trivial psychologizing. However, participation does need continuous theorizing (Okely, 1992: 13) and emotional or 'personal' experiences are an important route in such an endeavour (cf. e.g. McCarthy Brown, 1991; Dubisch, 1995). The point is that we do not learn about others by only observing and participating in their reality; we must go by way of how we experience our own. The attention one directs towards categories of informants as well as particular individuals in the field and one's mode of thinking about them is inextricably related, however complexly, to the reality embodied in oneself. It is this issue I wish to dwell on and link to meanings of place, home and involvement.

The field: its 'shifting locations' and relations

First a brief note on Swedish refugee policy, since it is one important reason why my 'field' is what it is.

The Swedish Parliament has unanimously declared that Swedish refugee policy should be 'generous, solidary and active' and those who are given asylum and therefore a residence permit should be encompassed by the general immigration policy goals of 'equality, freedom of choice and partnership'. To some Swedes this is promising too much; to others it is more political rhetoric that does not correspond to any real attempts to attain these goals.

In its present form, the definition and reception of refugees is regulated by the Swedish Immigration Act of 1989 (Utlänningslagen, 'The Act on Foreigners'). By the end of the 1980s there had been a substantial increase in the number of persons seeking asylum in Sweden and the Act was a means of more strictly regulating and handling the 'wave of refugees'.[6] The Act has been amended a number of times and there have also, in more recent years, been several sudden *ad hoc* political solutions to cope with unforeseen situations and consequences due to the regulations themselves, and the periodically high increase in the number of persons seeking asylum. In the 1950s and 1960s, and even in the early 1970s, most immigrants in Sweden had come as labour migrants (many of these were from Yugoslavia). Since that time, and especially since the early 1980s, almost the only way to apply for a residence permit is by seeking asylum. Sweden's economic difficulties and the subsequent high unemployment rate in the 1990s, as well as the reorganization and partial dismantling of the welfare system, has made labour migration to Sweden almost impossible for non-Europeans. Immigration based on flight is the only possibility. The dismal irony of this situation is that many who seek protection are not accepted as 'real' refugees and are either expelled or receive a residence permit on 'humanitarian grounds' (which does not lend them the status and thus the social and political recognition of 'refugee') only after years of appeals and anxious waiting. People are not given the right to define themselves or their situation, nor are they trusted to tell the truth about themselves. On the other hand, people do not necessarily identify with the category 'refugee'. They have come to seek a better, safer life, to join their families.

The National Bureau of Immigration is responsible for the investigation of all documents presented by each individual refugee upon arrival in the country and any other information he or she may wish to claim, in trying to judge their reliability and their right to receive a residence permit. This procedure is time-consuming and can take several years. During this time, while waiting for their verdict, the refugees, asylum-seekers as they are officially classified, are placed in reception centres located in different parts of the country.[7] During the prolonged period of waiting, each person receives subsidies of 71 crowns per day per adult to cover their expenses for food, clothing, bus fares, leisure activities and so on. They are also offered a variety of activities, the most important being that of Swedish language courses for adults and school for children. In later years participation is compulsory, otherwise the welfare benefit is withdrawn.

In the early 1990s, the great number of refugees in need of accommodation made the Immigration Bureau turn to municipalities in different parts of Sweden to establish local reception centres by renting empty apartments, mental hospitals that had been closed down, as well as hotels. At that time, there were many municipally owned housing areas lacking tenants due to economic changes and an accompanying population decrease in many regions. Renting out apartments to the

Immigration Bureau was deemed by local politicians to be a good economic solution. It was this situation which led to the establishment of a reception centre in a small town I call Gruvbo, situated in central Sweden.[8] Prior to and during this dramatic change I had been engaged intermittently in fieldwork in the town and municipality. That study concentrated on the meanings of place, the social production of ideas about local history and forms of belonging (cf. Norman, 1993, 1994). Shortly before, I had rented a small apartment in the public housing area originally built by a steel company for the benefit of the workers and their families, and later owned by the municipality. There were several apartments standing empty and it had not been difficult for me to find a small apartment to rent during my fieldwork. But neither I nor most of the other residents could then have anticipated that within a short time local politicians would let the empty apartments to the National Immigration Bureau for the establishment of a refugee reception centre, offering apartments in another housing area to those who wanted to move.

As the reception centre was established, I could look out from my kitchen window and see that my field site was changing. The large expanse of grass with the rundown playground by the birch trees had mostly seemed like an empty place, but now there were people wandering about everywhere. In the late summer afternoon, groups of women sat on the grass or strolled about while their children ran around playing or riding bicycles; men perched on the benches and children played on the swings nearby. Usually, a darkly dressed elderly woman walked ten steps behind the old man who was probably her husband.

All these people were refugees, mainly from the former Yugoslavia. This was in 1993. My fieldwork would be changing, that I knew, but I did not know how. I longed to go out and mingle with these foreign people, let myself be engulfed by the new and unknown. I felt the excitement surely common to most anthropologists when they are confronted with the possibilities of creating a new 'field'. Instead shyness and hesitation overcame me: I couldn't speak their languages, I felt painfully awkward, struck by an old, familiar feeling of being out of place, of not belonging. Many of the Swedish residents also gave expression to their feelings of estrangement, but they would also complain about it, that nothing was like it used to be. Hostility appeared to grow out of a sense among the Swedes that they were being forced out of their home and that home was being polluted. On my part, in the midst of my awkwardness, I rather felt the urge to start a new life, as it were, to find a new place to be.

For me this was an unsought opportunity to come close to the social and existential situation of refugees, confront experiences of exile, and learn how 'camp life' and bureaucracy were organized. I could not resist this even though I knew that I could not do full-time fieldwork. There were in particular a few Kosova Albanian families with whom I subsequently came into close contact, mainly because several of their members spoke Swedish quite well and because some of them were fairly active in the goings on at the reception centre and were interested in associating with me.[9] Kosova Albanians were, and still are, among those refugees most despised by many Swedes, and their fate moved me. This new field situation took hold of me emotionally as no other fieldwork ever has, and I expect that it will be difficult to give it up, especially since the situation in Kosova has taken such a violent turn and my informants live in a constant sense of distress. Since part of this fieldwork is 'at home' this is a practical possibility.

In less than a year the whole field situation changed again. The reception centre, the 'camp' as it was called by the refugees, was closed down almost as suddenly as it had appeared. Due to a diminishing number of refugees, the need for reception centres declined. Some refugees had already been expelled, others had received a residence permit, yet others had decided to move to larger cities and reside with relatives. The rest were relocated to other reception centres nearby or further away. For many of them this was frustrating and for me it was a depressing blow. I could not help feeling as if I had been abandoned. Gruvbo became a place without meaning. Fittingly, as it seemed to me at the time, most of the red-brick houses where we all had our apartments were demolished as part of local economic planning.[10] Within a few months there was no sign whatsoever of all that had happened. For a while I felt as if I could not really take an interest in Gruvbo and care about what was going on there. As it turned out I spent less time in Gruvbo, as often as possible going off to be with those Kosova Albanian families I knew who had been placed in a nearby town, here called town B, for short.[11] However, some families were placed in regions quite far away. One family ended up almost as far north as one can go in Sweden, more than 900 km away, and I simply could not keep up with them. We maintained contact by telephone, sent postcards and a few token gifts for the children at Christmas. After almost a year, they were transferred to a town near Gruvbo. However, after some months they moved again, of their own account, to Malmö, some 800 km south of Gruvbo. At the same time my 'core' family moved to town B and some of its members now live in another town, C. For several years then, everyone has been on the move, nothing seems predictable, and the field keeps changing boundaries, connecting several locations.

Those who have received permanent residence permits often choose to move to other places hoping to find a job or to get closer to friends and relatives. And those, mainly women and children, who still have valid passports go back to Kosova for visits of a month or two, or they may visit relatives in Germany. Since the outbreak of armed conflict in Kosova during the spring of 1998, few, if any, would dare such visits, unless they, i.e. the men, wish to join the UCK, the Kosova Albanian liberation army, operating in Kosova. Those without a permit who are still waiting, hoping or despairing are moved about to different places and apartments as reception centres are closed and reorganized. Off and on there have been rumours or news reports which have frightened people. Fearing that the police will come and send them back, some find yet other places and go into hiding there.[12]

Hope is another place

Through the following two examples I wish to consider experiences of place, home and belonging of two refugee women, mother and daughter, and their different ways of interpreting and coping with their situations. The emotions they evoke in me bear traces of my own experiences of loss and my ambivalent preoccupation with 'being at home or in other places'. This experience of their situation has led to certain forms of my involvement and intervention in their lives and thereby necessarily contributed to shaping the ethnography.

Fatbardha[13] is a middle-aged woman from Kosova who came to Sweden in 1992 with her three daughters and her youngest son, leaving her lost husband and her oldest son, who was in hiding in Macedonia, behind. The general structure of her life as a refugee, which is her main Swedish identity, resembles that of most other adult refugees in Sweden who apply for and finally receive a permanent residence permit. She was relocated to three different 'camps' until she received her permit, for which she had to wait two and a half years. She has completed part of the obligatory 700 hours of Swedish lessons and has intermittently been placed for a few months at a time in 'labour practice': sewing clothes for the Red Cross, helping out in a grocery store, baking bread and serving coffee at a local funeral home. Attendance in class and at the different assigned workplaces is compulsory, otherwise social welfare benefits are cut. Pay is in the form of subsidies, never income. Refugees have great difficulty finding regular employment and are very dependent on social welfare, which underscores their feelings of not belonging, of being a refugee, and disliked by Swedes.

Fatbardha now lives in town B where she has had three different apartments. One evening we were sitting in her kitchen after a late meal. Her young son and her half-grown children joined us from time to time. We exchanged some news but our conversation faltered and she had more difficulty than usual finding the right Swedish words. Then she suddenly said that they were going to move to town N, some 400 km away. I was dumbfounded. Even though many refugees choose to move south to the bigger cities once they have received their permits, I had thought that at least this family would stay on in town B. They had no reason to go anywhere else, as far as I was concerned. Fatbardha's married daughters lived in neighbouring towns, she did not have any relatives or close friends anywhere else in Sweden, and her chances of getting a job were nil.

Why hadn't she said anything about this before? After all we did talk on the phone quite often. She shrugged her shoulders and I felt the weight of her hopelessness fall over me. Her young son, Najm, saw my surprise and dismay and vented his fury at his mother for forcing him to move once more. He vowed that he would not go with her. I could not understand what she was trying to accomplish and again my own sense of loss made itself felt, as if she were leaving me, and my anger resounded with that of her son. Later, as she and I sat talking by ourselves, she told me that she hoped that her oldest son, who had finally arrived in Sweden seeking asylum some months earlier, would find a girl and get married, move to an apartment of his own, and leave her alone. He just sat around all day smoking, drinking beer and listening to Albanian music and kept nagging her for money. However happy and relieved she had been when he finally came, she now felt discouraged and frustrated. He could not understand the changes that had occurred to her and his sisters and he tried to meddle in how they now ran their lives. At the same time, he did not take any responsibility and she could not bear it any longer. And now she had signed the contract and sent it.

I felt that I just could not accept her solution, that she was continuing to flee and that nothing would change for the better just by moving to town N. I tried to convince her to change her mind. I reminded her that both her daughters living in and near town C needed her. One is seriously ill, the other has not received a residence permit and both live under extreme pressure which also strains their relations with their children and husbands. I also said that it would make life very difficult for her 10-year-old son who was finally growing accustomed to the school and seemed much happier and more confident than before. She was quiet, listened, sighed as I struggled to stick to the seemingly rational reasons while I felt like shouting at her that she was impossible, always running, just concerned about her own peace of mind, never trying to really understand what was going on around her, that she didn't take responsibility for her youngest child, and that she had no right leaving me like this. I was afraid and felt depressed. In a way I conflated the emotions of my own early memories with the experiences of her children. It was as if it would not be possible for me to see them in town N, which of course it would. I could not bear trying to incorporate yet one more place into my fieldwork and I fought her as if she were my mother, whom I never did fight. Exhausted, I realized that I had succeeded. She gave up, looked at me, smiled vaguely and said that they would stay. My feelings were mixed. I was relieved and glad, almost proud of my success. But I also had a vague feeling of guilt – had I done the right thing? In whose interest had I acted? I offered to call the landlord in town N and cancel the contract and see to it that they would not have to pay anything. But the rest, could I take care of that, too?

This was in 1995. Things have changed somewhat for the better, but was this because they stayed? I don't know. Her oldest son seems to get along a little better with the family. He has stopped drinking so much beer, he has cut down on his smoking, he has learned some Swedish and is friendlier and less bossy. But for him, town B was nothing, he did not know very much about the place. Town N would probably have been just as good. Perhaps even better, because later it dawned on me that they may have had plans to try to arrange a marriage with some girl who has a residence permit, which would give him a better chance of receiving one himself. This is what many young men do. Since he was over 18 when he came to Sweden he does not automatically get a residence permit just because his mother and sisters and brother have one. From a Swedish policy point of view, he is not a family member. He came on his own and is labelled a single male. None of them has directly talked in such terms, though they would most likely not have wanted to disclose such potential plans to me. Had I stopped them finding a solution to the boy's insecure position? Was I blinded by my own feelings and unaccounted-for motives? Cautiously I tried to find out if there had been any plans to arrange a marriage in order to get him a residence permit, but that kind of

deception is difficult to talk about since they would be mindful of the
risk of being detected by the authorities. More than a year later the
boy found a Finnish girl-friend, but he did not want to marry her or
anyone else. He wanted to be free, he said. So at least at that point he
had not taken the chance offered him to secure a permit to stay.

Fatbardha and the other family members do not relate any differently
to town B or show much more interest in the town than they did
before, except for Najm, the youngest son of Fatbardha. In November
1996, when I was driving them back from a long visit to town C,
Najm sat in the back, tired and hungry. As we were nearing town B he
suddenly exclaimed happily that 'B is the best place in the world'. For
Najm town B is a meaningful place. For Fatbardha it does not make
much difference whether she is in town B – or C or D or even in
Sweden, for that matter. She chose Sweden as a destination because at
the time it did not demand a visa and they were in a hurry to get out
of Kosova.

Fatbardha seeks solutions to 'problems' by going away or moving to
a different place. Her daughters have told me that they experienced this
tendency before in Kosova. So this is not solely a feature of refugee
identity, as one might assume. However, it is exacerbated by her status
as a refugee and the particular reception policy Sweden has in relation
to refugees in general, and from Kosova in particular. She does not
'know' the places she plans to move to and she does not seem to care.
This has a strong impact on my own sense of place as I do fieldwork.
She makes me feel as if town B is 'no place' and I realize that I have
great difficulty mustering the interest to make sense of life in the
town, even though I have been there many times. Kosova is the only
place that appears 'real' and knowable, even though she can be very
critical of 'Albanian culture'. I tend to identify with this 'absent reality',
yet hope that she will stay put and learn to think of the places around
her as worth knowing, make them 'real' for myself as well. For hope is
not always somewhere else. This is not a claim that fieldwork must be
in one locality. 'The field' may very well be wherever it takes me, as it
were. But this has had consequences with which I had not at first
reckoned.

Looking for home

One evening in the early summer of 1995, Marigona, Fatbardha's
youngest daughter who was unmarried and still living with her
mother, called me and declared that she was going to Kosova and

asked me to come along. She still had a valid passport, which her mother did not. She didn't care if it was dangerous, she declared defiantly. She had to go back to see what it was that she had been forced to leave behind three years ago when she was 16. As I interpret it, this was also a way of defying her mother, of wanting to recapture something her mother had almost brutally left, of finding her place in a life she had shared with her paternal grandparents whom her mother did not like. Fatbardha had always experienced considerable difficulties with many of her affinal kin, her mother-in-law especially. Marigona wanted me with her as a witness, as she said, a witness to the place and life that she missed so much. She felt that Sweden was nothing to her and that she was nothing to Sweden. If she could only go home, see Kosova, her grandparents, her aunts and uncles, her best friend, then she was sure that she could make a new start in Sweden. Her determination and hopefulness touched me deeply and I very much wanted to go with her. Her mother was at first very reluctant to let her go and I was afraid that she would feel pressured by me, as I was obviously willing. My accompaniment, as an adult and a Swedish citizen, was both reassuring to Fatbardha but also threatening since it meant that Marigona would most likely go. I could not really talk to Fatbardha about how she felt. She avoided my queries and I did not want to push her, partly because I did not want to hear her say definitely no.

Long before this event Fatbardha and I had sometimes talked about my accompanying her on a visit to Kosova. For me it had appeared more like wishful thinking than an actual possibility. At that time I did not know that many Albanians, primarily women and children, hired buses and returned for visits during Christmas and the summer vacation. This was not something anyone talked about or had confided to me. There were several reasons for this secretiveness, an important one being that people often do not wish to keep others informed about their plans and whereabouts. Perhaps as important was a wariness of Swedes in general and the fear that the social bureau would find out and cut off their economic support. The women would usually be away for a month or more and this could mean staying away from obligatory courses. It also implied spending money on things outside the range of purposes for which social welfare is designated. Her fears and worries were not only a matter of danger then, but also of expenses. Going to Kosova would cost a lot. She would have to borrow a large sum of money in order to take gifts of clothes and money for all relevant kin, quite a large number of people. Everyone in Kosova believes or is made to believe that their migrant kin – and almost every family has some member abroad – are economically well-off and it is impossible not to come home laden with clothes and money. Being a refugee or migrant means social and economic obligations and a continuous adherence to the common 'rules' of hospitality and exchange which bind people and places to each other.

We spent many hours on the phone the following three weeks discussing what to do, planning the trip, receiving advice from friends and relatives. For the sake of decency, as I saw it, and a wish to be a reciprocal part of this Kosova Albanian world, I helped finance the trip and the gifts but only to an extent which did not make me take over any initiative. I could not be sure where the limit of intervention was drawn and could not enquire, because to ask could have drawn attention to a possible infraction of hospitality codes. After all I was to be the guest, and a guest does not normally pay his or her way. I just had to feel my way through these sensitivities, drawing on my previous experiences, their indirect comments, gestures and facial expressions. However, it was first 'in place', in Kosova, that I sensed, and embodied, the meaning of the gift and the guest. For that, no telephone call in the world would have helped.

Finally we were on our way, and we spent a few weeks in the towns and villages that were central in Marigona's life; we met her grandparents, cousins, neighbours and friends; we met her relatives living in Germany, who are now slowly being incorporated into my fieldwork with the support of phone calls. Marigona alternated by being my interpreter and assistant and my quasi daughter or daughter-in-law. At times it was as if we were stranded together on an island in a troubled sea which none of us could really fathom; at other times I felt, quite childishly, stranded by her, when she sometimes would not help me if I did not understand or remember Albanian expressions or when she demonstrated certain 'silly Swedish traits', or when she 'used' me too much financially. I thought that she was perhaps angry about what I reminded her of, that other home, the inevitable return, that she was no longer just Kosova Albanian. Yet I was also the secure link back to her ongoing life, her mother, whom she missed very much. Marigona, who was so attended to by her relatives and friends, was also very much alone. She had changed, Kosova appeared different, and no one knew anything about the place she came from, about her Swedish life, partly because she, like so many other 'returnees', did not provide her kin or friends with much information about her situation in Sweden. I did know and could therefore be her quiet support. It is a strange feeling of being both a field and a fieldworker.

For me this trip gave some of the experiential resonance I was lacking in relation to all my informants in Sweden. I saw and felt some of the things and places they remembered and referred to, I was immersed in an interactive world they had known but which I did not. In some sense I felt that we became more real to each other. Marigona was almost tireless in her wish to associate with everyone, but she lost weight and was sometimes bewildered, sad and frustrated. For quite a long time afterwards, back in Sweden, she appeared depressed and was very angry with her mother for being in the wrong place, for being Albanian. I seemed to be, for a while, more important to her than her mother, perhaps because I shared in her experiences, perhaps because she missed the closeness that had developed between us and that now must take another turn.

Being involved in fieldwork

Involvement has many facets, in various ways dependent on the emotional involvement and problems of experience that I have been discussing and exemplifying, but not exclusively. Other dimensions of one's engagement also come to the fore such as one's social position and network outside 'the field', political inclinations, or specific knowledge to which one may have access. In both my examples, but specifically in respect to Fatbardha's attempt to move to town N, it is clear that I became involved in their lives in a way which induced me to intervene. Many times during this fieldwork I have been asked for my opinions on various matters, as I have been asked for help, advice and support. At other times I have given unsolicited advice or presented my interpretations of some event, and I have attempted to influence my informants' decisions and actions. I am still one of the few Swedes whom they know and associate with in their homes. Since I am a person with freedom, citizenship and a particular knowledge of 'how Sweden works', I can be useful. I have at times helped to fill in or explain official forms, written petitions, called social workers, contacted lawyers. But I can never disengage myself from the fact that I am doing fieldwork, so if places have 'porous boundaries' (Casey, 1996: 42), then so does fieldwork. Such acts and persons therefore all become part of 'the field' and expand my knowledge of how it is constituted. This kind of help and even interventions have been of value to my informants; I can nonetheless see that involvement of this kind is not unproblematic, for it can turn out to be based on misunderstandings of their actual situation and their real needs. I am sometimes pulled too strongly into their orbit of misery and complaints and cannot always think straight, advising in the wrong direction, or just worrying about them too much. In fieldwork, involvement in the form of 'help' can easily turn into a misguided show of authority and lack of sensitivity towards the competence and cultural specificity of the other. I am genuinely concerned about their well-being and I am prepared to help them, but 'help' can never be set apart from fieldwork, and I think that my greatest help is after all the interest I take in my informants and their lives, my willingness to listen and find ways to understand what concerns them.[14]

I am continuously placed within this range of conflicts between intervening and helping. While talking with Fatbardha recently, I half-jokingly asked her if she was going to move again. She had mentioned a month earlier that she might have to move to another apartment closer to her youngest son's school. The teacher had suggested, with the support of the social workers, that Fatbardha move closer to the school to ease the contact between home and school which was not deemed to be adequate. Fatbardha had not really wanted to move. She liked the new apartment they now had. The strain of moving, packing everything, carrying, refurnishing, all seemed too much to her. We dropped the subject. After a while she said, almost in passing, 'I might move to town S.' At first I did not understand what she said, a not quite conscious refusal to take it in. 'What do you mean, S?' 'A place near town S,' she said. 'Where is that?' 'Oh, it's 500 kilometers away!' 'But why town S, what do you know about that place?!' 'I don't know,' she said, she just wanted to move, to get away. I almost started laughing, for we were back on the same track again. But I did feel a moment of bewilderment about what to do. I could either try to convince her again that she must stay, or I could hear her out and try to understand what was bothering her, what she was looking or hoping for, what 'moving' means in her world. I am inclined to see the latter option as the more meaningful for both of us.

Places of home, exile and fieldwork

Place in the context of this chapter revolves around the complexity of place in terms of lived experience, our emplacement in the world, and the experience and meaning of place in relation to fieldwork and the import of field site, as well as the particular significance of places for the Albanian refugees in this study, who would in any general categorization be denoted as 'displaced persons'.

When I go to 'the field' I call first to say that I am coming. I want to check that those persons with whom I have most contact, Marigona and Fatbardha, will be there, or rather where they will be. We may talk about the order in which I should visit various persons or whether I should accompany the family I am staying with – most often Fatbardha's or a married daughter in a neighbouring town – on their visit to friends or to a sister or brother. Once I arrive, I usually find that plans have been changed, that we are going somewhere else or that we are not going anywhere or that we are going later, perhaps another day. Guests have sometimes preceded me and they must be taken care of. There are few spatial or practical obstacles for associating; much of people's time and energy is oriented towards receiving others as guests and helping each other out. I soon start floating along with them, being incorporated into their sphere of exchange and hospitality, enveloped by their concern for my own and others' well-being. It is a sensuous existence in their company, which can make it difficult to keep track of my more ambitious attempts at getting 'information' on various subjects. This does not mean that it is an idyll. On the contrary, it can often be difficult to understand, sometimes quite exasperating, even depressing. But I never feel bored, and especially never lonely or lost. Paradoxically, in the midst of their own insecurity in Sweden they induce in me a feeling of confidence, which finds expression in the sense that places do not matter, or that 'home' can be wherever you are.

During this prolonged fieldwork, the meaning of place has surfaced several times and I have sometimes felt as if I were asking 'Where are we?' while simultaneously thinking that they do not know where they/we are. I have not been able to rid myself of the feeling that 'place does not matter', well aware that place does matter. So I must ask myself to what extent this is simply my experience alone, to what extent does it depend on the specificity of this particular field/fieldwork or to what extent is it a sense communicated to me by my Albanian informants. By extension, these questions are related to more general underlying queries of the significance of 'place' for social experience, for fieldwork and the formation of anthropological knowledge.

'Place' is difficult to grasp since it is always there, as Geertz notes, so '(W)hoever discovered water, it was not a fish' (1996: 259). Our experience is always in relation to spatial horizons, depth, surface, closeness, distance. This is never just in general but is rather specifically placed – as our experience is always embodied so that we are always in, and of, place. 'Space is not the setting (real or logical) in which things are arranged, but the means whereby the position of things becomes possible' (Merleau-Ponty, 1962: 243). We live and move in specific spatial dimensions, in rooms, streets, landscapes, real or imagined. They are integral to the world we inhabit and the meanings we create. Having been children, we should know what force spatiality has in our lives, how much of our perceptions of the world relate back to the details of the places and bodies we knew as children (in whichever way we experienced our childhood years).[15]

Places are then integral to our experience, our thoughts and emotions. We cannot live 'placelessly' although we may feel 'out of place' or be seen by others as being out of place, and certain categories of persons, such as refugees, have come to be classified as displaced. Displacement, like 'refugee' and 'exile', is an especially problematic concept with its many political, emotional and theoretical implications. Malkki discusses the concept of displacement as being built on the assumption of our 'rootedness', the 'territorialization (of) our identi-ties', a 'peculiar sedentarism (which) enables a vision of territorial dis-placement as pathological' (1992: 31). From this point of view, being displaced is easily turned into a (negative) characteristic of the person rather than being seen as a consequence of a political and historical situation (cf. Shami, 1994) and as individually and collectively negoti-able. This is not to deny that forced migration and flight, or more generally moving to places not of one's choosing, can be a very painful, sad and frightening experience. Rather, it is an attempt to differentiate experiences of exile and of refugeeness, as well as the meaning of home and belonging, and of mobility more generally.

While we are all always located, dwelling in places, however transiently, the 'field' of our fieldwork is not reducible to the places where it is located. Neither is culture reducible to place. Anthro-pology's relation to place and culture is problematic, although not always problematized. As we know and as we are increasingly being reminded of in much recent writing (for example, Appadurai, 1988, 1992; Fog Olwig and Hastrup, 1997; Gupta and Ferguson, 1997), anthropologists have tended to equate cultures with particular geo-graphic places and also hailed the importance of regional expertise and thereby territorialized cultural difference (Fardon, 1990). But as has become all too apparent, politically, experientially, and so theoretically, 'culture' is not a bounded locality and to do fieldwork it is not enough to put our finger on a map, carve out a piece of territory and make it into a 'field'. Although doing fieldwork may place us, localize us, this does not mean that the locality is coterminous with the issues that concern us or the people whom we study. 'Generally, we may define the field, not primarily in terms of a locality, but as the field of relations which are of significance to the people involved in the study' (Fog Olwig and Hastrup, 1997: 8; see also Appadurai, 1995; Hannerz, 1996).

Places are about 'contexts of human experience, constructed in movement, memory, encounter and association' (Tilley, 1994: 15). Places become a part of our personal and cultural identities, but, as Tilley notes, '[P]laces are as diffuse and differentiated as the range of identities and significances accorded to them' (ibid.). What does that imply when you come to a new, unknown, place? With what means does a person orient herself? How do memories of other, earlier places relate to new places and the creation of a new space? Places one has no prior knowledge of, no experience, are 'senseless', as it were. They do not carry any memories, they have no story to tell. Points of reference are lacking, they must be created from assumptions which initially are from 'another place'. Unknown places may appear to stretch into the boundless, as Sweden seemed to do for Fatbardha and Marigona. Like my other Albanian informants, they must work at creating Swedish places, delimit them and give them meaning. As the crisis in Kosova has intensified, especially since the spring of 1998, their interest in Swedish places diminishes and Kosova seems to be more real but also more unreachable than ever.

At the beginning of my fieldwork Gruvbo seemed to me to be a 'definite', bounded place, although with a complexity of connotations for the people living there as for myself carrying out fieldwork there. Gruvbo has, like any lived space, an array of reference points and boundaries, for example, as a town, a municipality, as nature, as a place of work, as home, and all bearing names or other demarcations of identification. People have memories and show photographs of past events in particular known, remembered and named places. Then came the refugees for whom the meanings of the place of Gruvbo were completely arbitrary. They did not know where they were. For them Gruvbo was at first a backdrop, comparable only with other 'camp' locations they had already been to. Slowly, the refugees started to create this 'empty space' into a 'lived place' whereas for many Swedish residents Gruvbo threatened to become increasingly foreign and strange. The refugees soon learned where low-priced food and clothes could be bought and their sheer number stimulated immigrants from other towns to take their vans and set up markets in Gruvbo selling vegetables, flour, oil and other items at very low prices. A new dimension was added to the town square. The refugees made Gruvbo into a useful place for themselves, but they had very little contact with the Swedish population. As a particular place it was unknown and comparatively indifferent.

As long as the refugees were in Gruvbo, it felt like a very exciting and meaningful expansion of my fieldwork there. Then came the blow. The reception centre was closed, the refugees relocated to other towns. Where was I to go? What was I supposed to do? It is a painful experience when people in your field move away almost from one day to another. In the usual run of things, it is the anthropologist who suddenly leaves, perhaps never to return. Now it was the other way around and Gruvbo turned into a bleak place, almost like some empty space, as I perceived it. I did continue to maintain contact with my Swedish informants in Gruvbo, but the place had undeniably lost much of its emotional interest for me.

If 'the field' has conventionally been thought of as a locality, a place, this has changed for many anthropologists, while for some it has never been the case. Anthropologists, like the migrants and refugees they study today, become translocal, ethnographically and theoretically. This has repercussions for how fieldwork is experienced and conducted. In my case the field as a locality keeps changing. Instead of being in one place as before I am now moving between different places, and the meaning of 'a place' as a field site and as a source of experience and knowledge has changed in significance and general appeal. I take less interest in the places I am in which corresponds with how many of the refugees appear to relate to different places.

However, considering place and 'placelessness', the feeling that it does not make any difference where I or we are – which is not altogether an unpleasant feeling – the question arises as to what extent this is my feeling and to what extent my informants communicate it to me. We do not experience the world in general. As Hastrup writes, '[T]he world is always experienced from a particular point in social space' (1994: 234). Hearing my Albanian informants talk about Kosova it emerges as the only 'real' place; all others appear indistinct and interchangeable. I seem to identify with this feeling. The significance of going with Marigona to Kosova was that I had 'seen' the place, the people and spatial characteristics that make it into a meaningful place. Being in Kosova gave me a compass, it made it possible to locate and embody experiences immersed in the social life of a place. Events, actions, persons, became comprehensible, not from the perspective of knowing 'where it all came from' as some kind of matrix of their cultural origins, but rather more concretely and conditionally. I understood what and whom they were talking about. I had been in the houses where they had lived or visited, I had talked to people whom they missed. I was given access to their previous world of experiences and could share fragments of their memories (cf. Okely, 1994).

The emotional identification with informants during fieldwork has consequences for the kind of participant one becomes and the extent of practical involvement. This in turn influences the shifting boundaries of the field and fieldwork over time. As anthropologists have more consciously problematized the study of their own, often Western, societies or cultures – for which 'at home' is perhaps a misleading term – particular problems of participation and knowledge have been highlighted (cf. Jackson, 1987; Gefou-Madianou, 1993; Narayan, 1993). This links up with the discussions about experience (and reflexivity) and the reinvigorated interest in fieldwork practice; the return from culture as text to culture as fieldwork, as it were (cf. Handelman, 1994). However, relating one's own personal memories and experiences and the emotions they evoke may still seem out of place because it is difficult to make them theoretically relevant. They can easily be transformed into anecdotes or confessions. Personal experience and inner motives are nonetheless part of the anthropological project. My biography and experience alert me to certain aspects of life in exile. I may not be a better fieldworker for all that, but it does influence the way I act and the interpretations I make as I go along. Trying to be aware of this should make me more aware of how I delimit the field and formulate analytical problems, and the kind and degree of involvement I establish with my informants. The details of my life become connected with those of my informants, although it is not the 'story of my life' that is the important issue. It is rather the emotions and motives entrenched in this 'story' and how these veer and steer me towards others and what I want to know about them, how I am able or unable to perceive and understand the experiences of others. In my relationship with the refugee families, the complexity of this problem has become more obtrusive than during any other fieldwork in which I have been engaged. The preoccupation with 'home and other places' and the emotions this carries is, then, part of the logic of why I am attracted not only to doing fieldwork, but also to specific persons in the field. The relations many refugees have to different places have resonated quite strongly with my own ambivalent feelings about 'being at home' and 'going away'. That places appear interchangeable to them corresponds with places becoming emotionally indifferent to me.

This also gives me some insight into the meaning of their exile. Exile is not a static condition and not a place, but a process which involves experiences and memories of places and people. People change in and through what they experience in exile, while 'exile' as a way of life and set of meanings changes over time. The Kosova Albanians move, or are moved, from one place to another. Many hope that things will change and become better in a new place. But no one talks with particular interest about the place where they happen to be. In a way, they do not 'know' where they are or why they should prefer to go to one place rather than another. To the extent that I identify with them, then neither do I. Kosova is hailed as a 'true' place, however burdened with conflict and antagonism. It is a place that can be called home and many do go back and visit this waiting home. But some, like young Marigona, find that 'home' turns out to be where you aren't.

Notes

1 I wish to thank Moshe Shokeid for encouraging comments to a very first version of this chapter and Mona Rosendahl for valuable and detailed comments to a more recent version. Thanks also to a somewhat grumpy anonymous reviewer of *Culture, the Canadian Journal of Anthropology*, for useful comments.

2 'Informant' is not a very adequate term; it is too technical and emphasizes 'information' which is not what fieldwork is really about from the perspective of experience and interaction. However, I sometimes retain the term for want of a simpler and more convenient one. One could use 'friend' or some such term, but that also confounds problems inherent in forms of participant observation. I am close to many of the persons in my study and feel a strong friendship towards them, but the distance between us is there because the conditions of our relationship can never be completely ignored.

3 Spelling Kosova/o is not uncontroversial, and as the violence grows into war in Kosova/o, the spelling becomes a more obvious political stance. The Serbs spell it Kosova, the Albanians, Kosova and both categories make claims to the region by appealing to historical as well as present political/demographic conditions. In most English texts Kosovo is used, whether referring to the Albanian or the Serbian side; also because, historically, the province has not always had an Albanian majority (Malcolm, 1998). I have, however, used the Albanian spelling before and will retain it here since I am working with Albanians and this is how they pronounce it to each other. However, in relation to Swedes I have found that many have often said Kosovo, since this is how Kosovo is written and pronounced in the Swedish media.

4 As I wanted to choose a field site in Sweden for my very first fieldwork in the early 1970s, I was called in by a visiting professor to hear his warning

against such a foolish undertaking. I was told that first I should go abroad, preferably outside Europe, before considering doing fieldwork 'at home', so that I would have achieved a reasonable ability to be critical and comparative.

5 'Exile' and 'refugee' are problematic terms that can appear to rest on assumptions about undifferentiated experiences of loss, identity crises and total lack of contact with the homeland when instead forms and experiences of displacement are highly varied (for a critical discussion see Malkki, 1995; Eastmond, 1996; Shami, 1996). However, this is not the main focus of this chapter, but rather that of experiences of fieldwork among refugees within changing contexts.

6 In 1989, for example, about 30,000 persons sought asylum in Sweden, 'a new record' at the time. In 1992, about 84,000 persons arrived, mostly Bosnians and Albanians from former Yugoslavia. At that time Sweden did not demand visas, which was subsequently enforced and the number of new arrivals greatly diminished.

7 Since 1994, asylum-seekers may arrange their own accommodation if they wish and have the means. Each person can receive 500 Swedish Crowns per month to use as a payment for rent. Those who have relatives or friends who already have a residence permit can thereby stay with them and help pay the rent. The 500 crowns do not cover any real rent.

8 Gruvbo is a small town with about 7,000 inhabitants; the whole municipality has about 13,000 inhabitants. When the refugee reception centre opened it accommodated about 800 refugees (cf. Norman, 1995). Gruvbo is a region dominated by the steel industry while iron ore mining and foundries, forestry and farming have traditionally been the major forms of production. The industries employ almost exclusively men, whereas women are mainly employed by the municipally administered social service sector, that is, as caretakers of children, the aged and the handicapped. This is a common division of the labour market in Sweden; but it is iron production which is taken to be the essential creator of local identity, and in the local museums it is primarily the male-dominated iron production which is on display and in many tales of bygone days men are the cultural heroes. Since the late 1970s the region has faced serious economic difficulties and unemployment rates have been among the highest in Sweden. This is a different situation from that in the 1950s and 1960s when hardly anyone was unemployed and large numbers of Finns migrated to Sweden, and Gruvbo itself, to find work.

9 The number of Kosova Albanian refugees subsequently incorporated into my study comprises ten households which means about forty persons. The persons with whom I associate the most comprise five households. On the fringe of these households are quite a few people, mainly women, whom I meet in other people's homes or more often at the 'Albanian women's club'. However, the number of people varies from time to time depending on who has moved, when I have the opportunity to visit and how intensively I become involved in particular networks, especially that of Fatbardha, the main character in this chapter.

10 As a piece of interesting information relating to the economic and political changes going on in Sweden in the 1990s, about twenty-five apartment buildings have been demolished in Gruvbo since 1991.

11 I have retained the real names of the large, more well-known cities. For the names of the smaller or bigger towns I just use letters (e.g. 'town B', 'town C'). Mentioning the real names will risk identification of my informants. The towns are mainly located within the greater region called Bergslagen (the real name) where Gruvbo is also situated, along with several other municipalities. Using a letter instead of names also underlines the relative indifference and interchangeability of places which is a theme in this analysis.

12 This situation has changed somewhat since the upsurge of violence in February and March 1998. Shortly before this time and after prolonged negotiations, the Swedish government had signed an agreement with the Serbian government that both parties, Sweden and Yugoslavia, would take responsibility for any of their own citizens should they be sent back to their respective countries. The Serbian government would not ratify the agreement in the end. But for all practical purposes, Sweden acted as if the agreement was signed and working – that is, continuing to expel Albanian refugees, but not being able to effectuate it. Since March 1998, no one has been actually expelled and some refugees have finally received permanent residence permits. Others keep waiting, but need not at this point fear that they will be 'sent back'.

13 To protect the identity of the people in my study all names are pseudonyms. They would not have accepted it had I done otherwise.

14 For some anthropologists this may seem very meagre and even exploitative, since what I learn I can later use to advance my own career. This is a problem we are always confronted with and must keep trying to come to terms with. However, in considering the extreme difficulties many, if not most anthropologists around the world have of securing any kind of career and financing their projects, such arguments can end up being too simplistic and even opportunistic, at the same time denying the value anthropology has as a field of knowledge about the world in which we live. Who controls and has access to knowledge was, for example, debated at the fourth EASA conference in Barcelona, with a question posed by Marilyn Strathern, 'Should knowledge be free?').

15 Cf. Hart (1979) for an ethnographically detailed and fine study of children's experiences of place by a cultural geographer. Cf. Toren (1993) for an interesting analysis of children's perception of space in relation to hierarchy in Fiji.

References

Appadurai, Arjun (1988) Introduction: Place and Voice in Anthropological Theory. *Cultural Anthropology* 3 (1): 16–20.

—— (1995) The Production of Locality. In Richard Fardon (ed.) *Counterworks, Managing the Diversity of Knowledge*. London: Routledge, pp. 204–225.

Casey, Edward (1996) How to Get from Space to Place in a Fairly Short Stretch of Time: Phenomenological Prolegomena. In Steven Feld and Keith Basso (eds) *Senses of Place.* Santa Fe, New Mexico: School of American Research, pp. 13–52.

Clifford, James (1997) Spatial Practices: Fieldwork, Travel, and the Disciplining of Anthropology. In Akhil Gupta and James Ferguson (eds) *Anthropological Locations, Boundaries and Grounds of a Field Science.* Berkeley: University of California Press, pp. 185–222.

Cohen, Anthony and Nigel Rapport (1995) Introduction: Consciousness in Anthropology. In Anthony Cohen and Nigel Rapport (eds) *Questions of Consciousness.* ASA Monographs 33. London: Routledge, pp. 1–18.

Dubisch, Jill (1995) *In a Different Place: Pilgrimage, Gender, and Politics at a Greek Island Shrine.* Princeton, NJ: Princeton University Press.

Eastmond, Marita (1996) Luchar y Sufrir – Stories of Life and Exile: Reflections on the Ethnographic Process. *Ethnos* 61(3–4): 231–250.

Fardon, Richard (ed.) (1990) *Localizing Strategies: The Regionalization of Ethnographic Accounts.* Washington, DC: Smithsonian Institution Press.

Fog Olwig, Karen (1997) Cultural Sites: Sustaining a Home in a Deterritorialized World. In Karen Fog Olwig and Kirsten Hastrup (eds) *Siting Cultures, The Shifting Anthropological Object.* London: Routledge, pp. 17–38.

Fog Olwig, Karen and Kirsten Hastrup (eds) (1997) *Siting Cultures, The Shifting Anthropological Object.* London: Routledge.

Geertz, Clifford (1996) Afterword. In Steven Feld and Keith Basso (eds) *Senses of Place.* Santa Fe, New Mexico: School of American Research, pp. 259–262.

Gefou-Madianou, Dimitra (1993) Mirroring Ourselves through Western Texts: The Limits of an Indigenous Anthropology. In H. Driessen (ed.) *The Politics of Ethnographic Reading and Writing: Confrontations of Indigenous and Western Views.* Fort Lauderdale: Verlag Breitenbach Publishers, pp. 160–177.

Graham, Mark and Shahram Khosravi (1997) Home is Where You Make It: Repatriation and Diaspora Culture among Iranians in Sweden. *Journal of Refugee Studies* 10 (2): 115–133.

Gupta, Akhil and James Ferguson (eds) (1997) *Anthropological Locations. Boundaries and Grounds of a Field Science.* Berkeley: University of California Press.

Handelman, Don (1994) Critiques of Anthropology: Literary Turns, Slippery Bends. *Poetics Today* 15 (3): 341–381.

Hannerz, Ulf (1996) *Transnational Connections.* London: Routledge.

Hart, Roger (1979) *Children's Experience of Place.* New York: Irvington Publishers, Inc.

Hastrup, Kirsten (1994) *A Passage to Anthropology, Between Experience and Theory.* London: Routledge.

Hastrup, Kirsten and Peter Hervik (eds) (1994) Introduction to *Social Experience and Anthropological Knowledge.* London: Routledge, pp. 1–27.

Jackson, Anthony (ed.) (1987) *Anthropology at Home*. ASA Monographs 25. London: Tavistock Publications.

McCarthy Brown, Karen (1991) *Mama Lola, A Vodou Priestess in Brooklyn*. Princeton, NJ: Princeton University Press.

Malcolm, Noel (1998) *Kosovo, A Short History*. London: Macmillan.

Malkki, Lisa (1992) National Geographic: The Rooting of Peoples and the Territorialization of National Identity Among Scholars and Refugees. *Cultural Anthropology* 7 (1): 24–44.

—— (1995) Refugees and Exile: From 'Refugee Studies' to the National Order of Things. *Annual Review of Anthropology* 24: 95–117.

Merleau-Ponty, Maurice (1962) *Phenomenology of Perception*. London: Routledge & Kegan Paul.

Motzafi-Haller, Pnina (1997) Writing Birthright: On Native Anthropologists and the Politics of Representation. In Deborah Reed-Danahay (ed.) *Auto/Ethnography, Rewriting the Self and the Social*. Oxford: Berg, pp. 195–222.

Narayan, Kirin (1993) How Native is a 'Native' Anthropologist? *American Anthropologist* 95(3): 671–686.

Norman, Karin (1993) Controlling a Future by Admiring a Past: An Ecomuseum in Sweden. *Ethnos* 58(1–2): 37–51.

—— (1994) The Ironic Body: Obscene Joking Among Swedish Working-Class Women. *Ethnos* 59(3–4).

—— (1995) Refugees, Private Property, and Pollution: Conflicts of Belonging in a Swedish Small Town. Paper presented at the American Anthropological Association Annual Meeting, 19–22 November, Washington, DC.

Okely, Judith (1992) Anthropology and Autobiography: Participatory Experience and Embodied Knowledge. In Judith Okely and Helen Callaway (eds) *Anthropology and Autobiography*. ASA Monographs 29. London: Routledge, pp. 1–28.

—— (1994) Vicarious and Sensory Knowledge of Chronology and Change: Ageing in Rural France. In Kirsten Hastrup and Peter Hervik (eds) *Social Experience and Anthropological Knowledge*. London: Routledge, pp. 45–64.

Reed-Danahay, Deborah (ed.) (1997) *Auto/Ethnography, Rewriting the Self and the Social*. Oxford: Berg.

Shami, Seteney (1994) Mobility, Modernity and Misery: Population Displacement and Resettlement in the Middle East. In Seteney Shami (ed.) *Population Displacement and Resettlement, Development and Conflict in the Middle East*. New York: Center for Migration Studies, pp. 1–10.

—— (1996) Transnationalism and Refugee Studies: Rethinking Forced Migration and Identity in the Middle East. *Journal of Refugee Studies* 9(1): 3–26.

—— (1999) Circassian Encounters: The Self as Other and the Production of the Homeland in the North Caucasus. In B. Meyer and P. Geshiere (eds) *Globalization and Identity: Dialectics of Flow and Closure*. Oxford: Blackwell, pp. 17–46.

Strathern, Marilyn (1987) The Limits of Auto-anthropology. In Anthony Jackson (ed.) *Anthropology at Home*. ASA Monograph 25. London: Tavistock, pp. 16–37.

Tilley, Christopher (1994) *A Phenomenology of Landscape, Places, Paths and Monuments*. Oxford: Berg.

Toren, Christina (1993) Making History: The Significance of Childhood Cognition for a Comparative Anthropology of Mind. *Man* (n.s.) 28(3): 461–478.

Yamba, Bawa (1985) Other Cultures, Other Anthropologists: The Experiences of an African Fieldworker. *African Research and Documentation* No. 37.

Chapter 8

Access to a closed world

Methods for a multilocale study on ballet as a career

Helena Wulff

The ballet world is an intense, closed, highly specialized community that has reached across borders since its inception in the fourteenth century at Italian courts.[1] Dance historian and critic Joan Cass (1993) identifies ballet's international character by tracing it back to the first ballet production, the court ballet, *Ballet Comique de la Reine*, by Italian Balthasar de Beaujoyeulx in 1581 in Paris. Yet modern technologies of communication and transportation have increased the opportunities for mobility within a structure of new and old centres and peripheries. Today every major ballet production is a collaboration between people from a number of countries pooling national traditions and styles of choreography, composition, set and costume design.

In the relationships between culture and space from a macro perspective (cf. Appadurai, 1988; Gupta and Ferguson, 1992; Hannerz, 1992, 1996), the transnational ballet world is not only homogeneous in work practices (daily training, rehearsals, performances, basic steps) but also heterogeneous when it comes to national employment laws and funding systems. The transnational nature of the ballet world does not make national culture or the meaning of place obsolete. Ballet people are constantly negotiating transnational and national cultural processes. Sometimes one kind is more prominent than the other. There may be tensions between them, but also sparks of interchange. Ballet centres are characterized by national ballet styles, for example, which can be seen as one way to profile ballet companies and individual dancers transnationally.

By way of ethnography mainly from three national classical ballet companies – the Royal Swedish Ballet in Stockholm, the Royal Ballet in London, the American Ballet Theatre in New York, and to some extent the contemporary company Ballett Frankfurt in Frankfurt-am-Main – I will discuss how I gained access to this closed world, how I constructed my field by moving between the field locales in four countries, how I kept (and keep) in touch with informants in different field locales, and how they keep in touch with me. Exiting from the field presents different problems whether it is a field 'at home' or one 'away', not a part of the fieldworker's present, ordinary, everyday life. One prominent aspect of the mobility of the ballet world is touring, which meant from my point of view that the field was moving – and a few times I was able to go along with it. Tours are a kind of communitas, short-time fields that were very useful for my study, since certain cultural aspects are activated that are passive in the everyday life back in the theatre.

London is an old ballet centre where the Royal Ballet is cultivating its renowned style inspired by Kenneth MacMillan and Frederick Ashton. The English style is often described from other places in the ballet world as 'elegant, but slightly reserved'. New York is a multicultural ballet centre where the heritage of George Balanchine's neoclassical ballet with 'fast, even athletic technique', but also Martha Graham's modern technique and Alvin Ailey's African-American ballet, are explored in many ways. Frankfurt is a new ballet centre that the American choreographer William Forsythe has built up in a little over a decade, developing his own flowing movement vocabulary. Stockholm represents the periphery in the ballet world.

My units of study are thus demarcated by ballet centres of different kinds and peripheries, by the dancers' professional and personal networks, and by how dancers and other ballet people move between these localities that are consequently connected. There is, in fact, a history that goes back to the 1950s of mobility between the three classical companies, and since 1984 when William Forsythe took over Ballett Frankfurt, this company has been included in the transnational network. The four field locales were also divided into smaller sites. The theatres were the major arenas, apart from the American Ballet Theatre which did not have a theatre of its own, so I spent most of my time in its studios on lower Manhattan. The homes of my key informants also became recurring sites for fieldwork outside the theatres.

During the time of my fieldwork there was a certain amount of travelling by dancers, choreographers, coaches, conductors, composers and ballet directors between the companies I was studying. They came for a few guest performances or to work for a while with another company. I have thus, without planning it, met some of my informants in two countries – a few even in three countries – which gives a particular depth to the issue of transnationality. Some circumstances unexpectedly made sense in a transnational context.

It is obvious that the intrinsic transnationality of the ballet world calls for multilocale ethnography (cf. Marcus and Fischer, 1986; Clifford, 1997), or multi-sited ethnography, as Marcus (1995) has termed it more recently. In the ballet world there is a constant transnational awareness and communication with other places (cf. Marcus, 1989) through guesting, touring, competitions, galas, festivals and new technology, especially ballet video. Many ballet people possess both an active and a hidden web (that can be activated) of transnational experiences and connections. Personal encounters are often neglected in transnational studies; however, here, I will emphasize their importance. The ballet world is in large part connected by networks of choreographers, dancers and ballet masters who work together during weeks or months once a year, every other year or even more infrequently. But there is, typically, an assumption that ballet people from different countries will meet again.

'At home' and 'away' in the transnational ballet world

For more than two years I did a four-locale field study both 'at home' and 'away' in the transnational ballet world. As Kirsten Hastrup (1993: 151) points out, '"home" is a conceptual category with shifting references': since I grew up in the ballet world, conducting fieldwork there was, for me, like coming back home.[2] I danced classical ballet quite intensively for fifteen years, but had to stop in my late teens because of a back injury. (The fact that I used to dance with some of the people I study, that we have a shared past, is a rather unusual aspect of this fieldwork. It meant among other things that I was able to contextualize some of their biographical narratives.) My dancing experience is of analytical significance in two important ways: classical ballet is a non-verbal bodily type of work that is difficult to understand unless one has practised it.[3] Dancers moreover identify themselves as different from other people, more so than most groups. There are even conscious efforts to hide the exposed and sometimes painful work in run-down studios backstage, since a knowledge of that is believed to tarnish the ethereal illusion on stage. With the ballet steps, I also once learned the old-fashioned decorum that structures the ballet world. Slightly shocked that it was still there, I realized that a knowledge of it and an adherence to it proved useful in the field.

But if the notion of 'home' is a conceptual category with shifting references, so is that of 'away'. My home is 'away' for someone else, or in this case, the ballet world seems impenetrable and alien to many outsiders. Quite a few people, who do not go to performances or take an interest in ballet, assume that dancers are of the same relatively high social class as ballet audiences. This is not the case: most dancers are from upper working-class or lower to middle middle-class backgrounds. Those from upper strata of society tend to leave the ballet world unless they become principal dancers (which very few do).

Layers of acceptance, zones of access

The ballet world is fenced with security at electronically surveilled stage doors (entrances to the theatres) where visitors have to sign in a roster and obtain a visitor's tag. Inside the theatres there are signs saying 'No admittance' at doors leading to the stage. The pass door has a 'Private' sign in most theatres and is usually locked during performance. I was given ID cards to help me pass through security, and codes so that I was able to open locked doors and entrances. When there are Royals, presidential families and other dignitaries in the auditorium the security is heightened, with secret policemen backstage in electronic contact with their colleagues and bodyguards who might mingle with the audience. On these occasions, usually coinciding with important premières, the level of anxiety in the theatre was high among both directors and dancers.

I started my fieldwork in the ballet world by asking the director of the Royal Opera House in Stockholm for formal permission to spend one year with the Royal Swedish Ballet. When he had discussed my request with 'the leader's group' where the dancers have a representative, I met with the ballet director. Everyone responded positively to my request, but I was told not to create any disturbance in the studio, just to watch 'like a fly on the wall'. I was then immediately invited to watch a performance from the wings.

In August 1993 I began my daily contact with the ballet world at the Royal Opera House in Stockholm. With formal access I could observe company class, rehearsals and performances. The canteen was also a good place for participant observation, as were parties in the House and in the homes of the dancers. I started interviewing dancers and other personnel.

My relationship to the field, observational, participatory as well as dialogical, ran smoothly during the first two months of fieldwork.

I passed the usual initiation test by coping with one or two lies but also beliefs that I was there to recruit dancers to other companies. A tour to a provincial town during which I shared the dancers' strain and excitement in every detail marked the acceptance break for me, so I then moved on to deal with confidences like: 'What I'm going to tell you now, Helena, you mustn't write in your book, but . . .'.

Delighted that I had passed a significant threshold, I was well aware, however, that there was yet another zone that I had to penetrate in order to understand much of the goings-on: the dressing-rooms that were locked with codes. On a three-week tour to Japan, however, when I assisted as a dresser, I came to spend a lot of time in the dressing-rooms. This made it easier to hang around in the dressing-rooms at the Royal Opera House in Stockholm on our return. I was also invited there by dancers to look at pictures, have coffee, or just come in for a chat.

A reflexive comment on my presence at the Royal Swedish Ballet was performed in the sketch 'reviewing' major events of the season from the dancers' point of view at the annual spring party. This is one of only a few opportunities dancers have to release the intensity, constant judging and strict ranking of their career through structural rituals of rebellion (cf. Gluckman, 1982). Dressed up as the ballet management, including the coaches and the opera director, dancers made fun of their bosses and fellow dancers. Then 'the ethnographer' made her entrance in the sketch enacted by one of the dancers (incidentally a man). Dressed in trousers and a jacket, and with a wig looking like my hairstyle and hair colour 'I' stood shyly in the background radiating quiet interest. As the sketch moved on 'I' appeared here and there, sometimes quite unexpectedly, making my way towards the centre of activity, where 'I' found friends.

Increasingly, I noticed that some of my formulations and observations both about ballet and social life in the theatre 'came back' to me from the dancers. By then I had an idea about who was talking to whom about what, and I was able to trace my comments. Without striving for it, I had given the dancers words by verbalizing aspects of crucial ideas in the ballet world in a way that appealed to them.

At times dancers tried to use me as a pawn in intrigues. A male *corps de ballet* dancer, a jovial sort of person who had realized that his prospects for advancement in the company were not very good, enjoyed executing his story-telling talents in the canteen. This was where he really had an audience, especially of young *corps de ballet* dancers. One evening before performance he was in high spirits. 'You have to write this!' he urged me and indulged in a series of 'toilet stories' about an acclaimed female ex-dancer with the company who now has another prominent position in the ballet world. Encouraged by our roars of laughter, he set out on a new story by declaring: 'and this I know for sure!'

Marginal in the beginning, I was eventually able to move up and down in the social structure discreetly taking care of confessions from aspiring new *corps de ballet* dancers, tired principals and busy ballet directors. I comforted dancers with broken hearts, and homesick foreign dancers who missed their families and suffered cultural clashes. At times when a performance had not gone as well as it could have, or even occasionally had been downright disastrous, I was there to talk to. When bad reviews struck, I was sympathetic, as when there were set-backs in casting and upsetting social dramas, some of which I was also drawn into as a participant.

Fieldwork is often divided analytically into three phases. The first is characterized by a granting of formal access to hang around, the second which is the longest usually consists of more participation as well as observation, and the last is a hectic period of finalizing interview series and observational sequences to be followed by a reorientation back to the university. The transition between the first and second phase often takes the form of a dramatic event pushing the fieldworker deeper into the setting. One afternoon I became involved in a quarrel with the ballet director in a corridor at the Opera House. We were not shouting at each other, but there was obvious tension. He left quite upset. 'Now they will throw me out!' I thought, but instead I became more deeply involved in the ballet world. As I revealed my temper and sensitivity, it was confirmed that I was indeed one of their kind: a theatre person. A principal dancer who had witnessed the upheaval took me to the canteen to comfort me, and later I reconciled with the ballet director who became one of my key informants. It was through similar events that I obtained informal access and reached into the backstage of the backstage both spatially and mentally at the Royal Ballet in London, the American Ballet Theatre in New York, and Ballett Frankfurt in Frankfurt.

In the beginning of my fieldwork I sometimes forgot that the ballet world in general was more familiar to me than my presence was to people in the field locale I was in at that moment. Power structures, formal and informal, were not identical everywhere. Local power structure reflected national ballet culture and current alliances and antagonistic camps in daily politics. Since I had been watching performances from the wings at the Stockholm Opera innumerable times, I assumed that it was just a rhetorical question when I asked for permission to watch a performance from the wings at Covent Garden. After getting a polite 'No, I don't think that is possible' time after time, I realized that I had asked the wrong person, i.e. someone who did not have as much actual influence as her position seemed to entail. Later, I managed to get permission to watch from the wings from someone who had real power in the House. As I expanded my zones of access to the wings and the dressing-rooms at Covent Garden, I also learned the tacit House rules and which ones were broken by whom and how they were broken. One tacit rule was to sneak through the pass door from the auditorium to the backstage area and walk close to a wall during intermissions when the red light was flashing. This meant that entry to backstage was prohibited since a change of set was going on and there was a risk of serious accidents. One evening I was in a hurry because I had to make a telephone call during an intermission. I took the short cut, and as I was leaving the backstage area, I encountered not one, but two of the directors of the company. Blushing, I stammered: 'I've learned to break the rules the way you do!' One of the directors looked amused at my alarm, the other seemed worried and admonished me: 'Just don't walk across backstage!'

Ex-native anthropology

Native anthropology is a contradiction in terms, according to Kirsten Hastrup (1993). One is either an anthropologist or a native, she points out, identifying them as involved in 'different knowledge projects' (p. 154). The native is operating on a practical level, while the anthropologist in the end moves up to a theoretical understanding where the native's point of view and voice are included in the analysis, but are not the equivalent of it.

With modernization and increasing transnational connections there are not only new kinds of fieldworkers nowadays, more or less native (cf. Narayan, 1993), but the variation and range of natives are also different. I would suggest that the relationship between the anthropologist and the native has become more complex, at least in certain fields. All natives are not alike in their relationships to the anthropologist, not even in the same field. Natives may well possess an analytical talent – these are the ones who tend to become key informants – and nowadays may even be highly educated people. My anthropological training did not obliterate my native perspective. It does appear different through the anthropological lens, but is not distorted or useless for anthropological theorizing. This is not to say that I see myself as a native, just that my native experience from the past has been very useful in this field. In her comprehensive discussion on native anthropology, Kirin Narayan (1993) discards the separation between 'native' and 'non-native' anthropologists in favour of an exploration of shifting, multiplex identities in the field and in relation to theoretical issues.

Not only did I balance my status and experience as an ex-native in the ballet world; I also acquired a new form of nativeness: the form that comes with becoming a part of the setting on a daily basis. I could not have managed to cut off my own dancing experience when I was in the field, it was and still is too much a part of my personal self; and even if I could have cut it off, the dancers would have identified me as someone who was more native than most non-dancers, almost one of them. To me, there is an analytical significance in this: some anthropologists may define themselves, and be defined by the people in a particular field, as more native than others.

Getting around

Contrary to many other multilocale and transnational studies that consist of two or more short field studies conducted for the same length of time, I have one major field locale and three minor ones. My main field locale was at home at the Royal Opera House in Stockholm where the Royal Swedish Ballet, the national ballet company in Sweden, resides. I spent one year there, made frequent visits the year after and more scattered visits during the third year of my project, which makes this part of my fieldwork a conventional one in itself.

When my year with the Royal Swedish Ballet was drawing to an end, I asked the ballet management to connect me to the Royal Ballet in London and the American Ballet Theatre in New York. This they did through their personal and professional links. I already had some contact with dancers abroad, partly by way of Swedish informants who, for example, had introduced me via fax to a Swedish principal dancer at the American Ballet Theatre. When I met him, it turned out that we had attended the same ballet school as children in Stockholm.

After a few months of negotiations through mail, fax, telephone and personal meetings, I was welcomed to London and New York. Apart from the approval of the directors, their respective unions gave their agreements. The process for access was the same everywhere. I obtained permission myself from the fourth company, Ballett Frankfurt, by asking the director and choreographer William Forsythe when he was producing a new ballet, *Firstext*, at the Royal Ballet in London during my fieldwork there.

I had to handle suspicions everywhere that I was a critic, and attempts were made to hide issues that were considered sensitive, such as declines in famous dancers' careers, the use of drugs and the prevalence of AIDS. Then I reached a phase when my presence was taken for granted so much that I literally had to run from the last meetings with key informants both in New York and London in order not to miss my flights. During the second year of my fieldwork, my data continued to get denser, later events and processes illuminating early ones, sometimes providing clues I had been struggling to find and suddenly could discern because of my growing knowledge about contemporary ballet culture. And again, I saw certain things more clearly when I had grasped the transnational setting.

Exiting from the field

Access to the field has been dealt with at great length in the methodological literature as well as in stories and anthropological community lore, stressing initial hardships like marginality and cultural *faux pas* as a part of field socialization.[4] One difficult first encounter that has become somewhat classical is Napoleon A. Chagnon's (1968: 4–5) description of how, after travelling for days in a small, aluminium rowboat, he arrived, drenched in perspiration from the humidity and infested with insects, among the Yanomamö Indians in southern Venezuela. Chagnon met a group of the Indians, 'the fierce people' as he was going to call them, 'a dozen, burly, naked, filthy, hideous men staring at us down the shafts of their drawn arrows!' Exit from the field, on the other hand, has been regarded as more or less unproblematic. Fieldwork is traditionally constructed as a liminal period of time that the fieldworker is leaving behind and then returning to his or her 'real' life at the university. This is, however, clearly about to change. With the growing interest in anthropology at home, where it can be difficult to break off all contact with the field when the fieldwork is over, and with the prevalent use of technology like telephone, fax, video and even email, it may not be all that easy to leave a field 'away' completely either. What is more, the fieldworker may not want to cut off all communication. Even though it is customary to inform the people whom we study that we will eventually leave their everyday life, many fieldworkers have reported on phases when they have 'gone

native', been asked to stay permanently, and actually remember contemplating this as a possibility. Janet Siskind (1973: 17) reports on
her first six months of fieldwork among the Sharanahua Indians in the
Amazon jungle in eastern Peru as: 'at times exciting, often depressing,
a mixture of loneliness and satisfaction, exotic wonder and stifling bore-
dom'. On returning she confesses to have entered into the phase of 'the
romance of fieldwork'. This was when she really wanted to become a
Sharanahua and remain in the village. At some point, however, she
realized that it would be a limited existence for her so, of course, in
the end she left. Charges, even grief among informants about fieldworkers' departures, seem to be common. Some informants consider
how to make arrangements for fieldworkers to stay on in their worlds,
like the suggestion that I should train to become a choreologist (one
who notates, or writes down ballets). After a short repeat visit to
her field in a Bedouin community in Egypt's Western Desert, Lila
Abu-Lughod (1993) was about to return to the United States again.
The family she had lived with for two years pleaded with her to stay,
however. Her host, the man who was the head of the household, had
figured out the logistics around it: he would provide financial support
for a private school with Abu-Lughod as director. She declined, probably with some regret, and her host then drove her to the airport in
Cairo.[5] As upsetting, or bitter-sweet, as this field exit seems to have
been, there is at least some comfort in Evans-Pritchard's (1956: 79)
words that 'an anthropologist has failed unless, when he says good-
bye to the natives, there is on both sides the sorrow of parting'.

In a sense I had to make four exits from my fieldwork in the transnational ballet world, but one of them, the last, was more traumatic
than the others. Leaving the everyday life of the Royal Swedish Ballet
at the Royal Opera House in Stockholm was the hardest since I did
not know if I would ever return.

I had forewarned my informants that I only had seven days or
168 hours left with them. When the last day came with a performance
of a mixed programme, in the very last intermission, I said my good-
byes. I went back to my seat to watch the Czech choreographer Jiří
Kylián's one-act piece *Symphony in D* to music by Joseph Haydn. This
is a comic ballet, a veritable pearl in the Royal Swedish Ballet's repertory that by way of witty surprise steps makes fun of the characteristic
lines and language of classical ballet. Uninitiated audiences are usually
confused at first, then slightly embarrassed before a point when they
realize that they are allowed to laugh. I, however, was unable to laugh
that evening. Petrified, I wished the twenty minutes I knew the ballet

takes to dance would last for a lifetime. But the dancing finished, the music stopped, and when the curtain inevitably came down, the applause started. I rose, and stumbled in the darkness to the door of the box I was in. There were 'Bravo' shouts. The applause and the shouting grew stronger and as I ran backstage to get my jacket, I heard that it was unusually loud applause. Happy for the dancers, I yet struggled, overwhelmed with sadness, not to look back, not to be tempted to stay and take part in post-performance euphoria once again. Now I had to continue on my own. Outside the theatre, the white June night hit me with a blinding force, revealing my feeling of loss.[6]

Sooner or later, most fieldworkers do depart, carrying friendships and confidences with them, thereby sometimes worrying informants. There seems to be a qualitative difference between Janet Siskind's friendship links with her informants and those that Barbara Harrell-Bond had formed with the Western educated elite in Sierra Leone. Siskind (1973) states that she had true feelings for the people at Marcos, and Harrell-Bond (1981: 119) reveals that 'underlying the entire process was my realization that my intentions were mixed and that I had manipulated the relationships for the purpose of research'. It is significant that both kinds of field relationships actually exist, and not only the latter ones, especially with the growth of anthropology at home and long-term fieldwork.

During the course of my fieldwork in the ballet world I acquired key informants as a part of the expected process. This entailed an exchange of confidences which was the beginning of unexpected closeness with a handful of them distributed over the four companies. Most of these field friendships have survived the completion of my fieldwork.

Fieldwork is often not the kind of compartmentalized experience or practice it is presented as being. Harrell-Bond (1981) describes the ethical problems of leaving her field in Sierra Leone. Comparing with more traditional village studies where communication is broken after the fieldwork is completed, she presents a different situation with the elite whom she was studying. These people corresponded with her, even travelled to Europe and visited her. Once a woman from her field had a miscarriage during a visit to Britain. Harrell-Bond invited the woman into her home for a few days to recuperate. It turned out that the woman needed surgery, so she stayed in Harrell-Bond's home for five months, something which Harrell-Bond was in fact not too happy about.

In touch with the field

As I moved from one field locale to another I kept in touch with the other field locales, partly because I was moving back and forth to a certain extent. Having completed my fieldwork, I am still in touch with informants directly by way of telephone and mail, fax, email and indirectly by way of reviews and articles about them in newspapers and dance magazines, and videos and television programmes in which they perform. My informants are eager to tell me about company politics, casting, new productions, repertory, injuries, dismissals, reviews, audience reactions and personal news. They also ask me to provide such information and news about other companies with which they know I keep up to date. One Brazilian *corps de ballet* dancer wrote to me about her first solo:

> 'Oh! I nearly forgot to tell you a big news: I did my 1st solo with the company . . . I was covering Betty in a solo called 'the Odalisque' made by Tom Sapsford . . . I wasn't meant to do it unless something happened to her. But, Tom, seeing how much I had worked for it, decided to give me this chance. I was told only one week before 'the Day', so [it] caught me as a big surprise.
>
> I was so happy about it, so looking forward to do it, that I didn't feel nervous at all. Just wanted to do it and enjoy it. And so I did! . . . That moment on stage, during and after the solo, with all the flowers and applause, was one of the happiest in my life! Another dream coming true!!
>
> Are moments like this that keep me going, make me not give up yet!'

Conclusions: at home in a multilocale world

This chapter has dealt with the ballet world as a closed world and the strategies of access and exit as well as keeping in touch with the field which I used as an ex-native in my multilocale fieldwork among four interconnected ballet companies in Sweden, Britain, the United States and Germany. Despite the fact that the state of ex-nativeness is a very unusual situation, it was useful in this fieldwork about the non-verbal embodied practice of performing ballet. There has recently been some focus on the problems of studying non-verbal embodied practices ethnographically such as by French sociologist Loïc Wacquant (1995), who became an apprentice boxer for his study of boxers in Chicago; and Catherine Palmer's (1996) fieldwork on competitive cyclists in the Tour de France would probably not have come about unless she had been one herself.

Although the ballet world may appear to be set apart from the rest of society in many ways, the point of this chapter is really to show that the ballet world in fact illuminates certain general contemporary circumstances especially in relation to those quickly expanding transnational career networks that are anchored in multilocale structures of centres and peripheries. The ballet world is transnational by tradition, but other careers and communities are becoming transnational and new ones are emerging within many different fields. They will all have to deal with national versus transnational processes, as well as with cultural clashes within their transnational communications. Transnationality on the whole, but not least the kind of transnational links having to do with career networks, is thus an important contemporary social phenomenon that deserves more anthropological attention. This includes the practice of new methods such as multilocale fieldwork.

Acknowledgements

Some of the ideas in this chapter were first articulated at the seminar 'Translocal Field Studies' in the Department of Social Anthropology, Stockholm University, in 1996 and at a workshop on the same topic in 1998. I wish to thank my departmental colleagues for inspiring discussions on both of these occasions.

Notes

1 This chapter is part of a larger study on ballet as a transnational career. Some sections are a revised form of work which previously appeared in 'Studying Ballet as an Ex-Native: Dialogues of Life and Fieldwork' in *Kulturanthropologinnen im Dialog: Ein Buch für und mit Ina-Maria Greverus*, edited by Anne Clare Groffman, Beatrice Ploch, Ute Richel and Regina Römhild (Königstein: Ulrike Helmer Verlag, 1997). Some sections also appear in different versions in Helena Wulff, *Ballet across Borders: Career and Culture in the World of Dancers* (Oxford: Berg, 1998).

2 Marilyn Strathern (1987: 16–17) identifies the problem of 'how one knows when one is at home'. She suggests that personal credentials are not enough for this, there has to be cultural continuity in the eventual writings and accounts by the people about themselves.

3 See Maurice Bloch (1992: 130) on the problem of transferring mental models of informants to text and how this can be attained by learning a

culture through 'experience, practice, sights, and sensations', the way children are socialized. Growing up in the ballet world is a formative experience providing 'kinesthetic reference' (Novack, 1993: 36) that makes up for the fact that I was unable to dance like the people I was studying were dancing at the time of my fieldwork.

4 Discussing the social nature of learning, Lave and Wenger (1995) identify the importance of stories and community lore in apprentice learning. Such stories are often about mistakes, or when things go really wrong, they claim.

5 In the car, Abu-Lughod's host played a cassette of Bedouin love songs that had a local connection.

6 Looking back at this drama that occurred at the end of the 1995 season, I probably should confess by way of an epilogue that I have indeed found a way to stay on in the ballet world, both in the field locale at home and those away: I have started a new study on the social organization of 'dance and technology' (photography, television, video, CD-ROM). My multilocale field is turning into a long-term multilocale field, whereby I am after all avoiding exit from the field.

References

Abu-Lughod, L. (1993) Shifting Politics in Bedouin Love Poetry. In C.A. Lutz and L. Abu-Lughod (eds) *Language and the Politics of Emotion*. Cambridge: Cambridge University Press, pp. 24–45.

Appadurai, A. (1988) Putting Hierarchy in Its Place. *Cultural Anthropology* 3(1): 36–49.

Bloch, M. (1992) What Goes Without Saying: The Conceptualizing of Zafimaniry Society. In A. Kuper (ed.) *Conceptualizing Society*. London: Routledge, pp. 127–146.

Cass, J. (1993) *Dancing through History*. Englewood Cliffs, NJ: Prentice Hall.

Chagnon, N. A. (1968) *Yanomamö*. New York: Holt, Rinehart & Winston.

Clifford, J. (1997) *Routes*. Cambridge, MA: Harvard University Press.

Evans-Pritchard, E.E. (1956) Fieldwork and the Empirical Tradition. In *Social Anthropology*. London: Cohen and West Ltd, pp. 64–85.

Gluckman, M. (1982) *Custom and Conflict in Africa*. Oxford: Blackwell. First published 1956.

Gupta, A. and J. Ferguson (1992) Beyond 'Culture': Space, Identity, and the Politics of Difference. *Cultural Anthropology* 7(1): 6–23.

Hannerz, U. (1992) *Cultural Complexity: Studies in the Social Organization of Meaning*. New York: Columbia University Press.

—— (1996) *Transnational Connections*. London: Routledge.

Harrell-Bond, B. (1981) Studying Elites: Some Special Problems. In M.A. Rynkiewich and J.P. Spradley (eds) *Ethics and Anthropology*. Malabar, FL: Robert E. Krieger Publishing, pp. 110–122.

Hastrup, K. (1993) Native Anthropology: A Contradiction in Terms? *Folk* 35: 147–161.

Lave, J. and E. Wenger (1995) *Situated Learning*. Cambridge: Cambridge University Press.

Marcus, G.E. (1989) Imagining the Whole: Ethnography's Contemporary Efforts to Situate itself. *Critique of Anthropology* 9(3): 7–30.

—— (1995) Ethnography In/Of the World System: The Emergence of Multi-Sited Ethnography. *Annual Review of Anthropology* 24: 95–117.

Marcus, G.E. and M.J. Fischer (1986) *Anthropology as Cultural Critique: An Experimental Moment in the Human Sciences*. Chicago, IL: University of Chicago Press.

Narayan, K. (1993) How Native is a 'Native' Anthropologist? *American Anthropologist* 95(3): 671–686.

Novack, C.J. (1993) Ballet, Gender and Cultural Power. In H. Thomas (ed.) *Dance, Gender and Culture*. London: Macmilllan, pp. 34–48.

Palmer, C. (1996) A Life of Its Own. Unpublished Ph.D. thesis, University of Adelaide.

Siskind, J. (1973) *To Hunt in the Morning*. London: Oxford University Press.

Strathern, M. (1987) The Limits of Auto-Anthropology. In A. Jackson (ed.) *Anthropology at Home*. ASA Monographs 25. London: Routledge, pp. 16–37.

Wacquant, L.J.D. (1995) Pugs at Work: Bodily Capital and Labour Among Professional Boxers. *Body and Society* 1(1): 65–93.

Wulff, H. (1998) *Ballet across Borders: Career and Culture in the World of Dancers*. Oxford: Berg.

Chapter 9

Locating yoga

Ethnography and transnational practice

Sarah Strauss

Chicago, Illinois – September, 1993

Here I am, in 'The Field' again, trying to make sense of what's going on. Despite being in my native country, I feel nearly as overwhelmed as when I first arrived in India in 1990. Walking around at the opulent Palmer House Hotel in Chicago, peering into meeting rooms and watching the people rushing in all directions, it's hard to take it all in. The thick program for the second Parliament of the World's Religions – 100 years after the first – is astonishing in its breadth. In addition to lectures and films, there are well over fifty exhibitors offering courses, books, spiritual vacations, or simply lifestyle changes for the amassed participants. At the opening ceremonies a few days ago, the theme of unity and the fact that the Earth is 'the global home of one family,' as Swami Chidananda of the Divine Life Society in Rishikesh had put it in his address of the previous day, was everybody's mantra. Needing to get away from all of the talk, I wander off to a yoga demonstration by a man wearing the latest fashions in Patagonia outdoor wear and Teva sandals. Austrian by birth, he had grown up in England, Germany, and America, spent three years in India, of which a substantial part included Rishikesh as a home base, and then had come back to America to start a yoga school in Chicago; by the look of his clothes it was doing rather well.

Shifting terrain: multi-local ethnography in practice

The scene described above occurred about twenty months into a two-year project on the construction of yoga as transnational practice.[1]

I begin with this vignette to illustrate the kinds of situations encountered while pursuing dissertation research on a topic which spanned three continents and a century before I was done. As a graduate student embarking on my first fieldwork project, I did not originally set out to study yoga, but to understand what it means to be healthy. What constitutes health or illness for a given person, and how do such perceived states of being relate to everyday practices pursuant to broader life goals? Are understandings of personal well-being linked in any way to relationships extending beyond the person? How do such understandings differ across cultures? Questions like these brought me to India in 1990 for a brief visit, with the goal of making contacts for my initial proposed dissertation research, an investigation into how certain ideas and practices related to health were represented in an Himalayan town. Despite best intentions, the 'traditional' ethnography I had imagined myself completing did not materialize; instead I found myself following threads and trails of people, publications and practices that together told a story. This chapter addresses why I ended up conducting fieldwork at the Palmer House in Chicago in the footsteps of Swami Vivekananda of Calcutta, what that has to do with a study of yoga practice based in Rishikesh, India, and how such a project can illuminate the implementation of a new framework for ethnographic research.

In addition to its long-standing history as a major Hindu pilgrimage site on the banks of the holy Ganges River, the state of Uttar Pradesh and the government of India have proclaimed Rishikesh to be 'the place to go for yoga';[2] it is also the base for a number of adventure tourism organizations which take aspiring trekkers and white water rafters to the higher reaches of the Himalayan rivers and peaks. The main attraction for yoga practitioners is the Divine Life Society (also called the DLS or simply the Sivananda Ashram), founded in 1936 by Swami Sivananda. But the story of modern yoga that I am concerned with begins much earlier, with Swami Vivekananda, a young, unknown monk who left Calcutta for Chicago and the first Parliament of the World's Religions at the Chicago World's Fair in 1893. Vivekananda stayed in the West for four years, and during that time he wrote and distributed several books concerning yoga and Hinduism, and presented lectures in English to middle- and upper-class audiences thirsty for authentic Oriental wisdom.[3] This first 'export guru' (Narayan, 1983) was followed by many others, including Swami Sivananda, who developed his ashram and, later, his international organization, based on Vivekananda's model. As a physician, Sivananda focused his efforts on health improvement and promoted yoga as a method appropriate and indeed necessary for the health and well-being of Indians and others alike.

Although my first idea for field research did not require a site more specific than 'somewhere in Hindi-speaking north India, probably in the Himalayan foothills', various events, discussed below, led me to the town of Rishikesh at the beginning of 1992 and away from it again for a month in the middle of that year. At the end of 1992 I left India for another year of archival and ethnographic research in Europe and America. When I found myself going to Rishikesh, Sivananda and his organization presented a natural focus for my own health-related interests. As Gupta and Ferguson (1997: 11) point out, the choice of a particular field site is rarely due entirely to random luck as many ethnographic accounts seem to imply, but rather to certain ideological, structural and practical constraints which limit choices or create favourable opportunities. Yet failing to acknowledge that these very constraints are subject to external influences, and that they themselves are not necessarily stable, leads one to a false sense of inevitability. The chapters in this volume clearly demonstrate that events do indeed occur by chance as well as by design, and that such contingencies of illness, accident, and the unintended intersection of very different personal or institutional histories can radically alter the shape of the ethnographic field.

Much has been said about the importance of representation, the relative power of different voices and the impossibility of the task of ethnography; recently, more attention has been given to the fact that the 'Field' as traditionally conceived (a bounded, isolable, cultural whole) is not only unrealistic and inappropriate, but does not, and perhaps never did, exist. The actual process of 'constructing the field', the activities which lie between the observer's choice of a topic for ethnographic research and a representation of the history, settings and relationships that characterize the observed in written form, has been less of a focus. Each research project has a starting point, and, if not an ending point, at least a point of abandonment. How does the ethnographer make decisions about which lead to follow, and when is enough? Given that the privilege of movement in and out of the field is no longer only the prerogative of the ethnographer, how do we carve out meaningful slices of culture? In my study of yoga, I interacted with many people who saw themselves as 'world citizens' despite their varied countries of origin; they moved often, by flights both transoceanic and of imagination, and indeed embodied the deterritorialized world so frequently described by theorists of modernities, post and otherwise (e.g. Appadurai, 1991, 1996; Hannerz, 1996; Kaplan, 1997; Morley and Robins, 1996). Ethnographic settings like the Parliament described above are too planned to be quite the 'accidental communities of memory' of which Malkki (1997: 91) speaks, but they are certainly kin – neither are the sort of everyday, more-or-less permanent arenas of social interaction that anthropology has traditionally sought to address. One of the goals of this chapter is to suggest a way to frame historically grounded, transnationally dispersed anthropological research using a vocabulary that is capable of including a broad range of field locations, both grounded and virtual, without presupposing temporal, spatial or material boundaries.

In a recent article, George Marcus describes multi-local ethnography in terms of movement 'out from the single site and local situations of conventional ethnographic research designs to examine the circulation of cultural meanings, objects, and identities in diffuse time-space' (1995: 96). This review elaborates upon one of Marcus' essays of a decade earlier, in which he had set up the question of how we can understand the anthropological project of holism as both research and representational strategy 'once the line between the local worlds of subjects and the global world of systems becomes radically blurred' (Marcus, 1986: 171). At that time, Marcus suggested two possible ways of addressing this question ethnographically, either by using 'a single text to represent multiple, blindly interdependent locales, each explored ethnographically and mutually linked by the intended and unintended consequences of activities within them' (p. 171) or by 'construct[ing] the text around a strategically selected locale, treating the system as background, albeit without losing sight of the fact that it is integrally constitutive of cultural life within the bounded subject matter' (p. 172). For me, the decision to engage in multi-site ethnography was clearly a product of constraint and opportunity. In 1990, I had done preliminary research in a town about 150 kilometres from Rishikesh, but I was later told that a visa for research in that region would be hard to come by because of certain political problems in adjacent districts. A far less politically sensitive field site, an important official in New Delhi told me, would be the tourist town of Rishikesh. Following his advice, I applied for and received permission to carry out research in Rishikesh town on the subject of health and yoga. At that time, I fully expected to engage in a 'traditional' single-site ethnographic project, to be carried out not behind mud walls (*pace* Wiser and Wiser, 1971), but behind the colourful concrete walls of Swami

Sivananda's DLS ashram. In the usual manner of these things, it took a few weeks to get work underway at the ashram, and in that time I realized that such a fixed local ethnography would be insufficient to describe what was going on in Rishikesh, especially in terms of yoga. Instead, I began to see the possibilities in terms of movement through space and time.[4] My first fieldwork experience thus combined Marcus' two approaches, using Rishikesh as a single 'strategically selected locale' – which was nonetheless dictated by opportunity – to locate and orient a study which included other spheres of socio-cultural activity.

Sites and subjects: methodological concerns

As a pilgrimage town, Rishikesh is at any given time filled with residents of every state in India. In addition, one can always find a wide variety of international visitors; residents of Western Europe, North America, Japan and Australia dominate that population. The primary impression I received upon first wandering the streets of Rishikesh town was heterogeneity. Throughout the year, I found that I was using nearly as much German, and far more English, than Hindi in my interviews and interactions with the yoga practitioners, ashramites and townspeople who helped me to learn about this complex locale. I had studied German for several years in high school and college before taking up French, and later, specifically for fieldwork, Hindi. In his discussion of the methodological difficulties of multi-site ethnography, Marcus (1995: 101) points out that '[i]t is perhaps no accident that exemplars thus far of multi-sited fieldwork have been developed in monolingual (largely Anglo-American) contexts'. In another twist of fate, my husband was hired as a post-doctoral researcher in Zürich, Switzerland several months prior to beginning research in Rishikesh. Both of these circumstances made it possible for me to imagine and then follow through on a project involving a dispersed network of locations in a way which would otherwise have been linguistically and financially untenable.[5]

Marcus' observation that if translocal 'ethnography is to flourish in arenas that anthropology has defined as emblematic interests, it will soon have to *become* as multilingual as it is multi-sited' (Marcus, 1995: 101; my emphasis) demonstrates his own Anglo-American bias. For anthropologists from many other parts of the world – Switzerland and India certainly come immediately to mind – operating in a multilingual environment is simply business as usual. Indeed, the use of a 'local' language which usually constitutes one of the hallmarks of anthropological fieldwork was itself an issue; though I had prepared extensively and fully expected to make use of my training in Hindi, I found that the translocal politics of language use resulted in an almost equal utilization of Hindi, English and German. Because Sivananda was born in the southern state of Tamilnadu, many of the residents of the ashram, as well as visitors, spoke Tamil or Malayalam as a first language. Although most spoke Hindi as well as or better than I, the north–south politics of India, as well as the class concerns of many highly educated Indians, dictated that we speak English together. I also want to make the obvious point that there were many pathways I was not able to follow in conducting my research on yoga. These 'paths not taken' were determined not only by time, interest, assumed relevance and financial limitations, but also by my linguistic capabilities: in addition to the large numbers of German speakers whom I encountered in Rishikesh, there was also a highly visible population of young Japanese women, most of whom were travelling alone. I was intrigued by their reasons for studying yoga, but unable to obtain much information because their English was limited and my Japanese non-existent. Follow-up visits to Japan seemed improbable, and so I was unable to pursue what may well have been an extremely interesting and fruitful addition to my interpretation of yoga transnationally.

After my initial year of fieldwork based in Rishikesh, reflecting the traditional requisite for the anthropology Ph.D. at an American university (Gupta and Ferguson, 1997: 14), I pursued ethnographic research in a range of contexts across Germany, Switzerland and America for another fifteen months, making research trips of one to three weeks from my home in Zurich. 'My home', I say, because it was where I spent most of my days and nights, yet during that time most of my worldly possessions were in storage in three different places in the United States, and my parents were forwarding most of our bills. My husband and I, academic migrant labourers, were living out of suitcases and backpacks, and had been doing so for three years. Like many of my discussants, our professional practices took us into many different places, but in each, we found like-minded others with whom to share life. Paul Rabinow put it well when he described the condition of cosmopolitanism as 'an ethos of macro-interdependencies, with an acute consciousness (often forced upon people) of the inescapabilities and particularities of places, characters, historical trajectories, and fates' (1986: 258). One question I want to explore is how anthropology can incorporate the recognition that we are all, to one degree or another, now cosmopolitans in Rabinow's sense. We cannot place others in a locale, while we as ethnographers hover above, typing frantic representations into our laptop computers. That much has been clear for some time, at least since the mid-1980s and the publication of Clifford and Marcus' *Writing Culture* (1986), the volume in which Rabinow's definition appeared. More recently, Arjun Appadurai has worked to define the parameters of a new 'cosmopolitan ethnography' (1996: 52) which offers a new take on the old subject of micro–macro relations, highlighting the ways that the global and the local are ever intertwined and implicated in each other's pasts and futures.

This 'cosmopolitan ethnography' demands new ways of thinking about 'the field', and of actually doing fieldwork. I have come to think about the ways that my field experience developed in relation to a pair of linked concepts. These concepts help define the rather amorphous and sometimes ephemeral spaces – spheres of activity, as I called them earlier in this chapter – within which I conducted ethnographic research, and allow me to begin to map out the ways in which individuals, institutions, communities, ideas, practices and objects interacted in ways that made possible the transformation of yoga over the last century. The term I want to propose for such a 'sphere of activity' is a *matrix*. A matrix is comprised of two or more intersecting *vectors*. Drawing on the language of mathematics and physics, a *vector* is defined as a quantity having the properties of both direction and magnitude – force, mass, substance of any sort (*Oxford Desk Dictionary*); the standard definition of a matrix is a 'vector of vectors', that is, an array of intersecting directional forces, each with its own observable characteristics. In the context of ethnographic practice, such vectors can thus be understood as directional forces capable of transporting ideas, practices, objects or actors across specific pathways.

A matrix, then, is a set of linked or intersecting vectors. Matrices are by definition multidimensional, but the degree of dimensionality is infinite, as are, potentially, the boundaries of the matrix. The dimensions of a matrix are determined only by the number and scope of the vectors which comprise it. With these terms, we have a framework for defining non-geographically bounded sites of interactive research – field sites that are not *necessarily* anywhere, but do take place somewhere. The concept of a matrix allows us to describe contingent locations for social interaction, in which actors who call other places 'home' meet on regular or irregular bases, and create social worlds which in turn have implications for other arenas of sociocultural life, as well as more permanent kinds of locations. A matrix can be virtual or located in geographically defined space; using the terms *vector* and *matrix*, we can define any kind of socio-cultural form without resorting to the need for a physical boundary. The matrix is defined not only by the individual actors as one type of vector, but also by institutions, paradigms, products, and any other aspect of socio-cultural life that can be described; they are all vectors, because they all have magnitude and direction, both of which can change given interaction with other such forces.

The terms *vector* and *matrix*, though originating in mathematics, have been applied to a wide range of disciplines in different but related ways;[6] in mathematics, as noted above, the two terms are related, but in other fields they are more often used alone. One reason I have for introducing them into ethnography is as a way of building bridges across the drifting subfields of anthropology. Archaeologists use the concept of a matrix in a locational sense, to speak of the stuff within which artefacts and items of significance are found. They, like cultural anthropologists, also have an interest in defining locations for activity that are contingent, more transient than the traditional notion of a site (Binford, 1980: 9; Kelly and Todd, 1988), and for this purpose my definitions of vector and matrix may be useful. Geography, the most spatially oriented of social sciences, has also used the concepts of vector and matrix, but in a much more formal way and not always together, as part of an effort to quantify spatial relations according to mathematical and statistical models (e.g. Girardin, 1995; Harvey, 1969). In biological terms, a vector is the carrier of a disease-bearing agent (Benenson, 1985: 458); for example, the anopheles mosquito is the vector for certain types of malaria. But we can know something about the life cycle of a specific pathogen, and be reasonably certain about how it is transmitted from one host to another, yet still not be able to specify the exact reasons why one individual succumbs and another does not. Even without a completely clear understanding of mechanisms, however, an epidemiologist can collect a set of cases and begin to find patterns within it, patterns that will help to explain and create choices for shifts in patterns of thought or action. Without being morbid, the analogy of infection is not inappropriate when we are speaking of the transmission and transformation (not necessarily in that order) of socio-cultural ideas and practices, as with yoga. Some individuals or institutions will be more or less susceptible than others, depending on their own histories or circumstances of variable response to a given stimulus; we can describe these personal or local situations, but often only give meaning to them in relation to others. Most of the physical sciences use vectors to describe mathematically the properties of certain systems, whether at an atomic, molecular or larger scale. In physical chemistry, a matrix can be a solution within which the activity of specific molecular or atomic structures can be described using vector theory. In anthropology, the term has a history as well. In his last book, *The Concept of Cultural Systems,* Leslie White used the concept of cultural vectors as a building block for his theory of cultural systems (1975: 59). For White, however, vectors were institutional or ideological structures like the agricultural industry, professional organizations, ideology, language, or social classes. He allowed for a somewhat reduced level of subvectors, comprising things like hog farming, the gun control lobby, or determinist philosophy. Each vector or subvector has 'a magnitude, a force and a direction' (p. 91) or objective. For White, the individual could not be a vector, and the rigidity with which he defined a cultural system has little to do with the purpose I have in describing the notion of a matrix. Still, it is instructive to take note of White's use of the vector concept.

Using other terms, anthropologists and other social theorists have recently put forth a number of candidates for describing the shifting terrain of the 'postlocal' (Appadurai, 1997) world: Gupta and Ferguson (1997), Clifford (1997) and Kaplan (1997) have talked about locations; Appadurai (1996) has described cultures as non-Euclidean fractals comprised of various kinds of flows – scapes, localities and neighbourhoods; Auge (1995) presented the notion of non-place as the product of a supermodernity that has taken over large sectors of the modern world, though not completely displaced it; Martin (1997: 145) has suggested several metaphors – citadels, rhizomes and string figures – that contribute to a 'toolbox' of potential ways to imagine sections of the world that can be approached by ethnographic research; even the widely used virtual reality or community is part of this trend towards redefinition of old or acknowledgement of new socio-cultural forms. As I have defined them here, the terms *vector* and *matrix* can accommodate most, if not all, of these other concepts. I do not want to use vector and matrix as the building blocks for a mathematical model of the world, nor do I see them strictly as metaphors. Rather, I see them as something of a hermeneutic device which can help us to visualize, describe and understand the shape-shifting locations in which cosmopolitan ethnography takes place. Some of these locations are ephemeral, while others can more easily be revisited. They are all comprised of the constituent units that I call vectors which have certain identifiable characteristics – histories and futures, beliefs and goals, political, economic, social or ideological power that can be defined relative to each other, whether we are speaking of individual actors, institutions or other entities or objects. These vectors interact in the spaces I define as matrices; such matrices are both predictable and accidental, in ways that are shaped by the histories and trajectories of their constituent layers and tangents. Messy entities, these matrices yield infinite numbers of connections, but can of course always be truncated for purposes of analysis; they do not, however, assume bounded units. In the case of Sivananda and the DLS, I felt that I had begun to locate a relatively complete segment of the yoga story when I began to meet the same people and practices over and over again in different contexts, both historical and geographical.

In terms of methodology, the study of yoga has forced me to examine how we as anthropologists ought to constitute the object and circumscribe the location of our research, that is, how we 'construct the field'. I have found the concepts of vectors and matrices useful in this endeavour, because they allow me to think graphically about the ways that people's lives, as well as the 'social lives of things' (Appadurai, 1986), literally cross paths and shape practices. Because Swami Sivananda was a British-trained physician, an educated, middle-class professional who, like Vivekananda, used English as the primary medium for disseminating his teachings, his ideas were most available to a narrowly defined but internationally distributed population. Today, yoga appeals primarily to the educated or professional middle classes of both India and the West (Strauss, 1998) and as a result, the majority of my discussants are from socio-economic and educational backgrounds similar to my own: politically liberal, highly educated, and 'cosmopolitan' in Hannerz's (1992: 252–255) sense, with sufficient interest and discretionary income to travel regularly. Who, then, might I identify as the other so often sought in anthropological research? In addition, since my research led me to follow a network of matrices emanating from a hub in Rishikesh out to linked organizations, conferences, retreats, workshops, classes and individuals from New Delhi to Switzerland, Germany and North America, I found the question of distinguishing a 'field site' in the traditional sense of the term more than a little problematic. As this volume and other recent contributions (e.g. Appadurai, 1991; Clifford, 1997; Gupta and Ferguson, 1997; James et al., 1996; Marcus, 1995) demonstrate, the very notion of 'the field' has become a central problematic for anthropology and related disciplines. A field site can no longer be seen merely as a geographical location, but rather may be viewed as an intersection between people, practices and shifting terrains, both physical and virtual. The ability to observe ideas, images and practices, and pursue a network[7] of personal and institutional leads makes any location into 'the field'.

Another related methodological issue that this project has forced me to examine is the link between the history of academic research on a given topic, resting as it does on the life histories and personal contingencies of the scholars involved, and the history of the topic itself. In this case, the major existing scholarly treatment of yoga, a revision of Mircea Eliade's doctoral dissertation, was influenced by Eliade's own experiences while staying with Swami Sivananda in Rishikesh, which occurred in 1929, prior to the founding of the Divine Life Society. His book, *Yoga: Immortality and Freedom*, however, refers primarily to his textual research in Calcutta with the philosopher DasGupta. Although he acknowledges the fundamentally experiential and initiatory nature of yoga practice, Eliade mentions – but declines to comment on – his personal experiences (Eliade, 1969: xvii, xx, 57). He discusses them to some extent in the multiple volumes of his autobiography.[8] But those very personal experiences gave Eliade a particular understanding of yoga, and his book has in turn heavily influenced both scholarship and popular opinion of what constitutes yoga in the public imagination. This understanding was not just the result of 'objective' analysis of texts, but rather a very specific interpretation linked at least in part to Sivananda's particular 'brand' of neo-Hinduism (Eliade, 1982). Although this is not the place for an extended discussion of the Eliade project,[9] I think it is relevant to mention as an example of how the many researchers' own lives, with their particular goals and constraints, represent other vectors in a given matrix; the influence of Eliade on me as an ethnographer of Sivananda's world is related to, but different from, its influence on the practitioners of yoga I encountered, many of whom considered his book to be something of a bible. Indeed, Sivananda had told Eliade that he would be 'the next Vivekananda', bringing yoga to the West (Eliade, 1990: 190); through his efforts to experience yoga rather than merely study its texts, Eliade's life impacted that of Sivananda in a very direct way.

In my own research, participation was not merely a research strategy, it was absolutely essential to gaining not only credibility in the eyes of the community, but also the personal bodily understanding of the transformations which these practices make possible. 'Doing' and 'being' are at least as important – if not more so – as 'knowing'; Sivananda's oft-repeated formula for yogic life is 'Be Good, Do Good'.

I have made an effort in the following pages to discuss my own experiential knowledge of yoga, gained through the course of these two years of research, in terms of the explanations and representations collected from interviews and the media. The focus on practice, as both an empirical and theoretical imperative, was central to how I constructed a field that used Rishikesh as a focal point but was otherwise more easily described in terms of the vectors and matrices described above.

Globalizing yoga: linking matrices from Rishikesh to Chicago

Most of the non-Indian visitors to Rishikesh with whom I spoke learned about the town, and about yoga, primarily through the written word, while for most of the Indians, Rishikesh's fame as an extremely well-known and popular pilgrimage destination was linked directly to its mythological status as an ideal place for yoga, documented through the major epic tales of the *Mahabharata* and other well-known oral traditions. Yet this was not always the case. Although the region within which Rishikesh lies is part of the mythical Dev-Bhumi, the land of the gods wherein many of the episodes of the great Indian epics were said to have occurred, Rishikesh itself had very few visitors until quite late in the nineteenth century and no significant population base until after the Partition of British India in 1947. The popularization and name recognition of Rishikesh depended heavily on the activities of Sivananda. Like Swami Vivekananda in the nineteenth century, he relied heavily on the use of inexpensive printed pamphlets and books for the dissemination of his message. Distribution of print media is relatively inexpensive and allows broad coverage, but it often requires a catalyst of some sort to achieve the kind of authority which assures continuing attention. Sivananda's solution was to promote the 'export guru' as an authentic Indian product. The books capitalized on this tradition, by using informal language clearly directed at the individual seeking to better him- or herself. Sivananda encouraged his reading public to write to him for advice on their spiritual progress, enhancing the sense of one-to-one contact. He spent twenty years cultivating a crop of disciples capable of spreading his message. In the decade before his death, he began to send his young swamis on missions to other parts of India and the world. Although Sivananda himself rarely left Rishikesh, he had developed an international clientele through extensive distribution of print and audio media. In addition to sending material on request to individuals interested in yoga or Hinduism, Sivananda regularly mailed literature to people or institutions he considered important.[10]

The books, however, were not enough. While certainly central to the propagation of DLS ideology and yoga practices, the availability of publications worldwide only whetted the spiritual appetites of the reading public for 'the real thing'. Authenticity in Hindu spirituality and particularly in the practice of yoga depends on the physical presence of a teacher (Eliade, 1973; Juergensmeyer, 1991), so books, tapes and photographs remain only supplements. The traditional mode of knowledge transfer for yoga is the *guru–shishya* pair, which provides for direct one-to-one instruction, but does not reach mass audiences easily. Sivananda's disciples were therefore sent out from Rishikesh both on lecture tours and for the purpose of establishing DLS branches or, in some cases, their own organizations. While many of the more experienced disciples like Chidananda and Vishnudevananda were sent out in the late 1950s and early 1960s, others were sent or left of their own accord after Sivananda's passing. The sense of empire-building is difficult to escape. On one hand, more and more foreigners had been visiting Rishikesh since Indian Independence, and they asked Sivananda and his younger associates for help in continuing their education at home. On the other hand, Vivekananda's example as an ambassador of Hindu spirituality, and the related facts of increased availability of radio and mass media, as well as less expensive and faster travel, made short trips abroad a more feasible option. In addition, of course, since Independence there were ever-increasing numbers of expatriate Indians abroad, for whom the presence of Sivananda's emissaries might be comforting. Other branches of the DLS were founded in Europe, notably Germany and Holland, and in the United States.[11] Sivananda carefully covered all of the continents in his effort to create a universal community of yoga practitioners. The paths that my research on the transnational transformation of yoga took involved following various vectors that originated in Rishikesh and then moved around the world according to a variety of interests, needs and chance occurrences.

Reflecting Sivananda's substantial efforts, Rishikesh today draws an international clientele that defies description as belonging to one particular bounded cultural tradition. One effect the DLS has had on the dynamics of India's interactions with the rest of the world derives from its missionary zeal in sending young yoga teachers out from Rishikesh to colonize the West. Though on the surface this might appear to contradict the goals of the monistic ascetic tradition from which it derived, Sivananda's DLS focused on the development of the individual and therefore represented a related, if transformed, purpose. This globalizing process is important for understanding the ever-increasing market for yoga in both India and elsewhere. The DLS disciples who travelled out of India and set up yoga schools in Europe and America[12] were bringing what might be called 'authentic' – that is, local, situated, non-mechanically reproducible – yoga to new audiences. But this authentic product was itself developed out of the transnational flows of people and ideas beginning with Vivekananda. Rather than considering this an act of cultural creolization (Hannerz, 1992), implying a mixture of pure substances (Friedman, 1994), I see it rather as a process of mutual interactive practice; we can take a 'snapshot' at any time, but the motion never ceases. More importantly, the perception of that process differs depending on the observer. This is surely old hat in terms of theory, but it is important to remember when trying to explain the concrete fact that a particular, though admittedly fuzzy set of ideas and practices called yoga has become prevalent in parts of the world quite far from where it started.

In its global manifestations, we can view yoga as ideology, practice, lifestyle, metaphor, commodity and generator of a Turnerian emotive communitas which has come to substitute for the physically grounded communal co-presence now available only in fits and starts, filling in the interstices of modern cosmopolitan lives. The quest for communitas, spiritual 'oneness' without regard for socially imposed structural difference, while certainly a common ideal that is in many cases 'contradicted by easily observable empirical facts' (van der Veer, 1989: 60), can be viewed at a number of different levels in relation to other kinds of more materially globalizing processes. The alienating lifestyles borne of the requirements of late capitalism often leave a void which cannot always be replaced by the kinds of locally based social interactions of past centuries, not only in urban areas, but also – perhaps especially – in more isolated communities. While traditional ethnographic practice had as its goal documenting the varieties of Durkheimian social glue, Manchesterian social conflicts, or perhaps postmodern pastiches of meaning occurring within bounded socio-cultural and geographic units, acknowledging the impact of deterritorialization on such bounded units, whether imagined or not, leaves no option but to determine new ways of practising ethnography. The discourse on and practice of yoga has, since Vivekananda's reformulation in the nineteenth century, reflected an effort to achieve spiritual and social unity in the face of national and individual assertions of separate identities. To borrow Csordas' term, yoga is a 'somatic mode of attention' (1993) which can be used to generate communitas through practice, whether or not the individual practitioners are in the physical presence of others. It is a technique which both helps an individual cope with everyday stressors and also provides a basis for shared experience which can be drawn upon to help foster a sense of embeddedness in a community of like-minded others, even if those people are temporally or spatially disconnected from each other.

But what does this mean for the definition of an ethnographic field site? What made Rishikesh a good place to start, and why was it, in the end, insufficient by itself? Returning to the basic research problem I faced, how to understand the transformation of yoga from a regionally based religious tradition to a transnational, secular set of ideologies and practices, it became clear that the techniques I needed to use to understand this process must somehow reproduce the pathways taken to create the thing we know today as yoga. By following the routes taken by people, practices and representations related to Sivananda's version of yoga, I have tried to capture something of the complexity and continuity that has made this tradition, or sampradaya, a viable object of study. I have tried to avoid the suggestion of representing another bounded whole, but instead tried to tell a story that to me seems true to the events, experiences and interpretations of my discussants, their practices and their ideals.

Rishikesh, India – February, 1992

At sunrise, the rooftop garden of the hotel provided a beautiful and calm setting for Swamiji's yoga class. One other hotel guest and I sat on our mats, hands to our faces, alternately closing one nostril and then the other, breathing deeply of the crisp morning air. Swamiji taught classes whenever he was asked, sometimes morning and evening, or sometimes not at all. Each session was exactly the same, starting with alternate nostril breathing and a few prayers, moving on to a specific sequence of postures, from leg lifting to shoulderstand and a variety of forward and backward bending and twisting *asanas*, to headstand and then *shavasan*, the corpse pose, at the end. Swamiji's pace was slow and easy. In between the poses, Swamiji told stories about his life and people he had known, frequently punctuating his narrative with loud peals of laughter. Many stories poked fun at various yoga establishments; he once said that if he were to give anyone *sannyas*, he would name the person Swami Hypocritananda just to be up front about it. He said that he hated going out to walk around in town, because he invariably saw some friends, and all they wanted to do was gossip – better just to stay home and watch the football match on TV. Swamiji's classes were always in English; though he spoke fluent Hindi, he had grown up in southern India. In addition, his students came from all around the world, returning regularly to stay at the hotel and take classes with him.

Standardizing practice: the Rishikesh Reihe and Sivananda's twenty instructions

In addition to the cultural and linguistic complexity I encountered in Rishikesh, another factor which helped shift my research orientation from the local to the global – or, rather, from one locale to a global web of interrelated matrices – was a family health emergency which required me to leave India in the middle of the year. Counter to my fears, this proved disastrous neither on the personal nor on the professional front. Once the cause of my leave of absence from India was resolved, I was able to follow through on a number of leads in both the United States and Europe which provided new insights on the very institutions, people, practices and ideas I had begun to sort out in Rishikesh. In fact, I saw a number of the same people in two or more different locales and experienced most of the same practices in several different contexts, both inside and outside of India. Ever-present in all of the sites were the ubiquitous pamphlets, tapes and images that are the main stock-in-trade of both Sivananda's Divine Life Society and Vivekananda's Ramakrishna Mission/Vedanta Society. Elsewhere I have discussed extensively the notion of a 'community of practice' (Strauss, 1997, 1998) as a way of defining this dispersed but connected group of individuals. To illustrate what I mean by a shared community of practice, I want to make an excursion from Rishikesh town to Switzerland, and from there on to the east coast of the United States.

Although different yoga teachers have their own styles, favourite poses (*asanas*) and sequences of poses, many teachers trained by Sivananda or his disciples use a similar sequence known as the Rishikesh *Reihe* (series) of *asanas*. A number of the German speakers I met in Rishikesh had come there to learn yoga because they had encountered the Rishikesh Reihe through reading or classes at home in Europe. The name of the town was so firmly associated with the practice of yoga that it seemed to them absolutely natural to assume that one could only learn these authentic yoga practices in Rishikesh. The reality is that one individual, Swami Sivananda, who happened to have lived in Rishikesh, popularized this particular sequence through his extensive writings and large number of English-speaking, multinational disciples. Of course, the reason why Sivananda came to Rishikesh in the first place was far more than random coincidence; it was instead a choice made on the basis of mythological knowledge about the significance of the place, rather than the authenticity of local practice. Whether in Rishikesh, Zurich or Washington, the sequence of activities and specific yoga poses stays the same for many of these members of the Sivananda yoga community of practice.

The original version of the Rishikesh *Reihe* begins with shoulder-stand (*sarvangasana*), and continues through plough (*halasana*), fish (*matsyasana*), forward bend (*pashchimottanasana*), cobra (*bhujan-gasana*), locust (*shalabhasana*), bow (*dhanurasana*), spinal twist (*ardha-matsyendrasana*), and finally headstand (*sirsasana*). The rationale given for this particular sequence is one of opposition; the sequence begins and ends with an inverted posture, and the poses in the middle alter-nate between bending the spine forwards and backwards, and then to the side, which allows for the body to be stretched in all possible direc-tions. When asked about the rationale for such a sequence, people often mentioned balance; the idea is that failing to move the body equally in all directions will throw it out of balance. These shared practices are at one level understood to constitute a natural, logical sequence (van Lisabeth, 1992), but they are also a way to facilitate a shared state of mind, in lieu of a community held hostage to a fixed geographic locale. By knowing the poses and the sequences, I could join in with yoga practitioners anywhere in the world, and I, or anyone else who had attained a basic level of knowledge, would be accepted as a fellow traveller. The yoga postures themselves are understood to be tech-niques for achieving a certain state of mind (Eliade, 1973; Miller, 1996; Varenne, 1976). This state of mind in its most common inter-pretation[13] is a recognition of the fundamental unity of the cosmos, the notion that, echoing Chidananda's address to the Parliament of the World's Religions, we are all one.

Another set of practices which can be found anywhere the DLS version of yoga is found is Swami Sivananda's set of twenty instructions for spiritual success. These instructions have been reproduced in a number of different contexts around the DLS ashram: in books, pamphlets, signs, and a singular obelisk in the middle of a central plaza near the library and the main temple. They begin '1. Get up at

4 a.m. daily. Do Japa and Meditation' and continue to '20. Keep a daily spiritual diary. Stick to your routine'. At the bottom of the pillar, the reader is admonished that '[t]hese 20 spiritual instructions contain the essence of yoga and vedanta. Follow them all strictly. Do not be lenient to your mind. You will attain supreme happiness. –Swami Sivananda.' Those who stay overnight at the ashram receive a printed handbill with the daily schedule on it. These instructions, and the pattern of daily life encoded in them, are reproduced in nearly every place where Sivananda's presence is found. Together they provide Sivananda's prescription for a 'divine life' through yoga.[14]

In order to become a member of the community of practice, then, it is necessary to at least be familiar with these instructions or directives, even if one is not entirely successful at fulfilling all of them. At the DLS ashram in Rishikesh, for example, no one will force a visitor to wake up at 4 a.m. and participate in the programme, but most of the non-residents I met during stays there made sincere efforts to do just that. I saw the same basic programme in place at most of the Sivananda-affiliated institutions or programmes outside of Rishikesh, and many individuals who claim discipleship with someone of the Sivananda lineage also use this framework to help structure their personal lives. On the Sivananda Yoga Vedanta Centre's website, one can virtually visit a 'basic yoga class' or participate in a *Satsang* to pray and discuss points of spiritual interest through the medium of a chat room.

For example, one of the North American residents of the DLS ashram, when asked about the foreigners who regularly visited the ashram, suggested that I speak with Becki, a Swiss woman who had been visiting regularly for twenty years. Upon returning home to Zurich, I had the opportunity to visit Becki at her apartment. She was extremely excited to have contact with another person who had recently been physically present at the DLS ashram and who would understand her lifestyle, home decor and practices. When I arrived, I saw images of Sivananda and the current DLS president, Chidananda, on the walls, and was shown Becki's shrine and meditation room, as prescribed in Sivananda's instruction list. She told me that she did indeed get up early every day to meditate before work, maintained a sattvic vegetarian diet, and generally tried to follow Sivananda's rules. While showing me around, she repeatedly commented on how glad she was to have someone who 'really understood' visiting her, because she felt that no one in her local neighbourhood, a typical middle-class Swiss suburb, could understand her practices since they had not experienced such things themselves. As it happens, although there are a number of yoga schools and practitioners in the Zurich region, most of the Swiss who are affiliated in some way with Sivananda live in the western part of the country, around Geneva and Lausanne. Becki knew those people well, but saw them only rarely. Her comment about my experiences making understanding of her situation possible was not unusual – as I mentioned previously, many yoga practitioners are reluctant to discuss their practices in great detail with someone who has had no personal experience of them. An Indologist friend confirmed the importance of shared practice when he told me about his experiences in researching yoga in India. He said that the practitioners whom he consulted lauded his Sanskrit skills and ability to read the texts, but would not discuss their own practices because they felt he could not properly comprehend them (Peter Schreiner, personal communication, 1992). What Becki's experience demonstrates is that the shift from geographically based communities, still an extremely strong component of Swiss identity (Niederer, 1997), to deterritorialized, ideologically and praxis-centred communities, is underway, and it often leaves individuals caught in the middle, neither feeling fully a part of their local surroundings, nor yet always having the access to the dispersed community of fellow practitioners that would reduce their sense of alienation. Many forms of 'instant' communication, including telephone, fax and computer network – the basis for virtual community – exist, but whether they will prove up to the task of replacing everyday, localized, grounded (and not just electrically!) communities remains an open question.

Over the next few months we spoke occasionally on the telephone, and then Becki left for one of her nearly annual trips to Rishikesh and the DLS Ashram. The next time I saw her was in the United States, late in the summer of 1993. Swami Chidananda, Becki, and several other people associated with the DLS had gathered in rural Maryland for spiritual retreat which preceded the centenary celebration of the Parliament of the World's Religions in Chicago. The retreat, sponsored by the DLS of Maryland, provided an opportunity for seeing many old friends whom I had already interviewed in Europe or India and meeting others whom I would later interview at their homes on other continents. The schedule for the retreat closely followed that experienced by visitors and residents at the Rishikesh DLS Ashram, with meditation and hatha yoga early in the morning, followed by breakfast and lecture/*darsan* by the swami-in-residence. The yoga classes were led by various well-known disciples of Sivananda, including Lilias Folan, whose public television series on yoga is perhaps the best known public representation of yoga practice found in America today. Lilias, in the Preface to one of her many books, has also supported my classification of yoga practitioners by referring to her television and reading audience as a 'scattered community', suggesting a network of known and unknown participants in a shared project. The uncovering of this network provided the framework for my multi-matrix ethnography of yoga.

Follow the yellow brick road

Marcus points out that multi-site ethnography 'is designed around chains, paths, threads, conjunctions, or juxtapositions of locations in which the ethnographer establishes some form of literal, physical presence, with an explicit, posited logic of association or connection among sites that in fact defines the argument of the ethnography' (1995: 105). He suggests several possible ways to construct these chains of locations, including following people, things, metaphors, plots/stories, lives and conflicts. To this list I would add one more: follow the practice. While I did indeed follow some individual people from site to site, my effort to understand yoga in its transnational context has largely been a process of following the history and social life of a set of practices, like the Rishikesh *Reihe*, conveyed sometimes by people, sometimes by books, pamphlets or other printed texts, and sometimes by moving images like video or television. Within the schema I am proposing, each of these – as well as all the items on Marcus' list above – would constitute a vector, and the interactions among them can be used to define a matrix, which could be a permanent or ephemeral location, actual or virtual, in which observable social life is enacted. Understanding how yoga practices fit into the lives of people in disparate locales allows us to, as Appadurai suggests (1988), blur the boundaries between places and see the family resemblances as well as the distinctive features which cross-cut cultures. In this way, we can begin to see how the use of a vector–matrix framing of translocal ethnography can help anthropology avoid binding particular cultural forms to particular peoples and places. Rather than seeing Rishikesh as 'the place for yoga', or India as the place for caste or spirituality (as it has often been essentialized; see Appadurai, 1988), we see people engaged in practices that together comprise their lived experience in particular places. When the people move to different places their practices may change, or they may not; if they stay in one locale, the same may be true. The practices are used as means to construct social relationships that often cross-cut local and national boundaries. By highlighting the effects of translocally constituted practices on people living in disparate geographical spaces, we gain new insights on how to observe and understand peoples and cultures as fluid manifestations of specific historical configurations which may span not only temporal, but also spatial dimensions. Seen in this light, it becomes increasingly difficult to relegate them to the status of incarcerated natives bound to 'their' places by the authenticity of local cultural forms.

Refracting Rishikesh: creating community through practice

But if the group of people I studied in Rishikesh and elsewhere was not a bounded set defined by their own designated place, what was it? I have suggested that it is a community of practice, which can be described within a framework of vectors and matrices that occur in many dimensions, from temporospatial to virtual. Returning to Tönnies' 1887 definition of Gemeinschaft, we also find that he described many different types of community: of blood, of place and of mind. It is this last which provides the basis for a community of practice, for a community of mind:

> comes most easily into existence when crafts or callings are the same or of similar nature. Such a tie, however, must be made and maintained through easy and frequent meetings, which are most likely to take place in a town. . . . Such good spirit, therefore, is not bound to any place but lives in the conscience of its worshippers and accompanies them on their travels to foreign countries. Thus those who are brethren of such a common faith feel, like members of the same craft or rank, everywhere united by a spiritual bond and the co-operation in a common task . . . spiritual friendship forms a kind of invisible scene or meeting which has to be kept alive by artistic intuition and creative will.
>
> (Tönnies, 1957: 43)

Extending the definition from 'crafts and callings' – professions, religion, or rank – to other kinds of shared practice requires no artifice. Likewise, it takes little effort to imagine that while towns were the most obvious place for the 'easy and frequent meetings' required to maintain these relationships a century ago, new forms of communication and speeds of travel have permitted new ways of keeping such associations alive. While Tönnies may have been concerned with the differentiation between 'traditional' and 'modern' societies, giving the weight of Gemeinschaft to the former and of Gesellschaft to the latter, it seems fair at this point to suggest that a shift in orientation has occurred, and that new, composite forms of community (Etzioni, 1993) are being formed. Populations living under conditions of late or reflexive modernity often make self-conscious efforts to exert control, producing types of social groups which both retain the shared interests of society-based associations, and add back aspects of community-oriented shared meaning (Lash, 1994). Hybrid forms range from wholly one end to the other of this spectrum, as can be seen in the resurgence of intentional communities as well as the proliferation of multinational corporations and associations. As Hannerz demonstrates in his discussion of Robertson's (1992) reformulation of the concepts of Gemeinschaft and Gesellschaft, considering the effects of globalization requires a complete re-evaluation of the concept of community; no longer are communities inextricably bound to singular locales, and the notion of a transnational community 'is not a contradiction in terms' (Hannerz, 1996: 98). The bodily practices of yoga likewise generate many different types of communities; the ones with which I am concerned in this chapter are transnational, but intersect with many other more localized circles. Approaching community in this light does, however, force us to re-evaluate our criteria for valid ethnographic research, established as they were during the period when geographically isolated communities provided the basis for anthropological study. As Marcus (1995: 315) comments,

> The concept of community in the classic sense of shared values, shared identity, and thus shared culture has been mapped literally onto locality to define one basic frame of reference orienting ethnography. The connotations of solidity and homogeneity attaching to the notion of community, whether concentrated in a locale or dispersed, have been replaced in the framework of modernity by the idea that the situated production of identity – of a person, of a group, or even a whole society – does not depend . . . on the observable, concentrated activities within a particular locale or a diaspora. The identity of anyone or any group is produced simultaneously in many different locales of activity by many different agents for many different purposes.

Lash (1994: 114) quite rightfully points out that Tönnies' conception of Gemeinschaft depended upon shared meaning, and it is precisely through the sharing of practices that I argue, with Bourdieu (1984, 1987), that shared meaning is achieved. Yoga as a way of being in the world, and not merely a set of exercises or philosophical prescriptions, thus provides a good basis for a community of practice as a type of Gemeinschaft, in opposition to Tönnies' notion of Gesellschaft as 'the world itself' (Tönnies, 1957: 33). The role of personal experience in the production of cultural values within such a community provides another focus for both ethnographic evaluation (Urban, 1997) and the re-evaluation of ethnographic practice itself.

In Miller's analysis of Sivananda and the DLS, he focuses on the concept of the *sampradaya*, which he translates as 'teaching tradition', but to which I add the sense of community. According to Miller (1989: 82–83), the structure of a *sampradaya* consists of

> a pattern of ever and ever larger circles moving outward from the center, much as heat waves emanate from a blazing fire. Yet, at the same time the 'pull' or movement is toward the center. The guru is at the center. . . . The further one is from the center and from the guru, the less one feels the intimacy and warmth of the guru.

Miller takes up Bharati's idea of the modern Hindu renaissance as 'that kind of Hindu thinking that adopts the language of Western science and technology as a model of communication and persuasion without renouncing traditional religious values' (ibid.: 109) – he then adds to that the structural level of the sampradaya. I want to supplement this interpretation with another layer. The DLS *sampradaya* is a modern, ideological community grounded in shared practices which are based on the teachings of one individual, Sivananda; it can be viewed more abstractly as a matrix. But the disciples who left Rishikesh to found other related yoga institutions or to support international branches of the DLS maintained allegiance to Sivananda; rather than starting new *sampradayas*, their organizations function more as variants of the original, using nearly identical practices and rationales, the only difference being the packaging and catchwords – 'Integral Yoga' vs. 'Yoga of Synthesis', for example. What we have, then, are multiple intersecting matrices, forming concentric and overlapping circles, just as the ripples you might see upon throwing a handful of pebbles into a pond. On their return home, all the visiting yoga practitioners whom I met in Rishikesh continued their yoga practice by themselves, and some even taught yoga classes. They all continued to seek out other people who practised yoga, for both practical and spiritual support. One of my discussants, Beate, would visit the Sivananda Yoga Centre in Berlin for spiritual activities and attend an Iyengar-style class for technical practice. While World Wide Web access was not an option for them in 1993, I have seen an increasingly visible range of Web-based yoga communities developing since 1995.

Just as another discussant, Karen, had become uncomfortable with the Aryan yoga approach that she had been taught initially in southern Germany, I found that the people who had experienced yoga in Rishikesh often sought ideologically similar centres on their return home, whether or not they had been involved with such groups before their trip. Beate commented that she felt most 'at home' in India when she visited those ashrams and centres that followed Vivekananda's 'Science of Yoga' framework, promoting yoga as a rational set of practices that would help solve the problems of modern living, rather than a mystical ideology for removing oneself from society and its problems.

Is Rishikesh any more 'authentic' a locale for the practice of yoga than Philadelphia, Berlin or Delhi? Yes and no. For many reasons, Rishikesh has for centuries attracted individuals who sought to practice yoga. This local history carries weight in the ongoing process of redefining yoga. As I have shown, the specific life histories of Swamis Vivekananda and Sivananda have played significant roles in defining Rishikesh as a yoga destination *par excellence*, and so to base an ethnography of yoga practice in Rishikesh makes sense. Mary Des Chene concisely appraised her choice of a Nepali village as a fieldwork site for studying Gurkha pasts and presents by saying that '[t]his bounded locale, while an obvious and necessary site for speaking to [these men] . . . was in no sense a sufficient vantage point from which to understand' (1997: 73). Following Des Chene's logic, Rishikesh was a necessary place for me to base a study of Sivananda's yoga, but to have remained there without following at least some of the pathways taken by my discussants would have resulted in a less honest picture of the forces which continue to create the Rishikesh of the present. When I arrived in Rishikesh in 1992, I fully intended to produce a 'traditional' ethnography of yoga practice in an 'authentic' locale. Although I was familiar with transnational theory and the debates of the late 1980s over the representation of anthropological knowledge, I still somehow expected that I would find the situation in India to be relatively encapsulated, or at least that the boundaries of my subject, demarcated by the walls of the Sivananda ashram, would be reasonably clear. After a few weeks, however, I realized that although it would be possible to conduct such a geographically fixed research project, it would fail to completely describe or explain honestly what I was experiencing in Rishikesh. This ethnography, the product of a decision to pursue threads extending far beyond the geographical territory to which I had attached myself, still lacks many pieces of the puzzle. Still, it conveys a better sense of the complex interactions across time and space that have made yoga, and particularly Sivananda's 'brand' of yoga, a commonplace in many parts of the world, than it might had I focused my research only on Rishikesh. I make no claims about representing the 'truth' about the history, definition or practice of yoga, as experienced by any given individual. Yet I do think that my work in describing the transnational practice of yoga accurately represents those general trends and pathways of yoga's development in India and the Euro-American West that have made such individually experienced varieties possible.

Rishikesh – April, 1992

'Understand? Doubt is there?' Sumit asks us as the whole class stares at his notebook, where he has just diagrammed a *pranayama* (breathing) exercise. Everyone nods, and then we all trot off to our blankets, cover our eyes and ears with ace bandages, and try to execute the exercise for the next fifteen minutes or so. Sumit explains that we all need to experiment to see how long it would take each of us, individually, to complete a cycle of these breathing patterns. He says that sometimes, we might feel like doing more of one type of breathing than another, and that that was fine – the key was to experiment and find out what was most comfortable for ourselves. This was the same philosophy I had read in Vivekananda's works, and in Sivananda's writings as well. Swamiji, too, had told me that yoga is a science, and I must experiment with it, try things out for myself. The notion that no one else can tell someone how to feel or know what is best, that teachers are there only to suggest options, but that each person must decide how to do the practices for him or herself, resonated throughout my stay in Rishikesh.

Locating yoga

This chapter has used the ideas and practices of yoga as a tool with which to examine a number of themes. My discussion of doing field-work on the transnational practice of yoga contributes to the goal of this volume, an exploration of the ways that ethnographers have constructed their fields in the spaces between serendipity and structure, given circumstances that are far from the isolated and fixed field of the Malinowskian ideal. The crucial question for contemporary anthropology is how to demarcate the boundaries for appropriate study. Whether on a train travelling from Bombay to Delhi, practising yoga in Rishikesh, having a potluck supper in Maryland, visiting a friend and discussant in Germany, wandering the halls of the Palmer House, or even watching a yoga class on the World Wide Web, research for this project has forced me to negotiate a number of different circuits of association. Such a research strategy was not merely an interesting experiment, but absolutely fundamental to understanding the ways that yoga has been transformed over the past century.

How did the experiential knowledge gained through practising yoga help me to understand the process which I was studying? There is no question in my mind that my practice of yoga in Rishikesh, anywhere from one to five hours daily, along with the primarily vegetarian diet and relatively simple lifestyle (get up, do yoga, interview people, do more yoga, eat, read, write notes, sleep) contributed to my generally excellent physical health while in India. Although I have participated in many different kinds of athletic activities over the past few decades, from equestrian sports to running to rock climbing, I was certainly stronger, and had more stamina, than ever before. This experience gave me the opportunity to appreciate Eliade's evaluation of yoga as a set of techniques which provides one strategy for achieving a particular state of mind – ecstasy, in Eliade's case, and relaxation, in my own. The practice of yoga made me appreciate, in quite a visceral way, the reasons why my discussants found yoga to be a helpful component in their quests for a good and healthy life. But this very practice also made me aware that, in many ways, yoga is not at all unique. Rather, it is, as Eliade said, a methodology, a way of focusing the brain, calming the mind, relaxing and strengthening the body. And, of course, it made me into a member of Sivananda's community of practice.

The question of how to make use of such experiential knowledge is hardly a new one for anthropology (Hastrup and Hervik, 1994; Jackson, 1989); however, one of the problems I confront through the study of yoga is that of the determination of scholarly 'suitability', or the credibility of a research topic which depends on experiential data, and how to avoid straying from the narrow path which separates the 'popular' descriptions of practical experience from the 'academic' analyses of disembodied texts and reported speech. Eliade simply ignores this question; in his autobiography, he says that what he learned through practice had a profound impact on his understanding (1981: 190), but he would not discuss details, and, given the textual nature of his analysis, he didn't need to. My project, addressing the everyday implementation of yoga ideology and practice, entailed a more thorough treatment of the contribution of experiential knowledge. When I began the project, I was somewhat astonished to find that a subject which was so widely recognized in the public sphere had received so little scholarly attention, and that the work which had been done focused only on the textual tradition, completely ignoring the question of practice. Several years into the project, having myself been the subject of scepticism on all fronts, academic and experiential, I see more clearly the difficulties of walking such a tightrope. Yet it is important not only to engage in such research, but to discuss its impact explicitly. The very fears of blurring boundaries that such experiential knowledge engenders expose and clarify the entire process of anthropological data collection that earlier efforts only mystified.

In my pre-fieldwork imaginings, I saw the study of yoga practice as a contribution to understanding the relationship between the Hindu householders who came to visit the ashram and the renunciants who lived there, as well as a way to use a specific set of bodily practices and their accompanying 2,000-year-old textual tradition to understand how such philosophically based ideologies are actually enacted in everyday life. I assumed that the practice of yoga by these people was linked to their quest for health and a generally better life. I therefore expected to focus on the relationship between concepts of physical health and other levels of health – mental, social, spiritual, or however people wanted to define them. As originally conceived, the project assumed the viability of the mythical conditions of ethnographic research: a geographically and culturally circumscribed field site and community. Yet the extremely mobile situation I found in Rishikesh, as well as the responses of my discussants and the ubiquitous media representations of yoga which I encountered in India and the West, together influenced me to depart from some of the paths that anthropologists have more typically followed. I did not expect to be examining the way that the West took up the idea of yoga, nor did I expect to consider the way that American and German ideas about freedom and well-being would intersect with Hindu[15] ideas of *samsara* (the cycle of worldly life), *karma* (universal causality of actions), *dharma* (duty) and *moksa* (liberation from all of the above, which can be achieved through the practice of yoga). These were the paths I followed, but it would also have been possible for me to reject them as tangential, and to stick with the original plan of documenting ashram life, remaining within the preset boundaries. That 'traditional' ethnography was certainly within my grasp, would probably have been easier, would certainly have been sufficient for obtaining the Ph.D., and would also have failed completely to represent the Rishikesh which I experienced, knowable only with the context of movement and change.

Notes

1 Support for this project was provided by a Fulbright-Hays Doctoral Dissertation Research Award and a Travel Grant from the School of Arts and Sciences at the University of Pennsylvania. This chapter is derived from my 1997 dissertation for the Department of Anthropology at the University of Pennsylvania, *Re-Orienting Yoga: Transnational Flows from an Indian Center*, currently being revised for publication as *Balancing Acts: Yoga as Transnational Practice*. I am indebted to Vered Amit-Talai, Michael Harkin and Carrick Eggleston for helpful comments on earlier versions of this manuscript.

2 For example, the Government of India produces brochures about Rishikesh which refer to its value for students of yoga, as well as a poster and other supplementary materials promoting an annual International Yoga Week in Rishikesh, with leading yoga teachers from around the country participating.

3 See e.g. Vivekananda, 1989, 1990; for a discussion of Vivekananda's life, see Raychaudhuri, 1989.

4 I was also rather predisposed to such a theoretical shift because of my graduate training. Following mentors at the University of Pennsylvania who were firmly committed to an interdisciplinary area studies approach, I had been encouraged to seek out historical and geographical connections that would contextualize my fieldwork. In the late 1980s, as I was beginning my graduate training, Arjun Appadurai and Carol Breckenridge were developing the Center for Transnational Studies, and I benefited a great deal from participation in an interdisciplinary graduate student/faculty reading group which was grappling with questions of public culture in a deterritorializing world. Still, when I went to India, I had no plans to engage in anything but 'traditional' single-site ethnography. The situation I found, combined with the opportunities I was afforded because of my husband's job in Switzerland, made it both sensible and possible to undertake a multi-site project.

5 There is still an anthropological bias against working in Europe (Gupta and Ferguson, 1997:14), and first fieldwork funding for research there is nearly impossible to obtain, especially when one is officially considered a 'South Asianist' by training.

6 I am grateful to Carrick Eggleston, Marcel Kornfeld, Mary Lou Larson and Deb Paulson for extended discussions on the use of vector and matrix in physical science, archaeology and geography.

7 For a discussion of network theory in the ethnographic study of complex societies, see Hannerz (1980) as well as his later books (1992, 1996).

8 See especially the first volume: Eliade, 1981.

9 Elsewhere (Strauss, 1997) I have elaborated on these historical connections.

10 For example, upon arriving in London for archival research in 1993, I was surprised to find pamphlets inscribed 'To the British Museum' and signed by Sivananda among the extensive collection of Sivanandiana housed there. Similarly, libraries at many American universities, including Stanford and the University of Colorado, have inscribed copies of Sivananda literature in their collections.

11 Separate organizations were also created, and of those, several are still quite visible today. Swami Jyotirmayananda left the ashram in 1962 after an invitation from some students in Puerto Rico (DLS, 1987: 246); he later moved to Florida, where he continues to run a yoga school and research foundation, advertisements for which can be found in many new age magazines. Swami Shivapremananda, one of the mainstays of the editorial staff at the DLS, was sent to Milwaukee in 1961 at the request of an American devotee; he ran the Sivananda Yoga-Vedanta Centre there for three years, then moved to New York City to found another branch, moving in 1970 to Buenos Aires and developing Sivananda Yoga Vedanta Centres in Argentina, Uruguay and Chile (ibid.: 225). South Africa had long been a DLS branch location, first under the direction of Swami Sahajananda, and later, in 1961, under Swami Venkatesananda, who used that venue as a base for opening DLS centres in Madagascar, Mauritius and Australia. Another major DLS affiliate appeared in Malaysia in 1956, under the direction of Swami Sadananda, a former professor of history at Presidency College, Madras, who was extremely active in the Yoga-Vedanta Forest Academy, as well as the Sivananda Publication League (ibid.: 228–229). The other well-known disciple was Satchidananda, the American-based guru of popular physician Dean Ornish of *Dr. Dean Ornish's Program for Reversing Heart Disease* (1991) fame.

12 They also went to Africa, Australia and other parts of Asia, but these are beyond the scope of this research.

13 The monistic interpretation is not by any means the only way that yoga is viewed, but it has become the most prominent perspective, in part because of Vivekananda's influence; in other versions, a dualistic perspective is favoured.

14 Swami Vishnudevananda later took these twenty items and distilled them further into five basic directives: proper exercise, proper breathing, proper relaxation, proper diet, positive thinking and meditation. These 'five points of yoga' form the basis for Vishnudevananda's international net-

work of Sivananda Yoga-Vedanta centres and ashrams. Both Sivananda's twenty instructions and Vishnudevananda's five points of yoga can be found on the World Wide Web. For more information about these instructions, see http://www.sivananda.org for the five points and http://www.sivananda.org/teachings/lifestyle/20instr.htm for a complete listing.

15 On the subject of Hindu vs. Indian: while yogic traditions are also part of the 'heretical' traditions of Buddhism, Jainism, etc., and 'Hindu' ideas are not the only ones which have shaped the 'Indian' approach, I speak here of 'Hindu' thought to permit a focus on yoga as it relates to the representations of these ideas by such neo-Hindu thinkers as Vivekananda, Gandhi, Aurobindo and Radhakrishnan.

References

Appadurai, Arjun (ed.) (1986) *The Social Life of Things: Commodities in Cultural Perspective*. New York: Cambridge University Press.

—— (1988) Putting Hierarchy in its Place. *Cultural Anthropology* 3(1): 36–49.

—— (1991) Global Ethnoscapes. Notes and Queries for a Transnational Anthropology. In R.G. Fox (ed.) *Recapturing Anthropology: Working in the Present*. Santa Fe: School of American Research Press, pp. 191–210.

—— (1996) *Modernity at Large: Cultural Dimensions of Globalization*. Minneapolis: University of Minnesota Press.

—— (1997) Fieldwork in the Era of Globalization. *Anthropology and Humanism Quarterly* 22(1): 115–118.

Auge, Marc (1995) *Non-places: Introduction to an Anthropology of Supermodernity*, trans. John Howe. London: Verso.

Benenson, Abram S. (ed.) (1985) *Control of Communicable Diseases in Man*. Washington, DC: American Public Health Association.

Binford, Lewis (1980) Willow Smoke and Dogs' Tails: Hunter–Gatherer Settlement Systems and Archaeological Site Formation. *American Antiquity* 45(1): 4–20.

Bourdieu, Pierre (1984) *Distinction: A Social Critique of the Judgement of Taste*, trans. Richard Nice. Cambridge, MA: Harvard University Press.

—— (1987) *Outline of a Theory of Practice*. Cambridge Studies in Social Anthropology. Cambridge: Cambridge University Press.

Clifford, James (1997) *Routes*. Cambridge, MA: Harvard University Press.

Clifford, James and George E. Marcus (eds) (1986) *Writing Culture: The Poetics and Politics of Ethnography*. A School of American Research Advanced Seminar. Berkeley: University of California Press.

Csordas, Thomas J. (ed.) (1993) Somatic Modes of Attention. *Cultural Anthropology* 8: 135–156.

Des Chene, Mary (1997) Locating the Past. In Akhil Gupta and James Ferguson (eds) *Anthropological Locations*. Berkeley: University of California Press, pp. 66–85.

Divine Life Society (DLS) (1987) *The Master, His Mission and His Works.* Rishikesh: Divine Life Society.

Eliade, Mircea (1969) *Patanjali and Yoga,* trans. C.L. Markmann. New York: Funk & Wagnalls.

—— (1973) *Yoga: Immortality and Freedom,* trans. Willard R. Trask. Bollingen Series. Princeton, NJ: Princeton University Press. First published 1958.

—— (1981) *Autobiography. Volume I: 1907–1937 Journey East, Journey West,* trans. Mac L. Ricketts. San Francisco, CA: Harper & Row.

—— (1982) *Ordeal by Labyrinth: Conversations with Claude-Henri Rocquet,* trans. Derek Coltman. Chicago, IL: University of Chicago Press.

—— (1990) *Journal I, 1945–1955,* trans. Mac Linscott Ricketts. Chicago, IL: University of Chicago Press.

Etzioni, Amitai (1993) *The Spirit of Community.* New York: Crown Publishers.

Friedman, Jonathan (1994) *Cultural Identity and Global Process.* London: Sage.

Girardin, Luc (1995) Cyberspace Geography Visualization. Paper for the 5th International World Wide Web Conference, Paris, France, 6–10 May 1996. http://heiwww.unige.ch/girardin/cgv/abstract/index.html Accessed 14 September 1998.

Gupta, Akhil and James Ferguson (eds) (1997) *Anthropological Locations. Boundaries and Grounds of a Field Science.* Berkeley: University of California Press.

Hannerz, Ulf (1980) *Exploring the City.* New York: Columbia University Press.

—— (1992) *Cultural Complexity: Studies in the Social Organization of Meaning.* New York: Columbia University Press.

—— (1996) *Transnational Connections.* New York: Routledge.

Harvey, David (1969) *Explanation in Geography.* London: Edward Arnold.

Hastrup, Kirsten and Peter Hervik (eds) (1994) *Social Experience and Anthropological Knowledge.* European Association of Social Anthropologists. London: Routledge.

Jackson, Michael (ed.) (1989) *Paths Toward a Clearing: Radical Empiricism and Ethnographic Inquiry.* Bloomington: Indiana University Press.

James, Allison, Jenny Hockey and Andrew Dawson (eds) (1996) *After Writing Culture: Epistemology and Praxis in Contemporary Anthropology.* ASA Monograph 34. London: Routledge.

Juergensmeyer, Mark (1991) *Radhasoami Reality: The Logic of a Modern Faith.* Princeton, NJ: Princeton University Press.

Kaplan, Caren (1997) *Questions of Travel: Postmodern Discourses of Displacement.* Durham, NC: Duke University Press.

Kelly, Robert L. and Lawrence C. Todd (1988) Coming into the Country: Early Paleoindian Hunting and Mobility. *American Antiquity* 53(2): 231–244.

Lash, Scott (1994) Reflexivity and its Doubles. In Ulrich Beck, Anthony Giddens and Scott Lash (eds) *Reflexive Modernization*. Stanford, CA: Stanford University Press, pp. 110–173.

Malkki, Liisa (1997) News and Culture: Transitory Phenomena and the Field-work Tradition. In Akhil Gupta and James Ferguson (eds) *Anthropological Locations*. Berkeley: University of California Press, pp. 86–101.

Marcus, George E. (1986) Contemporary Problems of Ethnography in the Modern World System. In James Clifford and George E. Marcus (eds) *Writing Culture: The Poetics and Politics of Ethnography*. Berkeley: University of California Press, pp. 165–193.

—— (1995) Ethnography In/Of the World System: The Emergence of Multi-sited Ethnography. *Annual Review of Anthropology* 24: 95–117.

Martin, Emily (1997) Anthropology and the Cultural Study of Science: From Citadels to String Figures. In Akhil Gupta and James Ferguson (eds) *Anthropological Locations*. Berkeley: University of California Press, pp. 131–146.

Miller, Barbara Stoler (1996) *Yoga: Discipline of Freedom*. Berkeley: University of California Press.

Miller, David (1989) The Divine Life Society Movement. In R.D. Baird (ed.) *Religion in Modern India*, 2nd revised edn. Delhi: Manohar, pp. 81–112.

Morley, David and Kevin Robins (1996) *Spaces of Identity: Global Media, Electronic Landscapes and Cultural Boundaries*. London: Routledge.

Narayan, Kirin (1993) Refractions of the Field at Home: American Representa-tions of Hindu Holy Men in the 19th and 20th centuries. *Cultural Anthro-pology* 8(4): 476–509.

Niederer, Arnold (1997) *Alpine Alltagskultur zwischen Beharrung und Wandel*. Bern: Verlag Paul Haupt.

Ornish, Dean (1991) *Dr. Dean Ornish's Program for Reversing Heart Disease*. New York : Random House.

Rabinow, Paul (1986) Representations are Social Facts. In James Clifford and George E. Marcus (eds) *Writing Culture: The Poetics and Politics of Ethnography*. Berkeley: University of California Press.

Raychaudhuri, Tapan (1989) *Europe Reconsidered: Perceptions of the West in Nineteenth Century Bengal*. New Delhi: Oxford University Press.

Robbins, Bruce (1992) Comparative Cosmopolitanism. *Social Text* 31/32: 169–186.

Robertson, Roland (1992) *Globalization*. London: Sage.

Rouse, Roger (1992) Making Sense of Settlement. In Nina Glick Schiller, Linda Basch and Cristina Blanc–Szanton (eds) *Towards a Transnational Perspective on Migration: Race, Class, Ethnicity and Nationalism Reconsidered*. Annals of the New York Academy of Sciences, Vol. 645.

Strauss, Sarah (1997) Re-Orienting Yoga: Transnational Flows from an Indian Center. Ph.D. Dissertation, Department of Anthropology, University of Pennsylvania.

—— (1998) *Balancing Acts: Yoga as Transnational Practice*. Ms. under review.

Tönnies, Ferdinand (1957) *Community and Society*. ed. and trans. C.P. Loomis. East Lansing: Michigan State University Press. Originally published 1887.

Urban, Greg (1997) Culture: In and About the World. *Anthropology Newsletter* 38(2): 1, 7.

van der Veer, Peter (1989) *Gods on Earth: The Management of Religious Experience and Identity in a North Indian Pilgrimage Centre*. London School of Economics Monographs on Social Anthropology. Delhi: Oxford University Press.

—— (1994) *Religious Nationalism: Hindus and Muslims in India*. Berkeley: University of California Press.

van Lisabeth, Andre (1992) *Yoga Self Taught*. New Delhi: Tarang Paperbacks.

Varenne, Jean (1976) *Yoga and the Hindu Tradition*. Chicago, IL: University of Chicago Press.

Vivekananda, Swami (1989) *Memoirs of European Travel*, 3rd edn. Calcutta: Advaita Ashrama.

—— (1990) *Raja Yoga*, 19th edn. Calcutta: Advaita Ashrama.

White, Leslie (1975) *The Concept of Cultural Systems*. New York: Columbia University Press.

Wiser, William and Charlotte Wiser (1971) *Behind Mud Walls, 1930–1960. With a Sequel: The Village in 1970*. Berkeley: University of California Press.

Index

Abu-Lughod, Lila 89, 156
acceptance break 151
access 153, 154; informal 152; formal 150
alienating anthropology 48
Allpart, G. 89
Amit-Talai, Vered 26
anthropological research 'at home' 7, 11, 14–15, 25, 27–8, 32, 34, 36, 49, 63, 96, 101, 103, 106–7, 116, 121, 149, 158; see also fieldwork
anthropology: alienating 48; auto- 35; ex-native 153; 'insider' 34; native 153, 154; 'real' 28
Appaduri, Arjun 50, 73, 91, 168, 170
archetypes 2, 5
au pair 97–8, 104, 106, 109
Auge, Marc 90, 91, 170
'authentic' 175, 185
authenticity 19, 174, 182
auto-anthropology 35
autobiographical 116, 123; reflexivity 5
autobiography 6, 60–3, 99
'away' 25, 29, 149, 150, 155

ballet world 147, 149, 150, 152, 154, 158–60
Barthes, Roland 75
belonging 54, 56, 59, 60–7
Benenson, Abram S. 169
Bhabha, Homi 73

biography 40, 49, 100
Bloch, Maurice 159
Bourdieu, Pierre 184
Britain 9, 57–9, 61, 64–6, 103
Britishness 64, 65, 67
Bruner, J. 75
bullfighting 97, 98, 103

Callaway, Helen 3, 43, 56
Canterbury 97
Caputo, Virginia 4, 11
career 148, 151
Carter, Paul 92
Cass, Joan 147
Cayman Islands 9, 13, 14, 57; Grand Cayman 9
centres and peripheries 147
Chicago 162–3, 180
childhood 137
childrearing 45
children's sporting activities 38, 42, 47
children's sports 34, 37, 39, 45
citizenship 134
Clifford, James 19, 20, 29, 62, 67, 68, 73, 121, 168, 170
coach 43
cognitive 72–4, 85, 88, 90, 92
Cohen, Anthony P. 34, 100, 104, 121
communication 92
communications technology 14, 16, 73, 98, 100, 108, 109, 110–16, 180; on-line 100, 109, 110;

cyberspace 108, 110, 112, 114, 116; e-mail 108–14, 155, 158; World Wide Web 185, 187, 191
communities 40, 78, 88, 175, 180, 183
community 40, 50, 75, 178, 181, 183, 188
'community of practice' 8, 14, 178, 179, 182, 184, 187
community: sport 7; sports clubs 38
compression 73
comparative predispositions 48
competition 41
concept of culture 13, 21
conscious 77
consiousness 72, 75, 76, 90, 93, 94; experiencing 76
context 93
contextualization 89
contextualized 88
conversation 77–80, 88, 93
Cordoba 9, 97–8, 103, 107, 113
cosmopolitan 168
creolization 73
Crick, Malcolm 34
Crites, S. 89
Csordas, Thomas J. 176
culture 19

determined 90
deterritorialization 73
dislocated 90
dislocation 75, 76, 83
displaced persons 120, 135
displacement 72, 73, 122, 137
disciplinary authenticity 48
Divine Life Society 162–3, 166, 171, 174–5, 178–80
dramatic event 152
Durkheimian 175
Dyck, Noel 7

electronic communications *see* communications technology
Eliade, Mircea 100, 172, 187–8
ethnic lobbyists 11
ethics 2
ethnography; 'cosmopolitan' 168, 170; 'electronic' 107, 109; multi-

locale 149, 162, 165, 166, 181; 'practitioner' 59; 'processual' 74, 90; 'traditional' 163, 185, 189
Erben, Michael 68
Evans-Pritchards, E.E. 156
exile 142, 148, 155, 156
exiting 148, 155, 156
ex-native 154, 158
existential 90
experience 72–5, 82, 85, 89–93
experiential 73, 86, 88
experiential disjunctures 74
experiential knowledge 173, 187–8
'export guru' 163, 173

Fabian, J. 3, 91
fantasy 41
feminist anthropologists 25
Ferguson, James 1, 3, 19, 22, 54, 55, 61, 164, 170
field 19, 21–9, 36, 121, 164; 'the field' 4, 14, 23, 98, 131, 134, 136, 163–4, 171–2
fieldwork 1, 5, 16, 17, 19, 21–9, 36, 41, 58, 60–2, 67, 71–4, 93, 99, 115, 120, 122, 134–5, 140, 152, 154–9; 'away' 2, 11, 73, 74, 114; electronic 96; multi-locale 158–9, 160, 166; 'real' 21–2, 24, 26; 'retrospective' 99, 116; three phases of 52; 'traditional' 20, 25, 27
fieldworker 8, 27, 124, 133, 140, 156–7; 'at home' 28
Fine, Gary Alan 38
Finnegan, Ruth 50
Finnyan, Ruth 39
Folan, Lilias 180
form of life 72, 73, 90
Freeman, Mark 68
friendships 10, 40, 97, 102, 109, 115, 141
Frykman, Jonas 43

Garcia, Garcia J. 102
Geertz, Clifford 72, 91, 136
Giddens, Anthony 102
global 57, 73, 92, 175
globalism 91

graduate migrants 96, 98, 104
graduate migration 96, 101
Gruvbo 13, 126–7, 138–9, 142–3
Gupta, Akhil 1, 3, 19, 22, 54, 55, 61, 164, 170

Hammersley, Marlyn 59
Hannerz, Ulf 73, 171, 183
Harrell-Bond, Barbara 157
Hart, K. 91, 143
Hastrup, Kirsten 1, 5, 7, 11, 12, 14, 35, 36, 102, 108, 139, 149, 153
Hendry, Joy 10, 102
Hervik, Peter 1, 5, 11, 12, 14, 108
heterogeneous 147
hierarchy of field sites 22, 23
home 25, 29, 54, 74, 85, 88, 120, 124, 126, 137; 'home' 48, 50, 55, 75, 92, 98, 100, 116, 121–2, 136
homogeneous 147
Hoodfar, Homa 27
humanism 89
hybridization 73

identities 40
imagined selves 40
immerse 2, 67
immersion 1, 5–7, 10, 12
India 163, 166, 180, 188–9
individual 76–7, 87–94
individuality 88, 94
inter-referencing 73
interact 72
interaction 73, 77, 79, 88
interactional repertoire 41
interdisciplinary studies 40
interdisciplinary work 47
interpretations 76, 77, 89, 93

Kaplan, Caren 170
Kerby, A. 75
Knowles, Caroline 8
Kosova Albanians 13, 120, 123, 127, 133, 141–2
Kulick, D. 104, 111, 115–16
Kureishi, Hanif 64

language 72, 75–6, 90, 93
Lash, Scott 184
Lave, J. 161
Leach, Edmund 59
Levi-Strauss, C. 76, 77
'legitimate' field research 42
life course 74, 88, 90–1
literary turn 73
little league baseball 38
Lofgren, Orvar 43
Lower Mainland of British Colombia 7, 37

MacGregory, Roy 46
Malkki, Lisa 137
Marcus, George E. 54, 149, 165, 168, 181, 183
Martin, Emily 170
Massey, Doreen 62
massification 73
matrix 168–73, 177, 181–4
migrant 10, 62, 92, 100–1, 107
Miller, David 184
Mitchell, W. 111–14
mobility 147, 148
moment 71, 73, 76, 89, 92
Montreal 11, 58–9, 60–1, 68
Moore, Sally 71, 74, 90, 92
moral dimensions 46
movement 72, 88, 91
multilocale 8, 13, 154, 158; structures of centres and peripheries 159; study 148
multiple subjectivity 7
multi-sited ethnography 149
myths 76–7, 88, 91

Narayan, Kirin 154
narrates 88
narrative 12, 55, 57, 59, 71, 74–7, 83, 85–90, 96, 99, 101, 103, 106, 107, 114–16
narratives 55, 56, 62, 64, 66, 89, 93, 94
national culture 147
national versus transnational processes 159
native 7

'native' anthropologist 121
'nodes of communication' 77
non-academic readers 45
'non-places' 88, 91, 92
Norman, Karin 13, 15

Okely, Judith 1, 3, 5, 12, 34, 56,
    116, 123
'othering' 35, 36, 102–3
'otherness' 48
our personal biographies 49
'ourselves' as well as 'others' 34
'outsider' 34

Palmer, Catherine 159
Parliament of the World's Religions
    162, 163, 180
participant observation 2, 3, 5, 11,
    12, 101; or espionage 43
personal encounters 149
'phoning the field' 120
Pink, Sarah 9, 14, 15
place 19, 54, 55, 73, 74, 77, 82,
    88, 89, 91, 92, 136–9, 141, 147;
    'place' 25, 92
political: act 65; activity 64;
    autobiography, context, debate
    56; landscapes 58
politics of language 167
Poster, M. 100, 111, 117
power 25, 171
practice 181
predicaments 19
professional 96, 106, 107, 115
professional and personal networks
    148, 154
publishing 46

Rabinow, Paul 167, 168
race formation 56
racial landscape 60
racism 57, 67
Rapport, Nigel 6, 12, 74, 77, 91–3,
    100, 121
reflexiveness 64
reflexivity 56, 59
refugees 60, 122, 124–9, 131, 135,
    137–42
Renan, Ernest 66

Representation 73, 90–1, 164
rhetoric of parenting 33
Rishikesh 162, 163–7, 173, 176–8,
    180–9
Rishikesh Reihe 177, 181
Robertson, Roland 64
Rodman, Margaret 30

sampradaya 176, 184
'schizophrenic' 8, 11, 55–7, 67
self 56, 60–3, 76, 88, 90, 92, 115;
    identification 36; realization 36;
    transcedence 36; selves 75
serendipity 16
Shelley, P.B. 92
Siskand, Janet 156–7
sites 4, 58, 148, 164; 'field site'
    171, 176, 188
Sivananda Ashram 163
social construction of children's
    sport 42, 49
space 74, 78, 83, 90–1, 168–9
Spanish 10, 97–8, 102–5, 107–9,
    113
spatial 76, 165, 182; disjunctions 88
sports officials and parents 39
stasis 73
static 91, 93
stories 74, 89, 93; story 75–6, 88,
    91, 140
Stanley, Liz 68
Stoller, Paul 10
Strathern, Marilyn 35, 36, 121,
    143
Strauss, Sarah 8, 13–14
surburban community 37
Swami Sivananda 163–4, 167,
    171–80, 185–9
Swami Vivekananda 163, 171–5,
    185–6, 190–1
Sweden 13, 122–9, 131–4, 136,
    138
Switzerland 166, 189
symbolic 55
symbolism 55, 57
synchronicity 73

talking-partner 77, 88
'talking-relationships' 77, 89, 92

technology 149, 155
temporal 75–6, 85, 88, 165;
    temporality 90
Tilley, Christopher 138
time 71, 74, 75, 77, 83, 89, 91–3
Tönnies, Ferdinand 182, 184
Toronto 11, 60
touring 148
traditional ethnographic practice
    175
traditional practice 162, 186–7
transitions 85, 86, 90
transnational 8, 13, 14, 147, 155,
    159, 176, 183; career networks
    159; migration 62, 64; mobility
    62; network 148; practice 162;
    researcher 60, 61, 62, 67; studies
    154
transnationalism 54
transnationals 54, 56, 59
travelling 148
Turner, Bryan 68
Tyler, S. 91

unconsciously 91

value 19
vectors 168–74, 181–2

vector-matrix framing 181
video 155, 158

Wacquant, Loïc 158
Wagner, R. 91
Wallman, Sandra 15
Wanet, 12, 71, 72, 74, 75, 78,
    80–7, 92
Watson, L.B. 89, 93
Watson-Frank, M.B. 89, 93
Weiner, J. 89, 93, 94
Wenger, E. 161
White, Leslie 170
whiteness 61
Willson, M. 111, 115
Winant, Howard 56
Woolf, Virginia 92
world in motion 16, 71, 73, 74, 77,
    88
Wright, Patrick 65
writing 77, 88
Wulff, Helena 7, 8

yoga 162–3, 165–9, 171–89, 191
Young, Malcom 43
Yugoslavia 125–6, 143

Zurich 167, 180

DATE DUE